Dallas
UNCOVERED

Larenda Lyles Roberts

Republic of Texas Press
an imprint of
Wordware Publishing, Inc.

Library of Congress Cataloging-in-Publication Data

Roberts, Larenda Lyles.
    Dallas uncovered / Larenda Lyles Roberts.
        p.   cm.
    Includes index.
    ISBN 1-55622-378-1
    1. Dallas (Tex.)--Guidebooks.   2. Dallas (Tex.)--History.
    I. Title.
    F394.D213R63   1994
    917.64'28120463--dc20   94-11345
                                                                             CIP

Copyright © 1995, Larenda Lyles Roberts

All Rights Reserved

No part of this book may be reproduced in any form or by any means without permission in writing from Wordware Publishing, Inc.

Printed in the United States of America

ISBN 1-55622-378-1
10 9 8 7 6 5 4 3 2 1
9410

All inquiries for volume purchases of this book should be addressed to Wordware Publishing, Inc., at 1506 Capital Avenue, Plano, Texas 75074. Telephone inquiries may be made by calling:

(214) 423-0090

To Jack Roberts, Jr.,

*my husband and confidante,
a fine patron of the arts*

Contents

Acknowledgements ix
Introduction xii
Test Your Knowledge xiii

Section I
Uniquely Dallas 1

1. The Dallas Attitude and How to Develop It—
   A Crash Course 1
2. Highland Park Village Shopping Center 4
3. Deep Ellum 6
4. Park Cities and the Dallas Subculture—
   Life in the Bubble 11
5. That Famous Skyline 14
6. The Legacy of J.R. Ewing 17
7. Mobil Pegasus—*The Flying Red Horse* 20
8. High-Profile Crime 21
   Belle Starr 21
   Clyde Barrow & Bonnie Parker 25
   Walker Railey 34
9. Preston Road—*Cattle Trail Boulevard* 41
10. Texas Instruments—*Computer Chips,
    Doughnuts, and Jack Kilby* 42
11. West End Historic District—
    Frogs, People, and Partying 45
12. The Neiman Marcus Mystique 47
13. Dickey's Barbecue—*The Real Thing* 50
14. Dallas' Religious Roots—*Gamblers, Hogs, and
    Gun-Totin' Preachers* 52
15. Wilson Historic District 60
16. Lower Greenville 62

Contents

17. Shopping—*The Most Popular Sport in Dallas* ... 63
18. Dallas Culture—*Yes, Virginia, there is culture in Dallas* 65
    A. Museum Collections 65
    B. Performing Arts 70

Section II
Dallas Places 77

1. Adolphus Hotel 77
2. Freedman's Cemetery 81
3. The Old Red Courthouse 83
4. Log Cabin *(and a little pioneer history)* 86
5. Southfork Ranch 87
6. The Sixth Floor: John F. Kennedy and the Memory of a Nation 88
7. Dealey Plaza/Grassy Knoll 90
8. The Trinity River: Where is It? 92
9. Morton H. Meyerson Symphony Center 96
10. Frontiers of Flight Museum 99
11. Southern Methodist University 101
12. First Baptist Hard Rock Cafe 103
13. Pioneer Plaza 104

Section III
Dallas Legends—Ordinary Folks Who Made Good 107

1. H. Ross Perot—*The Best Little Billionaire in Texas* 107
2. John Neely Bryan 116
3. The Hunt Family—*Silver, Scandal, and Texas Tea* 121
4. Caroline Rose Hunt—*A Class of Her Own* 141
5. Mary Kay Ash 143
6. Anderson Bonner 145
7. Barney the Dinosaur 145
8. Alexander and Sarah Horton Cockrell 149

Contents

9. Henry Keller 151
10. George Mifflin Who? 152

Section IV
Dallas Remembers 155

1. La Reunion Colony 155
2. *Dallas Times Herald* 159
3. The Day Dallas Burned 160
4. Freedman's Towns 162
5. *Dallas Express* 167
6. Clock Tower Atop the Old Red Courthouse 169
7. Elks' Arch 172
8. Braniff's Colorful Jets 172
9. Routh Street Cafe 173
10. *D* Magazine 174

Section V
The Sports Page 177

1. Da Boyz—*Those Incredible Dallas Cowboys* . . . 177
2. Those Equally Incredible Dallas
   Cowboys Cheerleaders 190
3. Texas Rangers—*Baseball, Not Outlaw* 194
4. Nolan Ryan—*The Legend Lives On* 198
5. Basketball—*From Diamonds to Mavericks* 203
6. Of Ice Hockey and Dallas Stars 207
7. Cotton Bowl 210

Section VI
**Dallas No-No's: Twelve Things
You Should Never Do in Dallas** 211

Section VII
**Amazing Dallas Trivia: Twenty Little-
Known Facts About the Big D** 215

Contents

Section VIII
Why Is That? Answers to Ten Petty Questions About Dallas 221

Section IX
Dallas Brags 233

Section X
Dallas Lists 237
1. Notable Names 237
2. Unusual Dallas Outings 244
3. Dallas Firsts 247
4. Dallas Chronology 249

Section XI
Dallas Secrets 261
1. Where the Rich and Famous Live 262
2. Best-Kept Secret Bargain Stores 264
3. Where The Snobbiest Sales Clerks Work 266
4. Where The Friendliest Sales Clerks Work 266
5. You Haven't Lived Until You've… 268

Sources 269
Index 271

Acknowledgements

This section is usually a dull piece where the author complains and whines about how much trouble it is to write a book and how he or she had to make great sacrifices to do so, all in hopes of getting you, the reader, to feel sorry for him or her.

But I won't do that. I got all my complaining and whining out the last nine months. Just ask my family and the two friends I have left.

Seriously, I had great fun writing this book and assistance from many people. First of all, I am grateful to my spies and undercover agents out there, although I won't mention them by name. You'll see why if you read this book. They know who they are.

Especially helpful and enthusiastic were Jimm Foster and the gang at the Texas Archives Division of the Dallas Public Library, Gaylon at the Dallas Historical Society, my cousin Jeri Beth Bohannan and her coworkers at Jones Day Law Firm, Joyce Lebovitz of Community Introductions, Fred Ligon and staff at Sedgwick James, and Barbara Lacy and the gang at Crown Sterling Suites Management.

I also wish to extend my gratitude to Mary Goldman, my editor, for giving me this opportunity. Thanks go to David Finfrock, meteorologist at Channel 5, to Ana Szafranski, who accompanied me to Deep Ellum late one Saturday night for "research" and to Nina Kelly and Shirley Wilson, for helping me get through a cross-country move. Appreciation goes to a special friend, Don Hooker, without whom I would not have had this opportunity.

I am grateful to my father and brother, George Lyles and Bob Lyles, of Accu-Tech Computer Services, for forcing me against my will into the computer age and then answering

Acknowledgements

all my "911" calls. I seem to suffer from a chronic case of that modern malady, computer hysterics. Also, I appreciate John Nastasi's calm instructions during the many crises.

From the time I first visited Dallas at the age of 14, I have been in love with the city and dreamed of living there someday. Fortunately, I was able to do so not many years later. Dallas is a great city, and I hope anyone who picks up this book, whether it's to browse, read one section or the entire book, will enjoy reading it as much as I enjoyed writing it.

Introduction

◆ ◆ ◆

Dallas. Think the word, and feel the powerful vastness, the endless legends, wrapped in a spirit of innovation that shaped the American frontier. This spirit thrives today in one of the world's favorite cities.

From the lone rancher gazing across flat terrain to the entrepreneur looking out of a tower of dark glass and glistening steel, Dallas has come to represent America's maverick city. Dallas is bigger, brasher, and glitzier than other cities and proud of it. You don't have to be well-bred or well-educated to make it in Dallas, but you do have to be brave. If it's new and different, Dallas will try it.

In a mere five generations, Dallas sprang from a small group of primitive cabins on a muddy riverbank to a huge, sprawling city of skyscrapers and modern offices that rise out of the prairie like a high-tech mirage, visible for miles. It has often been said that the people who settled this area known as "Dallas" pulled themselves up by their own bootstraps.

Certainly, it was no accident that two major railroads crossed here in the 1800s and that Dallas, without any oil fields of its own, managed to become the financial center of the Southwest, generating funds for oil exploration and development of the vast petroleum industry. Likewise, it was not by chance that Dallas became a major aviation hub with the second busiest airport in the world, the Dallas/Fort Worth International Airport, providing travelers with three-hour connections to any city in the continental U.S.

Introduction

With dreams of greatness, the men and women of Dallas visualized the future. They struggled, fought, and worked, risking their lives and fortunes. Often in their battles, they lost and failed, but even in defeat, they never gave up their vision of a great city in this raw, untamed land known as Dallas, Texas.

How Much Do You Really Know About Dallas?

TEST YOUR KNOWLEDGE

1. In the 1930s, the area called "Deep Ellum" was known for what?
   A. Cocaine dealers.
   B. Blues singers.
   C. Black magic.
   D. All of the above.
2. Which is the worst time to visit Dallas?
   A. Texas-Oklahoma University football weekend.
   B. August.
   C. Cotton Bowl weekend.
   D. State Fair month.
3. What should you never, ever do in Dallas?
   A. Eat chili at a cafeteria.
   B. Announce that you're from Fort Worth.
   C. Wear sequins to the symphony.
   D. Criticize the Dallas Cowboys.
4. Reunion Arena derives its name from which of the following:
   A. A wild horse that once roamed the prairies.
   B. A colony of French utopians.
   C. A name given to Southern family get-togethers.
   D. None of the above; developer Ray Hunt merely liked the name.

Test Your Knowldege

5. Why is there an ongoing feud between Dallas and Fort Worth?
   A. Because Fort Worth says Dallas is a snooty town.
   B. Because Dallas says Fort Worth is nothing but a big cowtown.
   C. Because Fort Worth has better art museums than Dallas.
   D. Because Dallas beat Fort Worth in a football game in 1891.
   E. All of the above.

6. Why were 20,000 people jamming the streets of Dallas in the last week of May 1934?
   A. To watch the Rodeo parade.
   B. To celebrate Texas' Centennial.
   C. To view the bodies of Bonnie Parker and Clyde Barrow.
   D. To watch the *Hindenburg* fly over Dallas.

7. What did Jack Kilby do in Dallas in 1958?
   A. Designed the Dallas freeway system.
   B. Decided to give the freeways names instead of numbers.
   C. Designed a multivibrator that formed a complete circuit.
   D. Designed the largest doughnut machine ever made.

8. What did Dallas civic leaders do when they determined that the Trinity River was not navigable?
   A. Built numerous bridges and turnpike systems across it.
   B. Decided to navigate it anyway, no matter how many boats sank.
   C. Built a huge dam and blocked the river.
   D. Moved the river three-and-one-half miles over.

Test Your Knowldege

9. Which statement is most likely to blow a business deal in Dallas?
   A. Troy Aikman is not the best quarterback in the whole world, ever.
   B. Dallas women are overdressed and wear too much makeup.
   C. Art in Dallas? Come on.
   D. People in Highland Park think they're better than people in University Park.

10. What does the term "Hot Pan Men" refer to?
    A. Panhandlers in Deep Ellum.
    B. Domestic workers at the Adolphus Hotel.
    C. Unemployed men who courted domestic workers.
    D. Cooks on cattle trail chuck wagons.

11. Why do some Dallasites get nervous—and excited—every year on June 27th?
    A. Because it is the anniversary of Texas' Independence from Mexico.
    B. Because there is a superstition that the 27th of June is unlucky for you if you're in Dallas.
    C. June 27th is the date of SMU's graduation ceremonies.
    D. Because it is Ross Perot's birthday, and he's been known to make startling announcements on this date.

12. What is Valley Ranch?
    A. A massive estate built by Dallas billionaire H.L. Hunt.
    B. A working Dallas ranch that allows visitors to tour it.
    C. The training center for the Dallas Cowboys.
    D. A salad dressing invented in Dallas.

◆ ◆ ◆ ◆ ◆

Test Your Knowldege

ANSWERS

1. D   pp. 7-8
2. A   pp. 46, 78, 210
3. C   p. 212
4. B   pp. 15, 136, 155
5. E   pp. 221-224
6. C   pp. 34, 216-217
7. C   p. 43
8. D   pp. 92-96
9. C   p. 65
10. C   p. 165
11. D   pp. 190-110
12. C   p. 182

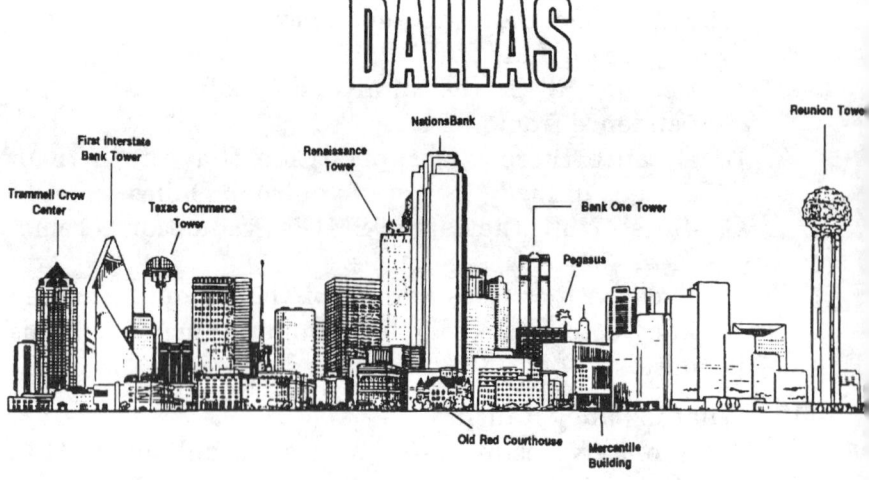

Dallas Skyline (Courtesy of the Dallas Convention & Visitors Bureau.)

SECTION I

Uniquely Dallas

1:
The Dallas Attitude and How to Develop It — *A Crash Course*

Part I—Attitude Adjustment

Newcomers to Dallas often think to themselves that they've never seen such a boastful, cocky, and overdressed group of people as the residents of Dallas. Along with big hair, Dallasites tend to have big heads, the new guys in town notice. And didn't their mothers teach them that polite people aren't supposed to brag?

These newcomers get pretty annoyed—and rightly so—when they visit Dallas and realize that when it comes to "biggest and best," Dallas claims to outshine them all, no matter what the subject may be. Everything in Dallas seems to be greater and grander than anyone else's, and Dallasites take great pride in pointing this out to guests. The visitor then starts to wonder, "Who do these Dallas people think they are, anyway?"

Trouble is, after they've been here awhile—at least 24 hours—the newcomers tend to start playing the game themselves. They begin striding around the city (Dallasites don't walk—they stride) with a certain long, forward gait reflecting a self-assured cockiness that says, "I am strong. I know what I want and how to get it" (even if they don't).

After all, if John Neely Bryan could stake his claim the minute he set eyes on the place, why can't they? So what if he didn't have a legal right to the land yet. He figured out a way eventually, right?

Then a few days later, these same people—no longer newcomers—find that they are worrying about such things as *image* and *accessories*. They start thinking that they are pretty great individuals and that Dallas is one remarkable place, after all. Soon, they discover that it's fun and even a little self-satisfying to brag about one's chosen city.

They start pointing out to more recent arrivals and relatives who phone that Dallas is headquarters for the world's largest providers of information and technology, as well as the world's largest oil company, Exxon Corporation. They boast to New Yorkers that the Greater Dallas/Fort Worth International Airport is larger than the *en-tire* island of Manhattan *and* that Dallas is the only major U.S. city with a AAA bond rating from Standard & Poor. And did you know that Dallas, they tell relatives who wonder what's gotten into them, has more shopping centers per capita than any major U.S. city? *And* that the Dallas Market Center is the world's largest wholesale trade complex?

Before long, these new Dallasites are sporting boots and bumper-stickers that read, "I wasn't born in Texas, but I got here as soon as I could." They get chills when they spot the downtown Dallas skyline at night. All those things that annoyed them when they first rode into town, like the "DON'T MESS WITH TEXAS" signs posted everywhere, now make them hold their heads a little higher. Well, it's only civic pride, after all. But the best civic pride found anywhere, of course!

So don't feel guilty when it happens to you.

Part II—Your Comeuppance

Once you've acquired the Dallas State of Mind, it's time to come down a peg or two. Self-confidence is great, but Texans, even Dallasites, don't take kindly to snobbery. Even if your mother did move to Highland Park and graduate from Hockaday after her daddy struck oil in Odessa, you're still just folks, and don't you forget it.

Courtesy and down-to-earth friendliness are prerequisites for popularity in Dallas. People from outside the South may be surprised at the openness of Dallas citizens, even the old-money socialites. Although there are exceptions, Dallas doesn't tend toward snootiness (unless, of course, you're talking about Fort Worth).

Keep in mind that oil isn't the only thing that gushes in this part of the country—Texans like to talk, so don't be offended if a total stranger strikes up an intimate conversation with you. The polite response is to offer to share your own life history as well.

There are several reasons why Dallas, in spite of all the bragging that goes on, isn't considered snobbish. For one thing, Dallas is a very young city, and as such, most of the "old guard" aren't all that old. Tracing one's roots all the way back to 1922—or even 1872—when the population was around 7,000—isn't terribly impressive. And after all, if you *can* trace your roots back that far, chances are that your great-great granddaddy was a railroad worker, a freed slave, or even a cattle rustler.

Dallas is considered a sophisticated, savvy city, particularly for such a young Southern city. Corporations headquartered in Dallas attract highly educated people, many of whom become involved in the arts and cultural life. You will, however, find people in Dallas with all types of backgrounds—from the proper Highland Park matron to the struggling blue-collar worker who moved to Dallas with the hope of finding a better life for his family. From the nouveau riche to nouveau poor, Dallas has them all.

Now, you may find a few people who tend to get a mite uppity, just because they have lots of money, live in the right places, shop only in exclusive stores, and contribute vast sums to the arts. But don't be intimidated by these people. If you run across one of them, remind yourself that she gets her hair bleached one strand at a time, just like everyone else.

And that one of these days, she'll get her comeuppance, too.

2.
Highland Park Village Shopping Center

Can you imagine a grocery store that offers valet parking? The shoppers in Highland Park Village can. Old-world charm of Spanish mission architecture, combined with exquisite merchandise, the little necessities of life, and merchants who know their customers by name, make this prestigious shopping center a popular gathering place for the Park Cities crowd.

Opened in 1931, at the corner of Mockingbird Lane and Preston Road, Highland Park Village has the distinction of being the country's first "shopping center" in which stores faced inward, away from the surrounding streets, developed as part of a unified management. A Beverly Hills designer, David Cook, designed the Village, along with developer Hugh Prather and architect James Cheek.

Prather and Cheek visited southern California in 1928 to study Spanish missions and in 1929 went to Barcelona, where they found designs for the intricate facades, balconies, light fixtures, and arches that give Highland Park Village its warmth, color, and charm. Hugh Prather visualized a "town square" setting, where residents of the community could shop for groceries, buy stamps, purchase both casual and fine apparel, dine with the family, and have their shoes resoled—all at one stop. The buildings were kept low so that shoppers could leisurely stroll from one shop to another.

Completion of Highland Park Village required twenty years. Work on the theater unit, the first luxury suburban movie theater in Texas, was begun in 1935.

During the 1960s, malls began competing with shopping centers, and the Village went into a period of regression and deterioration. Power lines obscured red-tiled roofs, storefronts were incongruous, and architectural control began eroding. Eventually, the ornate towers and elaborate facades were in disrepair, and many tenants left the premises.

In 1976 Henry S. Miller Jr. and Associates bought the Village and took over its management. Restoration was a long process and was greatly impeded when a fire in 1979 caused extensive damage. Efforts were concentrated on restoring the Village to its original grandeur while replacing the community flavor that had been lost as well.

In spite of Highland Park Village's location in an affluent residential area, the Miller Group felt it was very important that neighborhood service-oriented shops, such as grocers, shoe repair, and dry cleaners, be retained, along with Hermes, Harold's, and other exclusive stores.

The restoration was a success, and today the Village boasts 80 retail and 12 office tenants. Crisscrossing power lines are gone, and the original ambience of a Spanish mission is evident from the red-tiled roofs to the open courtyards and abundance of flowers and greenery.

Highland Park Village services not only the elite clientele that one might expect, but also many original residents of the Dallas area. Stop for lunch at the Celebrity Restaurant and Bakery, and you will likely see prominent Dallas businessmen and businesswomen dining outdoors, but go early for coffee and homemade pastries, and you will meet the friendly older citizens of Park Cities, who are greeted by name.

Section I

The current Village management works along with shop merchants to maintain the community texture that was the original intent of Hugh Prather, attracting affordable stores such as Gap and Express to fill the spaces between internationally renowned boutiques like Chanel, Calvin Klein, and Polo/Ralph Lauren.

Particularly on a sunny day, shopping is once again the pleasant experience envisioned by Prather, as one drifts through flowering courtyards and down clay tile steps while classical music filters through the air. Power lunches are conducted on the sidewalk as neighbors greet one another. Hugh Prather would be proud to see the ancient Chevrolets and Buicks parked alongside Lexuses and Mercedes.

But it's still wise to bring your credit card collection.

Corner of Mockingbird Lane and Preston Road

3.
Deep Ellum

If the idea of avant garde nightclubs, eclectic stores, and highly unusual people attracts you, then you should definitely make a trip into the area known as "Deep Ellum." Located on Elm Street east of Central Expressway, Deep Ellum derives its name from the way "Elm" was pronounced by jazz singers and the original residents of this area.

Freed slaves first settled in Deep Ellum during the 1860s, when it was one of the "Freedman's Towns" that grew up after the Civil War. *(see Sec. IV:4.)* The early residents of Deep Ellum were laborers who lived and worked along the railroad tracks that were being built in Dallas. As time passed, the area became a notorious entertainment district. Pawn shops, hotels, cafes, tattoo studios, and secondhand clothing stores sprang up, along with the Cotton Club and gun shops.

Almost anything could be found in Deep Ellum, from a "threadbare cloth-of-gold dress to a collapsible bathtub," according to one observer. Along with merchandise, popular food stands serving such favorites as barbecue, fried catfish, and collard greens drew people to the neighborhood of Deep Ellum.

J.H. Owens ("Old Ironsides"), a black columnist, wrote the following about Deep Ellum in 1937:

> Down on "Deep Ellum" in Dallas, where Central Avenue empties into Elm street is where Ethiopia stretches forth her hands. It is the one spot in the city that needs no daylight saving time because there is no bedtime, and working hours have no limits. The only place recorded on earth where business, religion, hoodooism, gambling and stealing goes on at the same time without friction.... Last Saturday a prophet held the best audience in this "Madison Square Garden" in announcing that Jesus Christ would come to Dallas in person in 1939. At the same time a pickpocket was lifting a week's wages from another guy's pocket, who stood with open mouth to hear the prophesy.... (*Dallas Gazette*, July 3, 1937).

In addition to the preaching that went on, there was plenty of drug dealing and black magic. Many blacks continued to believe in the supernatural and carried on folklore traditions taught them by their ancestors. In Deep Ellum, they could obtain love potions, philters (aphrodisiacs), incense, magnetic lodestones for poker players, and Van Van oil to shake off a jinx.

One establishment, the Wish-I-Wish Company, featured special New Orleans lucky bags, purported to be effective for a full year. This particular company was run by a white man, whose patrons referred to him as "Doctor," and who was credited with the power to read potent policy numbers in the smoke of incense.

The area attracted many black folk and jazz singers, such as Blind Lemon Jefferson and Huddie "Leadbelly" Ledbetter. There was no bedtime in Deep Ellum, and its streets were often crowded with cocaine and marijuana dealers, sidewalk preachers, card sharps, and blues singers. Marijuana, which was called the "loco weed," was easily cultivated in Texas backyards and sold by the "reefer man" on the streets. Addicts were referred to as "muggle smokers." The Cotton Club, which was closed by 1940, was a popular cabaret club that featured swing music. Muscular attendants searched guests for weapons, and white people could visit only by appointment.

One writer, in describing some of the people walking Deep Ellum's streets in the 1930s, wrote:

> Con men—"pigeon droppers"—the reefer man, the card sharp, the too-lucky crap shooter, and the dusky lilies of the field, faces powdered to a cadaverous blue dinginess, tight-fitting gowns supplemented by five-and-dime costume jewelry, hair groomed by the hot-iron straightening process, rub shoulders in the evenings with those innocently bent on spending their wages for a touch of night life.

After Central Expressway was completed in the 1940s, Deep Ellum was severed from downtown Dallas, and it began a long decline. However, in the late 1970s, artists began opening studios in the area, which was by then mostly manufacturing plants, mechanic shops, and boarded-up buildings. It wasn't long before cafes and clubs followed. The Dallas Blues Society, founded in the mid-1980s by Dallas blues-lover and musician Chuck Nevitt, began showcasing local talent and guest artists at J & J Blues Bar and other clubs that line the famous street.

Today, Deep Ellum carries on its tradition of cutting-edge diversions with a curious and often bizarre collection

Uniquely Dallas

of nightclubs, restaurants, tattoo parlors, jewelry stores, trendy furniture shops, and art galleries. Establishments with such names as "The Bone," "Club Dada," "Left Brain, Right Brain," "Wild at Heart," and "2826" line the streets. Twenty-one clubs, twenty-seven restaurants, and at least fifty-two retail shops make up the district.

Street scene from Deep Ellum Gypsy Tea Room Cafe, c. 1939. (From the collections of the Texas/Dallas History and Archives Division, Dallas Public Library.)

Section I

Elm Street, looking west from near St. Paul. c. 1905. (From the collections of the Texas/Dallas History and Archives Division, Dallas Public Library.)

Although its streets still never sleep, Deep Ellum really comes alive after ten o'clock at night, when live music ranging from original country blues to heavy metal can be heard coming from clubs, and smells of incense fill the night air. Deep Ellum, however, is not for the faint of heart. Do stick to the main street and well-lighted areas.

When you go down on Deep Ellum,
To have a little fun
Have your sixteen dollars ready
When that policeman comes.

Chorus

Oh, sweet mama, your daddy's got them
Deep Ellum Blues.
Oh, sweet mama, your daddy's got them
Deep Ellum Blues.

Uniquely Dallas

> *Once I knew a preacher,*
> *Preached the Bible thru and thru,*
> *Till he went down on Deep Ellum,*
> *Now his preaching days are thru.*
>
> *(Chorus)*
>
> *When you go down on Deep Ellum,*
> *Put your money in your socks,*
> *'Cause them Women on Deep Ellum*
> *Sho' will throw you on the rocks.*
>
> *(Chorus)*
>
> *Once I had a sweetheart,*
> *And she meant the world to me*
> *Till she hung around Deep Ellum,*
> *Now she's not what she used to be.*
>
> *Deep Ellum Blues*

Elm St. between Central Expressway (U.S. 75) and Missouri-Pacific railroad tracks
Weekly Update—214-747-DEEP

4.
Park Cities and the Dallas Subculture — *Life in the Bubble*

A newspaper columnist in Houston once wrote, "There is Highland Park and there is heaven, although occasionally the locals get the two mixed up." If you want to get the feel of an ideal American town, such as one might see in *It's A Wonderful Life,* all you have to do is take a walk through the streets of Highland Park. In Dallas, there is no more prestigious address than Highland Park, a name that is synonymous with old money, old values, and proud old houses.

In 1906 John S. Armstrong, a Dallas developer, began a suburban development north of town, which he named Highland Park. Hugh E. Prather, Armstrong's son-in-law and business partner, hired Beverly Hills architect David Cook to design a model plan for their community. Armstrong died two years later, but the project was continued by Prather, who incorporated Highland Park as a city in 1913, with its own municipal government.

Eventually, University Park grew up adjacent to Highland Park, around Southern Methodist University. Known as the "Park Cities," Highland Park and University Park are both incorporated cities within the city of Dallas. Each "city" has its own police and fire departments, and the two share the same school district. On the wall of Highland Park's small city council hall are the words:

> A haven for home and fireside—undisturbed by conflict of commercial or political interest. The function of government in Highland Park is protection of the home. Citizens who cherish their homes will vigilantly preserve their heritage of self-government.

Many of the distinctive houses lining Highland Park's shady streets are historical reproductions of Mediterranean villas, French chateaux, and Tudor mansions. An early advertisement for the development states, "Distinctive Architectural Types Find Their Proper Environment in Highland Park."

In addition to having their own public school district, (Highland Park School District operates independently of other Dallas public schools), residents of the Park Cities feel they are sheltered from crime and other urban ills; hence the term "life in the bubble." Likewise, inhabitants have access to exclusive shopping centers, such as Highland Park Village and Crescent Court.

The visitor will find some of Dallas' most beautiful homes along Turtle Creek, which flows through the two neighborhoods on its way to the Trinity River. The oldest areas in Highland Park were developed first because of their proximity to the trolley stop. Many other homes in Highland Park, particularly the multimillion-dollar mansions along Beverly Drive, were built during the oil boom in Dallas in the 1920s and '30s.

The isolation of the Park Cities and their proximity to SMU have given rise to a unique culture. There are no bars or liquor stores in Highland Park, because the founders wanted to keep their neighborhood free of drinking. There are a few to be found in University Park, however. Also, there are no churches in Highland Park, but you will find many churches that incorporate "Highland Park" into their names. Every year, there is a festive Fourth of July parade, complete with floats, balloons, lollipops, and antique fire engines.

Residents of Highland Park and University Park work very hard to maintain their image and lifestyles. In the spring, the area is famous for its gorgeous azaleas that bloom along the banks of Turtle Creek and in the exquisitely manicured lawns. Growing azaleas is a feat in itself. Dallas' soil is alkaline—being on the blackland prairie—and therefore resistant to azaleas. However, in the mid-thirties, a horticulturist named Joe Lambert Jr. figured out a way to grow the showy bushes by replacing soil with peat moss and sandy loam and keeping the bushes well-watered and mulched with a special type of much.

Mr. Lambert planted hundreds of azalea bushes along Turtle Creek, creating a Dallas gardening phenomenon. Although the cost was prohibitive, socialite wives up and down Turtle Creek wanted the plants, and it became a status symbol to have a row of the costly, lavish blooms lining your drive. As a result, in mid-March, traffic is unusually slow in the Park Cities because of motorists stopping to gasp at the masses of pink and white blooms.

Section I

Drive through the Park Cities on any given day, and you will likely see a parade of maids, servants, gardeners, and chauffeurs coming and going among the estates. Walk its streets and you will find hidden stone bridges, gurgling ponds, squirrels, and fireflies, along with a pleasant sense of safety and well-being. If you look closely enough, you can still see small rusted iron rings embedded in the curbs where horses were once hitched.

Critics say that the Park Cities are elitist and can no longer ignore or keep out the sprawling city, massive freeways, and urban blight that surround them. They say that life in the bubble is unreal and that the Park Cities will soon be swallowed up by the bigger city. But the residents of Highland Park and University Park continue to prove them wrong.

Bounded by Northwest Highway, Central Expressway, Dallas North Tollway, and Wycliffe

5.
That Famous Skyline

Ever since a pilot made the claim that he could spot Pegasus, the famous lighted red horse that soared atop the Magnolia Building, all the way from Waco, Dallas developers have rushed to erect the tallest, most spectacular building in downtown Dallas. The result of their efforts is a dramatic outline of illuminated superstructures whose glistening forms against a western sky cannot fail to awe even the world's most seasoned traveler.

The once-proud Pegasus has long been dwarfed by such buildings as NationsBank Plaza that rises 72 stories and is outlined at night with over two miles of green argon. One of

Uniquely Dallas

Pegasus at night. Pegasus will fly forever across downtown Dallas, thanks to its designation in 1973 as a City Landmark. Erected in 1934 as the corporate symbol of Magnolia Oil Company, the "flying red horse" has become the symbol of Dallas' "can do" spirit and once was visible for 25 miles. (Courtesy of the Dallas Convention & Visitors Bureau.)

the more noticeable skyscrapers is Reunion Tower, a 52-story building completed by developer Ray Hunt in 1978 and described by one reporter as a "giant dandelion." This futuristic structure, lighted at night as a sphere, contains an observatory on the 50th floor that provides a spectacular view of Dallas and the Trinity River. A revolving restaurant and bar make up the top floors. Adjacent to the tower is Reunion Arena, which is site of many of the city's sports and entertainment events.

The Reunion Complex, which consists of Reunion Tower, Reunion Arena, and the Hyatt Regency Hotel, a set of four-leveled mirrored cubist peaks, has become the symbol of Dallas as the city approaches the 21st century. Ray Hunt chose the name "Reunion" to honor the French and Swiss colonists who came to Dallas in the 1850s as part of the failed "La Reunion" colony on the banks of the Trinity River not far from the new tower *(see Sec. IV:1)*.

Although the artists and intellectuals who came to Texas were practicing a form of socialism known as "Fourierism," and Ray Hunt was a capitalist, his name choice proved both ironic and prophetic. "Reunion" also stood for the uncommon synergism of government and private enterprise that took place in order to build the development. When asked why he did not name his project "Hunt Plaza," Ray Hunt replied, "I don't believe in monuments."

The Reunion Complex was seen as a tremendous boost to downtown Dallas and civic pride. The long-awaited opening on April 15, 1978, featured a spectacular light show on the new tower and a massive fireworks display that brought freeway traffic all over the city to a halt as motorists watched the night sky celebration.

Buildings that once claimed the title of tallest include the Mercantile National Bank Building, Republic Bank (forty stories with a revolving search light), the Southland Life Building, First National Bank in Dallas, and First

International (56 stories). Currently, the winner is the NationsBank Building at 72 stories.

Reunion Tower
300 Reunion Blvd.
214-651-1234
Event Information—214-670-1395

Sec. I:7—Mobil Pegasus
Sec. III:3—The Hunt Family
Sec. IV:1—La Reunion Colony

6.
The Legacy of J.R. Ewing

The debut of the CBS television series "Dallas" in 1978 marked the beginning of a new era for the city. J.R. Ewing, the show's main character played by Larry Hagman, came to epitomize the mythical rich and powerful American businessman.

Although J.R. Ewing was only a fictional character, his wheelings and dealings inspired a whole generation of businessmen and women during the scandal-ridden, greed-driven eighties. A shady, devious, and downright mean oil baron, rancher, and entrepreneur, J.R. Ewing almost overnight became a hot topic and a source of controversy in offices, homes, and even classrooms across the country. Why was America so fascinated by this man who gladly betrayed his friends, cheated on his wife, defrauded his business partners, and took the law into his own hands—all with a gutsy laugh and a shrug of the shoulders that displayed his lack of remorse?

In its height of popularity, the show took the country by storm. Even college professors debated America's love-hate

Section I

relationship with J.R. Ewing. Some speculated that fans admired J.R. because he dared to do what viewers only fantasized of doing, while others said it was because he represented power and control. Maybe, though, it was because deep down, J.R. was just a good ole boy who minded his mama, listened to his daddy, and cared about his family, even though that family happened to be a backstabbing, dysfunctional group of millionaires living in a mansion called "Southfork." Plus, it was somehow comforting for viewers to see that the rich and famous led miserable lives.

But whether it was to savor J.R.'s latest exploit or merely to get an update on the newest fashions and hairstyles, or just to forget about their own problems for a little while, millions of viewers tuned in every Friday night for a total of twelve seasons, spawning a new pop culture of Dallasmania. In beauty salons around the country, women asked for "Pam Ewing" or "Suellen" haircuts, and clients in fashion boutiques added shoulder pads and adjusted their silhouettes to reflect those of the Ewing clan.

Although critics claimed "Dallas" was nothing more than a glorified soap opera, the show continued to draw viewers with its slick production and controversial themes of adultery and underhanded business dealings. Whenever J.R. suffered a defeat, viewers expressed sympathy for him as they would a mischievous little boy.

The city of Dallas relished its newfound fame, particularly after enduring so much negative publicity following the Kennedy assassination. Dallas was now seen as the embodiment of the new American city—sophisticated, bold, powerful, and rich. Tourists flocked to Dallas as never before, and so many drove out to see Southfork Ranch that the original residents were forced to move in order to protect their privacy.

"Dallas" seemed to fit well with the eighties decade, blending glitz and glamour with a new finesse that included and celebrated America's western roots, even though most of the "Dallas" duels were fought in skyscrapers rather than

Uniquely Dallas

corrals. Country music was suddenly "in," along with cowboy boots, large belt buckles, and ten-gallon hats.

In fact, it has been noted that "Dallas" changed social habits, as many fans turned down Friday night engagements and rushed through dinner in order to gather around

Larry Hagman as J.R. Ewing (Used by permission)

the television with the family, eat the newly invented microwave popcorn, and see what evil schemes old J.R. had up his sleeve that week. Even church groups reluctantly rescheduled Bible studies so their members wouldn't miss an episode. (Remember, this was before most people had VCRs.)

The show became such a phenomenon that the episode in which J.R. was shot in 1980, a cliffhanger, ranked as one of the most-watched shows in television history. When the last showing of "Dallas" aired in 1990, the mythical gates of Southfork closed, and J.R. Ewing rode off into television history and reruns, leaving behind his trademark white hat, his famous smirk, and a lasting place in the gallery of America's favorite bad boys.

See Section II:5—Southfork Ranch

7.
Mobil Pegasus—*The Flying Red Horse*

Pegasus, the beloved flying red horse that rotates atop the Magnolia Petroleum Building, has been a Dallas landmark since it was first lit on November 8, 1934. The winged horse of Greek mythology, Pegasus symbolized speed, power, and imagination and was the corporate symbol of Magnolia Petroleum, the company that eventually became Mobil Oil.

In 1922 Magnolia Petroleum built its 29-story headquarters at the corner of Akard and Commerce streets. For twenty years, it was Dallas' tallest building. When, in 1934, the company placed a massive five-story revolving red horse on the building, it became an instant landmark. Lighted by neon, the graceful, glowing shape of the horse was visible for miles around and came to symbolize the imaginative spirit of the Dallas people.

J.B. McMath designed and erected Pegasus for the Texlite Sign Company. Pegasus stands thirty feet tall and thirty feet long and weighs fifteen tons. As a tribute to the horse, Dallas artists Robert Trammell and Alison Kraft organized an art exhibit in 1981, "The Flying Red Horse Show." Over forty area artists were invited to enter works inspired by the winged steed as a symbol for the city of Dallas.

Today, the flying horse is almost obscured by the taller buildings that tower around it, but to true Dallas lovers, Pegasus will always be Number One. Both Pegasus and the Magnolia Petroleum Building are now protected historical landmarks.

Corner Akard and Commerce Streets

8.
High-Profile Crime

Belle Starr (1848-1889)

The notorious "Bandit Queen" and "female Jesse James," as she was known, lived in Dallas during a portion of her exploits in a section that is now in the Pleasant Grove-Pleasant Mound area on Scyene Road. Myra Maybelle Shirley first rode through Dallas from Missouri in the 1860s with her parents, John and Eliza Shirley, and siblings. The Shirleys settled above Mesquite Creek, about a mile east of Scyene, which was later incorporated into Dallas.

The daughter of a gentleman farmer and hotelier, Maybelle or "Belle," as she was known, was educated in a private school and spent her formative years at her father's hotel in Carthage, Missouri, where she listened to tales of the Confederate guerrilla bands that roamed the area. An accomplished equestrienne, she often rode through the night carrying messages to the guerrillas. One of her brothers, "John A.M." or "Bud," as he was called, joined these forces and was later killed in an ambush. Belle vowed to avenge his death, and legend has it that she promised to marry the first man who tracked down and killed the soldier who murdered her brother.

After their move to Texas, the Shirleys continued to provide lodging for a number of their acquaintances, many of whom were war-hardened Confederate refugees. John Shirley opened another tavern and hotel that became a popular stop-off for these "outlaws." Like a number of others, the Shirleys felt the unlawful actions against Northern enterprises were justified, so they offered them food and protection when possible, and were at various times hosts to such desperadoes as William Quantrill's band, Frank and Jesse James, and the Younger brothers, to name only a few.

The legend of Belle Starr is such that it is difficult, if not impossible, to separate fact from fiction, but there is no doubt that Belle was a strong-willed, rambunctious, wild woman, who delighted in the danger and excitement offered by the Wild West. An expert marksman, she rode through the muddy streets of Dallas splendidly dressed in velvet and a plumed hat, her trusty pistols proudly displayed in their holsters, often stopping at the saloons to dance, play the piano, or just to prop her riding boots on the table and converse with the locals, using all the vulgarities common to ranchhands.

Belle's shocking behavior made her a target for the local gossips, but her acquaintances were quick to point out her generosity and kindness. She was especially good to care for sick neighbors and doted on her daughter, Pearl. Belle was

Uniquely Dallas

married at least three times and was reputed to have lovers as well. Her first husband, Jim Reed, was a known horse thief and stage robber who was killed in 1874 near Paris, Texas, by a bounty hunter. Two children, Pearl and James Edwin ("Eddie") were born of this union.

The story is told that Belle rode to McKinney, Texas, to identify and claim her husband's body. She looked at the body, turned to the bounty hunter and law officers and said, "If you want the reward for Jim Reed, you will have to kill Jim Reed. This is not my husband." She then returned home, leaving the body, which was buried in a potter's field, and a very disappointed bounty hunter.

Belle was arrested and tried in Dallas on charges of arson and horse thievery, but the charges were dropped for lack of evidence. Eventually, Belle moved to the Cherokee Nation in northeastern Oklahoma, where she married Sam Starr, son of the infamous Cherokee bandit Tom Starr.

Except for a nine-month incarceration for horse thievery, Belle spent most of the remainder of her life living at Younger's Bend, a particularly perilous bend in the South Canadian River (in Oklahoma), where the Starrs had headquartered. Here she raised her children and sheltered outlaws, commuting back and forth to Fort Smith, Arkansas, on occasion to answer various charges brought against her. Sam Starr was killed in 1886 as a result of a duel with Frank West, an old enemy of the Starrs.

Belle next married Bill July, alias James July Starr, a sort of adopted son of Tom Starr. On February 3, 1889, as she rode home from a neighbor's house, Belle Starr was shot and killed near Younger's Bend, allegedly by Edgar Watson, a disgruntled sharecropper who had had some quarrels with Belle, his landlord. Neighboring women dressed Belle in her favorite black velvet riding dress, placed her in a lace-lined pine coffin, and crossed her arms with one hand holding her favorite revolver. She was buried at Younger's Bend.

Section I

Hangmen. Sheriff Dan Harston (on left) and unidentified assistant in front of gallows in Dallas County Jail, c. 1923. (From the collections of the Texas/Dallas History and Archives Division, Dallas Public Library.)

Clyde Barrow & Bonnie Parker

During the Great Depression of the 1930s, the unpaved streets of West Dallas gave rise to two people who would go down as the twentieth century's most notorious criminal couple: Bonnie Parker and Clyde Barrow. Born in 1909 in rural Telico, Texas, to an illiterate tenant farmer, Clyde Barrow moved with his family to Dallas in 1922 at the age of 13. It was in the poor white neighborhoods of Dallas that Barrow was introduced to a life of crime. The family first lived in an area known as the "Bog," due to its proximity to the Trinity River, which often overflowed into the muddy yards. Eventually, they moved to a combination gas station and house on Eagle Ford Road (now Singleton Blvd.).

Bonnie Parker (From the collections of the Texas/Dallas History and Archives Division, Dallas Public Library.)

Section I

At one time, Clyde worked in a mirror shop on Swiss Avenue. By 1926 he had clashed with the law and was running with a group of car thieves and smalltime robbers. He was a member of the "Root Square Gang," that specialized in stealing tires, selling them, and getting drunk with the profits.

Bonnie Parker was born in Rowena, Texas, in 1910 to a bricklayer and moved to Dallas in 1914 after her father died. Emma Parker, Bonnie's mother, was forced to work outside the home and leave her three children in the care of their grandmother. The Parkers resided in Cement City, an area on the outskirts of Dallas that had become one of the toughest parts of the city and a haunt of criminals.

An intelligent but rowdy girl, Bonnie was known for her exhibitionism and a propensity for fighting. She fell in love with a fellow pupil at the Cement City School, Roy Thornton, and married him when she was sixteen, after having his name tattooed on her thigh. The marriage was short-lived, and Bonnie took a job at a cafe near the Dallas courthouse, where she was popular with the lawyers and "courthouse bums" who frequented the place. The cafe eventually closed, and Bonnie went to work for another cafe on Houston Street, where the lively 4-foot-10-inch waitress came to know many Dallas citizens, including Ted Hinton, a young postal worker who would later participate in her demise.

The economic malaise gripping the country brought with it despair and a rise in crime. Bonnie met Clyde Barrow, a small man with sharp features and prominent ears, in West Dallas in 1930 and fell in love with him almost immediately. At the time, Clyde was wanted for burglaries in Waco and Sherman. Clyde was arrested at the home of Bonnie's mother within a few days of their meeting, and Bonnie, according to Mrs. Parker, "…screamed and cried, beat her hands on the wall, begged the officers not to take him." It was the beginning of her obsession with Clyde Barrow.

Clyde was incarcerated in Dallas, awaiting trial, and was frequently visited by Bonnie. Eventually, he was taken by the Denton police to Waco, where he was held for trial. When Bonnie discovered that her lover had been taken away, she wrote, "I was so blue and mad and discouraged, I just had to cry. I had Maybelline on my eyes and it began to stream down my face.... I laid my head down on the steering wheel and sure did boohoo." She even contemplated crashing her car or hanging herself.

The miserable Bonnie headed to Denton and then to Waco, where she secured a gun and smuggled it to Clyde when she visited him in the Waco jail. Although in her letters to him Bonnie expressed a desire to lead a normal life and stated, "I want you to be a man, honey, and not a thug[,]" she was eager to help him escape.

Clyde broke out of the Waco jail but was recaptured within a week and sent to the state penitentiary in Huntsville. At the Huntsville prison, Clyde, seeking to escape work, had a fellow convict amputate two of his toes. While recovering from this mutilation, he learned that he was being given parole and left Huntsville on February 2, 1932, on crutches.

Clyde returned to the home of his sister in Dallas, bought a new outfit, and went to see the elated Bonnie. He took a job in Massachusetts but worked for only two weeks before returning to Dallas. Within the month, Clyde, accompanied by Bonnie, stole a car to use in a robbery attempt. They were pursued by the police and were forced to abandon the car and flee on foot when the car became stuck in mud. Clyde was able to escape, but Bonnie was captured and jailed in Kaufman, Texas.

A sympathetic jury released Bonnie on June 17, 1932, and within weeks, Bonnie had joined her thieving lover and his companion, Raymond Hamilton, in Wichita Falls. Clyde had not been idle during Bonnie's brief incarceration; he and Hamilton were busy attempting various robberies in and around West Dallas. In addition to the robberies,

Section I

Barrow and his accomplice were identified as the murderers of John Bucher, an elderly grocer and respected citizen of the small town of Hillsboro who was shot on April 27, 1932, while his terrified wife looked on.

Thus began the two-year escapade of Bonnie and Clyde as they successfully eluded law enforcement officers, engaged in fierce gun battles, and shocked the nation with their wild, erratic behavior. The legends that grew around the duo were mostly false; they were not skilled criminals nor advocates of the poor, as they are often depicted, but rather a sociopath and his obsessed lover, both of whom despised authority and killed with little or no provocation, sometimes laughing as they "finished off" a victim.

Bonnie and Clyde, however, did strike a chord among the American public with their rebelliousness and knack for showmanship. They let it be known that they would not be captured but intended to die together—shooting. Newspapers ran photos of the stylish couple, who made it a point to always be well-dressed, even while living in their stolen cars. The photos enthralled the nation and maddened helpless law officials. Bonnie was portrayed as the ultimate cigar-smoking moll (although she insisted she did not smoke cigars) who loved her man even to death, while Clyde was seen as a dashing fugitive fleeing from an unfair judicial system.

In truth, most of the pair's attempted robberies were bungled affairs that often ended in death for the innocent victim. The pair are credited with at least twelve murders, several kidnappings, and numerous robberies, many in the Dallas area. In one instance, they ambushed a work gang at the Eastham Prison Farm in Huntsville, killing a guard and freeing Raymond Hamilton, their former cohort, as well as other prisoners.

Clyde's driving skills and his extensive knowledge of the backroads of Texas, Oklahoma, Kansas, Missouri, and Louisiana enabled the two to elude authorities, who were becoming increasingly frustrated with the situation. Also,

Clyde insisted on stealing Ford V-8s, which easily outran most police cars. Clyde even wrote a letter to Henry Ford which was printed in papers around the country, complimenting him on his "dandy car" and noting that, "I have drove Fords exclusively when I could get away with one."

Having killed a man on Christmas Day while attempting to steal his car from his home in Temple, Clyde was lying low in a rented apartment in Joplin, Missouri, in April of 1933. In Dallas, he and Bonnie had been joined by a West Dallas teenager, W.D. Jones, who claimed to be good with cars and longed to be a member of the Barrow gang. Also with them in Missouri were Clyde's recently paroled brother, Buck, and his wife, Blanche.

In Joplin, the group spent two weeks cooking, playing cards, reading magazines, and talking. Neighbors, however, noticed an alarming number of weapons being carried into the apartment, along with license plates. This information was reported to law officers, who decided to investigate the matter. There was a shoot-out on April 13, 1933, wounding Clyde and W.D. Jones and leaving a detective and a constable dead. All members of the Barrow gang managed to escape, and Bonnie dug a ricocheted bullet out of Clyde's chest with a hairpin.

What the Joplin police found in the abandoned apartment only further enhanced the legend of the criminal couple. The Joplin paper reported that "A mass of clippings and writings in the bag indicated that the killer's wife was a lover of morbid and gangster poetry. In fact she was composing such a poem, entitled *Suicide Sal*, when the shooting started, for the unfinished poem, with pen and ink near by, was found on a writing table in the apartment."

In the poem, Bonnie told of being the "pal of a killer" and of her love for him, despite the reckless life she was leading.

A stanza from the lengthy poem reads:

> *From Irving to West Dallas viaduct*
> *Is known as the Great Divide,*

Section I

> *Where the women are kin,*
> *And the men are men,*
> *And they won't "stool" on Bonnie and Clyde.*

The final stanza was written as follows:

> *Some day they'll go down together;*
> *And they'll bury them side by side;*
> *To few it'll be grief—*
> *To the law a relief—*
> *But it's death for Bonnie and Clyde.*

Bonnie Parker

Also found in the Joplin apartment were two rolls of camera film, which, when developed, showed pictures of Bonnie and Clyde in various poses holding revolvers. The photographs were quickly picked up and run by newspapers around the country.

As the gang, with varying accomplices, crisscrossed the Southwest, they kept in close contact with their families back in Dallas through postcards, letters, and secret meetings. Bonnie was extremely attached to her mother and insisted on seeing her often. Frequent Barrow and Parker family rendezvous were set up, with the code words being that they were "having red beans for supper" (Bonnie's favorite dish). When this phrase was passed throughout the streets of Dallas, it meant that a clandestine meeting had been arranged, usually near ravines off one of the lonely country roads that surrounded Dallas. Their last family meeting supposedly took place on Preston Road north of Dallas.

Bonnie would recount the hardships they endured living on canned beans and biscuits, sleeping in the car, and being forced to bathe in cold streams. The two were fastidious about their appearance, Clyde insisting on having his suits cleaned and pressed and his shirts and underwear laundered and Bonnie often manicuring her nails. Blanche

Barrow was usually the one who carried laundry and food back and forth, since she was the only member of the Barrow gang whose picture had not been circulated in the newspapers.

Clyde's sister, Nell Cowan, recorded that when she asked Clyde how he felt after killing a man, he replied, "Like I always felt—sick inside, sick and cold and weak—and a sort of dull wishing that I'd never been born." Mrs. Parker tried desperately to get Bonnie to give herself up, but she said that she loved Clyde and would stay with him to the end.

Their nomadic existence continued, and in June 1933, as they drove across the high plains of Texas' panhandle, Clyde swerved to avoid a bridge that was closed, causing his car to crash down an embankment and explode in flames, trapping Bonnie inside. Clyde was able to free the hysterical Bonnie, who was severely burned and in such agony that she begged him to shoot her. They were assisted by two farmers who happened by and carried Bonnie to one of their homes, where she was treated by the farmer's wife.

Since they couldn't risk calling an ambulance or doctor, Bonnie was forced to endure horrible pain. The farmers' suspicions were aroused, particularly in light of the arsenal of weapons that had fallen from the car, and one of the farmers slipped away to call the sheriff. A daughter-in-law of one farmer knocked on the door and was shot in the hand by W.D. Jones. Pandemonium ensued as Bonnie staggered out of the house, followed by Clyde and W.D. A sheriff and town marshal, who were outside approaching the house, were surprised by Clyde and W.D., who handcuffed them and forced them into the car. The two law officers were taken on a ride across the Texas border to Oklahoma, where a Barrow gang reunion was planned.

The officers were released unharmed, but Bonnie was badly in need of medical treatment. They met up with Buck and Blanche Barrow and drove to Fort Smith, Arkansas, where they hid in a tourist camp. A doctor was eventually called, and he suggested that Bonnie's mother be sent for, because he feared the patient would not live much longer. Clyde drove to Dallas and brought back Bonnie's sister, Billie, who nursed her to health, although Bonnie continued to suffer from the burns for the remaining time that she lived.

The escapades of the Barrow gang continued, and in July 1933, a shoot-out with police near Platte City, Missouri, left Buck Barrow mortally wounded. Clyde managed to get away with his injured brother and the others, all of whom were wounded, save W.D. Jones. He drove to Iowa and there, in a secluded field, they set up camp. Police soon caught up with them, there was another gun battle, and Buck, who was now near death, was taken into custody along with his wife, Blanche. Again, Bonnie, Clyde, and W.D. managed to escape.

Meanwhile, as the robberies and killings continued, a new player came quietly into the picture: former Texas Ranger Frank A. Hamer, who was asked to track the killers. On February 10, 1934, Hamer began a slow, methodical process of following his prey by studying their habits, talking to those who knew them, and finally locating their hideouts and "post offices," where the killers secreted messages.

The massive manhunt came to a grisly end on the hot morning of May 23, 1934, in Gibsland, Louisiana, where Hamer and five other lawmen, including Ted Hinton, were waiting. Although Hamer had hoped to take the two alive, they immediately grabbed their weapons at the command to "Stick 'em up." The ambush left dozens of bullets in the bodies, shooting away Bonnie's hand and causing the back of Clyde's head to explode.

By dusk, the roads into and out of Arcadia, a small town nearby where the bodies had been taken, were jammed with hundreds of cars containing reporters and sightseers. The morbidly curious crowd, estimated at six thousand, became mad to secure ghoulish souvenirs from the slain couple.

Uniquely Dallas

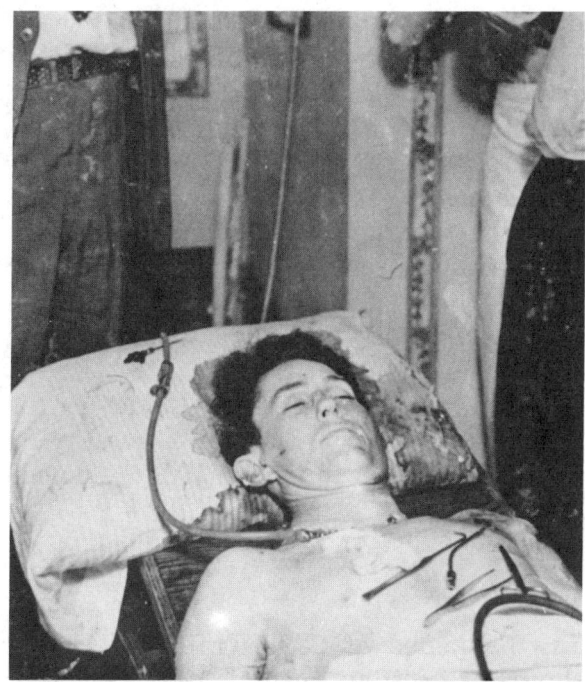

Clyde Barrow at the time of his inquest, May 23, 1934. (From the collections of the Texas/Dallas History and Archives Division, Dallas Public Library.)

Bonnie Parker's funeral, Dallas, May 26, 1934. (From the collections of the Texas/Dallas History and Archives Division, Dallas Public Library.)

Doors of the undertaking parlor where the bodies lay were torn off their hinges as the mob sought to glimpse the bodies of the duo. Bits and pieces of clothing, stained with blood and flesh, were taken from the bullet-riddled gray Ford sedan that was the couple's death car.

The bodies were claimed by family members and taken back to Dallas, where they lay in state as huge crowds filed past to view the multiple murderer and the woman who died at his side. Bonnie's body was in a silver casket, clad in a blue silk negligee. Her hair was "marcelled" (waved), and her fingernails polished.

Clyde was buried in Western Heights Cemetery in Dallas. Bonnie Parker was buried in Fishtrap Cemetery in West Dallas but later was moved to Crown Hill Memorial Park, near Love Field.

Walker Railey

A terrible thing happened at 9328 Trail Hill Drive, Dallas, in the last hours of Tuesday, April 21, 1987. However one chooses to judge the violent incident that took place on Trail Hill Drive, when it was over, two persons' lives were changed forever. One of them, Margaret "Peggy" Railey, lies in a nursing home in Tyler, Texas, in frozen horror, her condition described by doctors as "a persistent vegetative state."

The other person, Walker L. Railey, lives in California, alternately working as a counselor or funeral consultant, while attempting to return to his former ministerial profession by passing out fliers advertising that he is available to preach or teach religious classes. Such a cataclysmic downfall of the once-prominent senior pastor of the First United Methodist Church of Dallas is nothing short of Shakespearean in its tragic scope.

When Walker Railey stood before a capacity crowd of 2,000 on Easter Sunday, April 19, 1987, few of those attending the service knew that he was wearing a bullet-proof vest or that undercover police officers were guarding the minister and his wife, who sat in the audience, or that Dr. Railey's ministerial staff had begged him not to preach. Peggy Railey, the minister's wife, was an attractive, intelligent woman, considered cold and distant by some, but to others, a loyal minister's wife, a skilled musician, and a disciplined woman with a quick wit and sense of humor.

The cause of the apprehension on that Easter Sunday was a series of threatening letters received by Walker Railey, one of which had warned, "On Easter Christ arose from the dead. And on this day you are going down." Other letters accused him of being a "nigger lover" and stated that, "You have a beautiful home, a beautiful wife and two beautiful children—but not for long." When the service ended without incident, there was great relief and rejoicing in the minister's office. Maybe things would finally return to normal around the church.

On Tuesday evening following Easter Sunday, Peggy Railey was at home with her small children, five-year-old Ryan and Megan, age two. Walker came home around 6:00 p.m. and, according to his account, shared a glass of wine with Peggy and left around 6:30, saying he wasn't hungry and had to do research at the SMU library that evening.

At least two other people spoke with Peggy Tuesday night: Adeline Oakley, a family friend, who was concerned for the Railey family safety in light of the threatening letters, and Peggy's mother, Billie Jo Nicolai. Mrs. Nicolai likewise expressed concern that Walker had left his wife and children alone in the house, but Peggy assured her that the security system had recently been checked, and she and the children were perfectly safe.

Peggy and her mother discussed the threatening letters, Peggy's recent visit to her parents' home in Tyler, and various family concerns. At 9:27 p.m., Billie Jo told her daughter she loved her and hung up the phone.

On Wednesday, April 22, at 12:43 a.m., a 911 dispatcher answered the following call.

"Dallas Emergency—"
"This is Walker Railey. I'm at 9328 Trail Hill Drive..."
"What is the problem, sir?"
"I've just come into the house, and my wife is in the ki—...garage—and...and somebody has done something to her. Send the paramedics and send the police—please, please..."
"Stay on the line with me. What street crosses Trail Hill on the corner?" the dispatcher asked.
"Uh, it's uh...uh; it's between Audelia and, uh, White Rock Trail."
"Is it a house or an apartment?"
"It's a house. It's about four blocks north of Lake Highlands High School."
"Okay. What's your name, sir?"
"Walker Railey. R-A-I-L-E-Y."
"Okay. We'll get them out there."
"Please hurry. Please."

Railey next called Diane Yarrington, whose husband John was the church choir director, and asked them to come over right away. He then went next door and awakened a neighbor, Charles Massoud.

Paramedics arriving less than five minutes later found Peggy Railey lying on the floor of the garage, in front of her car, in a decerebrate position, which indicates a rigidity characteristic of brain stem damage. It appeared that she had been hanged or possibly strangled; her face and neck were a swollen blue mass, blood vessels were broken in her cheek, and deep red marks, indicative of a ligature, were evident around her throat.

Peggy Railey was not dead, however. Saliva foamed out of her mouth as she convulsed and struggled for air. No signs of a struggle were immediately evident; the only obvious scratches on the victim were her bleeding elbows that had been scraped when instinctive gasping caused her to rise and fall on the concrete floor.

Peggy Railey's hair was neatly combed, and she was wearing eyeglasses. Charles Massoud, the paramedics, and the police, who also arrived, all noted the peculiar behavior of Railey, who smelled of alcohol and paced back and forth in the living room, where his traumatized children sat. They noted that he had not covered his wife, nor did he touch her. When she was taken away in the ambulance, he voluntarily stayed behind, talking with the police for about an hour.

From the beginning, the police suspected Dr. Railey had tried to strangle his wife. The liquor on his breath, his strange behavior, and the fact that the spouse is usually the first suspect in domestic violence, caused the police to question Railey extensively that night.

In the meantime, news of Peggy's condition spread like wildfire throughout the congregation. By morning, church members, friends, and Peggy's parents, Bill and Billie Jo Nicolai, had gathered in the hospital to await word of her condition and offer what comfort they could to the distraught minister.

Dallas citizens, as they learned of the attack, were shocked and outraged. Certainly, in spite of the racial strife present in the city, it seemed implausible to think that even a white supremist group would attack a minister's wife. Three thousand people attended an interfaith prayer service for Peggy Railey, held in Thanksgiving Square in downtown Dallas.

The police, meanwhile, had uncovered evidence of an extramarital affair Dr. Railey was having with a Dallas psychologist, Dr. Lucy Papillon. Papillon, the twice-divorced daughter of a Methodist bishop, was an attractive woman in her mid-forties, who had formerly lived in California. Blonde and always well-dressed, she was described as glamorous and flamboyant. After a "spiritual awakening" following her second divorce and the death of her father, Bishop Robert E. Goodrich Jr., Lucy had changed her last name to "Papillon," which means "butterfly" in French. The reason given for this name change was that she had undergone a metamorphosis from a lowly caterpillar into a free, beautiful butterfly.

Other facts were surfacing as well. A family friend and the Railey children's pediatrician, Dr. George Monroe, examined Ryan and Megan at the Yarringtons' house on the morning following the attack and noticed bruises on five-year-old Ryan's neck, throat, and behind his ear. Apparently, no one had seen marks on the child the night before, possibly because bruises are more noticeable later in time.

Doctor Monroe concluded from the marks that the child had probably been choked into unconsciousness. Police believed Ryan witnessed the attack on his mother, and when questioned alternately identified the attacker as "Jim," "Jim's daddy," and "Daddy."

Using mobile phone records, police determined that Railey was not where he said he was on the night of the attack on Mrs. Railey. Although he had made appearances at SMU's Fondren and Bridwell libraries, Railey had also been at the home of Lucy Papillon.

On Saturday, May 2, 1987, security officers at a motel found Walker Railey unconscious in his suite. An empty bottle of prescription drugs and a four-page handwritten letter were nearby. In the letter, Railey confessed to having a "demon inside my soul" which "tries to lead me down paths I do not want to follow."

Although Railey did not admit to anything specifically, his suicide letter was a confession of a desperate man. Railey supporters saw the letters as an admission of his adulterous affair, while others saw it as a confession that he indeed attempted to murder his wife. After a brief hospital stay, Railey was admitted to Timberlawn, a psychiatric hospital, where he remained several weeks.

On July 29, Railey was called before a Dallas grand jury to answer questions about his whereabouts on April 21, 1987. Acting on the advice of his attorney, Doug Mulder, he took the Fifth Amendment forty-three times. By this time,

Mrs. Railey, whose condition remained unchanged, had been transferred to a nursing home in nearby Tyler, Texas, where her parents lived.

Dallas police continued to be frustrated by Railey's unwillingness to cooperate with them, although he freely gave interviews to the press. Assistant District Attorney Norman Kinne eventually concluded there was not enough evidence to bring the case to trial. Although many church members and friends continued to support Railey, who had resigned from his ministerial duties, a growing number of Dallas citizens were outraged that he had not been arrested.

In November of 1987, Railey moved to San Francisco, accompanied by Lucy Papillon, leaving his two children in the care of John and Diane Yarrington. The Nicolais, Mrs. Railey's parents, filed a civil suit against their son-in-law in an attempt to see that their daughter would continue to receive the care she needed.

During the civil proceeding, a videotape was shown of a young, talented Peggy Railey playing the harpsichord. It was made only a few weeks before the attack. The videotape then showed the horribly disfigured woman Peggy Railey now was, her body contorted, her eyes moving without seeing, the occasional inhuman howls that came from her. Several spectators were so disturbed by the sight that they left the courtroom. Railey did not appear, although Lucy Papillon testified about their relationship. The court found in favor of the Nicolais and awarded them an $18 million judgment.

As the months became years, the *Dallas Morning News* from time to time published articles about the unsolved attack, often accompanied by a photograph of Mrs. Railey in the Tyler nursing home and an interview with her parents, who continued to visit and care for her daily.

On March 11, 1988, ABC featured the Railey story on its news program, "20/20," in a segment titled, "A Fall From Grace." John and Diane Yarrington, who had moved to Little Rock, Arkansas, and been awarded custody of the

Railey children, were shown celebrating Christmas with Dr. Railey in their home. Assistant District Attorney Norman Kinne was interviewed, along with others connected to the mysterious case.

In 1992, five years after the crime, Norman Kinne was removed from the case, and it was turned over to Assistant Prosecuting District Attorney Cecil Emerson. In August 1992 Walker Railey was arrested in Los Angeles, where he was employed by the Emmanuel Presbyterian Church, extradited to Dallas, and indicted for attempted murder on the basis of "new evidence" gathered by the prosecutors. Doug Mulder, Railey's attorney, was granted his request for a change of venue, and the proceeding was moved to San Antonio.

The four-week trial took place during the latter part of March and early April 1993 and was broadcast on "Court TV." Cecil Emerson and his team of prosecutors used mobile phone records to prove Railey was not where he said he was on the night of April 21, 1987. The phone records, which were the "new evidence," indicated Railey's whereabouts by the cellular signal sent, and prosecutors claimed this technology had only recently become available. Prosecutors also brought in FBI experts who testified that the threatening letters had been typed on a church typewriter and that saliva samples taken from Railey matched saliva on the envelopes of the letters.

Railey's attorneys attempted to prove that a dark-skinned man seen in the neighborhood that night had committed the crime, and that Railey's lies about his whereabouts the night of the attack were made to cover up his extramarital affair. They pointed out that the evidence was entirely circumstantial and could easily be misinterpreted. Lucy Papillon testified that she was with Railey early that evening, but that he left her house and went to the SMU libraries. Various people who noticed Railey in the two libraries gave conflicting and confusing accounts of his dress and the time span during which they saw him.

Finally, Walker Railey himself took the stand and, facing the jury, denied having anything to do with the attack on his wife. In his highly emotional testimony, Railey confessed to an affair with Lucy Papillon and stated that he was overwhelmed with shame that he had not protected his family that night and was instead with his mistress. The room was still as the former minister read his suicide note aloud, pausing to wipe away tears. During jury deliberations, it was reported that Railey and others sat around and speculated which actors might play him and others in a movie, assuming one would be made of this true-life drama. Three days after beginning deliberations, jurors found Railey not guilty of the attack on his wife.

Following his acquittal, Railey filed for divorce and returned to California. Mrs. Railey remains in the nursing home, where she is cared for by the staff and her elderly parents, who continue to visit her daily.

9.
Preston Road—*Cattle Trail Boulevard*

Originally a Shawnee Indian trail, what is known today as Preston Road (State Highway 289) was the route taken by John Neely Bryan in 1841 on his first excursion to the bluff at the Trinity River. The founder of Dallas had stopped for a while at Preston Bend on the Red River, at a trading post known as "Coffee's Trading Station."

It was while clerking at Coffee's Trading Station, from listening to the Indians and other travelers, that Bryan learned about the Three Forks area of the Trinity. In November of 1841, he headed south on the old Indian trail, accompanied by an Indian friend, Ned, a dog, Tubby, and a horse named Neshoba (Gray Wolf). Bryan followed the trail until he reached the bluff of the Trinity, where he staked his

Section I

claim and decided to start a town. The north-south route of Preston Road grew in status as it became a major cattle trail.

Later in the history of Dallas, Preston Road became known as the spine of the "Golden Corridor," the area beginning in prestigious Highland Park and reaching through North Dallas, Richardson, and Plano. The old Indian trail played a major role in the rapid growth of Plano, a town just north of Dallas, that was once a farming community and is now home to such major corporations as EDS, J.C. Penney, and Frito-Lay. The southern section of Preston Road in Highland Park is still marked by the expensive homes and country clubs that line the route once taken by Indians and cattle drivers. Coffee's Trading Station is now at the bottom of Lake Texoma.

Sec. II:13—Pioneer Plaza
Sec. III:2—John Neely Bryan

10.
Texas Instruments—*Computer Chips, Doughnuts, and Jack Kilby*

The next time you rush into a supermarket to buy a calculator for school, turn on your personal computer, await the results of a CAT-scan, fax a document, or talk on a cellular phone, take a minute to remember a discouraged young scientist who was working alone in a laboratory one hot Texas summer day.

His name was Jack S. Kilby, a recently hired Texas Instruments engineer, who was working even though the plant had closed for its annual two-week vacation. As a new employee, Kilby had not yet accrued any vacation time.

Jack Kilby completed work on an IF amplifier prototype, as well as a production cost analysis, to be used in the Micro-Module program. He was dismayed because it was obvious the design would not be cost-effective unless the entire product concept were changed.

At the time, the electronics industry was grappling with a serious problem. Although transistors had made it possible to design devices of increasing complexity, the difficulty of interconnecting large numbers of transistors and other discrete components had become extremely frustrating. Wiring thousands of units almost entirely by hand was not only costly and time-consuming, but inefficient and unreliable as well.

Kilby, in his solitude, sketched a design for a multivibrator that formed a complete semiconductor. This early success led to the first integrated circuit on germanium wafers and the creation of what is known today as a "microchip." The year was 1958, and Jack Kilby had just solved the "tyranny of numbers" and ushered in the computer age.

It was 1967 before Texas Instruments invented its first electronic handheld calculator using integrated circuits, designed by engineers Kilby, Jerry D. Merryman, and James H. Van Tassel. Although Texas Instruments had become an international corporation in the late fifties, TI's beginnings had nothing to do with semiconductors, but rather with the search for oil.

Started in 1930 as "Geophysical Service," the company specialized in the reflection seismograph method of exploration, used primarily in the petroleum industry. Its founders were J. Clarence ("Doc") Karcher and Eugene McDermott.

In 1939 the name was changed to Coronado Corporation, with GSI as its subsidiary, and in 1941 GSI was purchased by Cecil Green, Erik Jonsson (who later served as mayor of Dallas), McDermott, and H.B. Peacock. GSI branched into areas of national defense with the invention of submarine detection devices, airborne radar systems, and other increasingly sophisticated electronic equipment.

In 1950 total revenues were $7.6 million; employees 1,128. The company's name was changed to Texas Instruments Incorporated in 1951. Thanks to the genius of Kilby and other innovators, TI mushroomed in the next four decades and was for many years Dallas' largest employer. Until the late sixties, TI, a close-knit company, was still small enough to do such things as provide its employees with free doughnuts and coffee.

At one time the company even had the distinction of owning and operating the largest doughnut machine in Texas. The machinery was necessary to keep up with employee demand for free doughnuts. At each morning and afternoon break, cafeteria workers rolled out huge carts holding urns of coffee and trays of doughnuts—some glazed and some cake.

With the continued growth of semiconductor manufacturing, the advent of terrain-following radar (1958), and TI's pivotal role in national defense and space exploration, the company's growth was so rapid that new plants were opening all over the world. Eventually, TI was forced to change a few company policies, among them the free doughnuts provided to employees.

It was a sad day at Texas Instruments in late 1968, when the company announced it would cease giving away doughnuts. Two TI employees, Bob Lockett and Jim Stocks, decided to save their last free doughnuts—both of the cake variety. In a company report dated October 1988, the two men are pictured with their twenty-year-old doughnuts— Bob's prize encased in acrylic plastic and Jim's final freebie in a box that he reports had become badly discolored from the grease.

Today, Texas Instruments continues to produce many innovative products and remains a leader in the high-tech field of electronics, with approximately 60,000 employees in over thirty countries and computer systems that bounce information around the world via satellite. The company has manufactured over 24 billion chips, facilitating communication worldwide, strengthening national defense, revitalizing manufacturing, and enabling medical professionals to image heart valves and unborn babies.

But what lies ahead? Mark Shepherd Jr., retired chairman of TI, sees such developments as computers activated by voice command, the merging of publishing and communication companies into a single industry, and home computers that not only regulate temperature, but monitor and order household supplies. Predictions are that the design complexity of a single chip will soon be similar to that of a street map of the entire North American continent.

Today, Jack Kilby works as a consultant from his Dallas office, and a historical marker at the TI plant on Central Expressway marks the site of his revolutionary discovery.

11.
West End Historic District—*Frogs, People, and Partying*

Tourists visiting Dallas inevitably end up in West End, a historic part of Dallas that was a section of the original city platted in 1846. The boundaries of the 20-block district are Woodall Rogers Freeway, Commerce Street, Lamar, and the MKT Railroad tracks. In the early part of the 1900s, the West End was a busy collection of warehouses for railroad lines that crossed here. This area, low river bottom land, was also part of "Frogtown," one of the freedman's towns that sprung up after slave emancipation. It was so named because of the numerous frogs that gathered there at night to croak at the Dallas lights.

Today, the warehouses have been renovated and serve as restaurants, shops, pubs, and nightclubs. You will find red brick streets, vintage street lamps, turn-of-the-century architecture, and horse-drawn carriages in the West End. The West End Marketplace contains 80 specialty shops and a dozen eateries, as well as Dallas Alley, a hotspot for nightlife, where you can access seven nightclubs for one cover charge.

The West End is also famous for the notorious University of Texas-Oklahoma University football feuding and brawling that goes on every year on the second weekend in October. Known as the "Texas-OU" game, it is played on Saturday at the Cotton Bowl Stadium, a neutral site halfway between Norman, Oklahoma, and Austin, Texas, where the two schools are located. Traditionally, Commerce Street comes alive on Friday night with partying Texas Longhorn and Oklahoma Sooner fans, who hold a pregame rally and confrontation. On Saturday night, after the game, the partying is done mostly by the winner.

In years past, UT fans, while chugging beer and screaming, tossed chairs and couches from the windows of the Adolphus Hotel. There was plenty of beer, fans, and shouts of "Hook 'em Horns!" In the sixties, police would make as many as seven hundred arrests during the weekend, mostly from fistfights and drunkenness.

Unfortunately, the police report that fights now tend to be settled with knives and guns, rather than duking it out, so they have had to clamp down on things. In 1992 a Carrollton man was shot to death and several others were shot, stabbed, and assaulted. The past few Texas-OU celebrations have been very calm and controlled by hundreds of police officers, but due to congestion and inebriated fans, most Dallasites know to avoid the West End during the second weekend in October.

1801 N. Lamar St.; Dallas 75201
214-720-7107

Uniquely Dallas

Everything is bigger and better in the Big D, especially the good times. An unlimited variety of dining, nightlife, and entertainment possibilities make it easy to have a hot time in the old town any night. (Courtesy of the Dallas Convention & Visitors Bureau.)

12.
The Neiman Marcus Mystique

Even though the locals like to refer to it as "Needless Markup," this world-famous store has long been a Dallas tradition. Founded in 1907 by Herbert Marcus Sr., his sister Carrie Marcus Neiman, and her husband, A.L. Neiman, the store was touted as an "exclusive shopping place for fashionable women."

Located downtown at the corner of Elm and Murphy, the first Neiman Marcus was begun with $25,000 revenue from a sales promotion business the trio had in Atlanta. The

47

buyers had offered the Marcus family either $25,000 cash or the Missouri franchise for a new bottled drink: Coca-Cola. It became a family joke that Neiman Marcus was founded on poor business judgment.

The small specialty store soon became known for its attention to customers and its innovative sales techniques. In 1909 a Christmas card inviting clients to come into the store was mailed out, and by 1915 the "card" had expanded into a six-page booklet, featuring Christmas gift suggestions such as perfumes, fur coats, handbags, and lingerie.

The store's remarkable rise to international acclaim is credited to the aggressive marketing ideas of Stanley Marcus, son of Herbert Marcus. In the thirties, when it started purchasing ads in *Vogue*, Neiman Marcus became the first store outside of New York to advertise on a national scale.

In 1938 the marketing genius came up with the idea of the Neiman Marcus Award of Distinguished Service in the Field of Fashion. Suddenly, the world's top designers, such as Christian Dior and Coco Chanel, were traveling to *Texas*, of all places, to claim fashion awards. Neiman Marcus' reputation was growing, and the fashion world started to pay attention to this arrogant little store in a place called "Dallas."

Marcus' insistence on customer satisfaction became legendary as well. The story is told of a Kansas woman who ordered twenty $5 gift-wrapped items to be used as dinner party favors. The gifts arrived—unwrapped—and the woman called the store.

"It was our mistake," Stanley Marcus admits. "So we chartered a plane and flew someone from giftwrap to the woman's home. What started out as a $100 purchase cost the store several hundred dollars."

On another occasion a wealthy Texas oilman came into the store stating that he never spent more than $1 for Christmas gifts. After some searching, Stanley Marcus produced a jar of imported jam for $1. The oilman continued to call for his one-dollar Christmas gifts each year, and Marcus continued to produce them. Eventually, the customer decided to purchase a $30,000 sable coat as a gift to his wife.

A devastating fire during the 1960s destroyed much of the downtown store. Always looking out for his customers, Stanley Marcus, after seeing that the firemen were fed, began making arrangements to fly designers in from New York to help replace wedding gowns destroyed in the fire.

Perhaps Neiman Marcus is best known for its Christmas Book, which gained the store instant notoriety in the press with its outrageous His and Hers gifts, a feature that began in 1960. Over the years, offerings have included His and Hers robots, Beechcraft airplanes, Chinese junks, camels, and mummy cases. Believe it or not, orders were received and filled for many of these items.

Today, Neiman Marcus continues its trend-setting reputation with 27 stores in 24 cities, as well as an expanding mail-order operation. It is currently owned and operated by the Neiman Marcus Group, Inc., a publicly owned specialty retailer headquartered in Chestnut Hill, Massachusetts.

Walk into a Neiman Marcus store today, and you will likely find not only the latest fashions and unique gifts, but a store that resembles a fine home, complete with skylights, wood flooring, and dressing rooms where shoppers can try on clothes in natural light and rest on designer furniture while sipping beverages provided by the attentive staff.

Of course, Neiman's larger-than-average sales staff is creative and helpful as ever, anxious to assist every client. Although the store would never admit to *following* trends, there is a new social consciousness that is reflected in the growing number of community benefits Neiman Marcus sponsors and an emphasis on such things as recycled shopping bags.

Alas, Neiman's (as the locals also call it) is not for the frugal-minded. If the idea of His and Her dirigibles doesn't appeal to you, then you might be better off shopping at one of the mainstream department stores. In fact, the truly thrifty shopper might risk a coronary merely by browsing at NM. However, if you are positively discriminating, willing to pay a little more for pampering and quality (okay, maybe a lot more), and you want a gift that's really special, then Neiman Marcus is the place to go.

Dallas Locations:
Downtown—214-741-6911
Northpark Mall—214-363-8311
Prestonwood Mall—214-233-1100

13.
Dickey's Barbecue—*The Real Thing*

You aren't likely to find Dickey's Barbecue listed in any of the fancy visitor guides or tourist books, and you probably won't see ads for Dickey's on Dallas billboards. That's because T.D. Dickey, his brother Roland, and T.D.'s son, T.D. Dickey III, don't have time to think about advertising. They are too busy working with Texas ranchers and restaurant managers to be sure the 100,000 pounds of beef they use each month are smoked 18-20 hours over East Texas hickory wood—a process that goes on every night at each Dickey's Barbecue—and that the taste is moist and juicy enough to please their customers.

In 1941 Travis D. Dickey, Sr. bought a beer joint next to the Houston & Texas Central railroad tracks (now Central Expressway and Knox-Henderson). One of the first things he did was hire a black friend he knew in East Texas to come over for a week or so and show him how to cook meat. And that's exactly what T.D. Dickey started doing—cooking meat, the finest grade of beef, smoked for hours to succulent perfection and topped with his secret sauce.

T.D. and his wife, Ollie, kept the restaurant by the railroad tracks running for many years, and people kept coming back to taste the barbecue they cooked. An artist's drawing of the original Dickey's Barbecue shows a small building under a large tree. In front of the building is a bin that was used to collect pots, pans, and scrap metal for making ammunition during World War II. The original restaurant was eventually torn down and a new one built in 1951, when the old railroad tracks were taken up and Central Expressway was constructed in their place.

In 1967 Mr. Dickey died, and Ollie carried on the family barbecue tradition. Her sons, T.D., Jr. and Roland, were involved in other business pursuits, but they wanted to help their mother out and started looking after the business for her. A second restaurant was opened in 1968, and the two boys soon found that the taste of brisket was in their blood.

As the family business grew, dishes such as homemade (from scratch) pies, fruit cobblers, potato salad, cole slaw, and baked beans were added to the menu. When the public became more health-conscious, Dickey's began offering fruit salad, low-fat vegetables, and leaner cuts of meat. Eventually, there were 11 Dickey's barbecue pits in the metroplex, as far away as Plano, Garland, and Grand Prairie, employing a total of 135 people. Many of T.D.'s super-friendly employees started with Dickey's over twenty years ago.

Dickey's most famous patron is H. Ross Perot, who frequents the Forest Lane location so much that, during the 1992 presidential campaign, he received mail and packages there. Reporters and journalists from all over the country got to sample Dallas' best while waiting for Perot during that hotly contested, colorful summer race. (WARNING: HRP does *not* want to be disturbed while he dines at Dickey's. Even though you're his biggest fan, let the man eat his barbecue in peace. Otherwise, T.D. may have to set up shop at the Perot estate, because Ross can't go long without his Dickey's barbecue.)

After celebrating 50 years with the same family, Dickey's knows how to barbecue. Dining at Dickey's is an authentic Dallas experience. As high-profile chain restaurants sprout around them, the Dickey family and their employees have proven that good old-fashioned cooking and just-folks friendliness work magic every time.

Dallas Locations:
14885 Inwood Road
7770 Forest Lane
14999 Preston Road
2445 Northwest Highway
Central Expwy. at Knox-Henderson

14.
Dallas' Religious Roots—*Gamblers, Hogs, and Gun-Totin' Preachers*

Not many major American cities consider a pastor's resignation over at First Baptist Church a newsworthy event, but when Dr. Joel Gregory resigned on September 30, 1992, it not only made the front page of the *Dallas Morning News*, it headlined local television newscasts as well. Churches, religion, and religious leaders often make the news in Dallas, due to the city's long history of religious traditions. From the time Dallas was first settled by hard-working, God-fearing pioneers, the area has been known for religion and religious people. It is often said that Dallas is located in "the buckle" of the "Bible belt," a term that refers to the stretch of Southern states populated by fundamentalist Christians.

John Billingsley, one of the first settlers of Dallas, came to the area with his brother in November 1842, and there he found John Neely Bryan and three or four others living in a solitary log cabin on the banks of the Trinity River. Billingsley kept a colorful journal about his life in the struggling settlement. Here he describes early religious gatherings:

> When preachers first came to the border line of Texas we had no houses for them to preach in, only the houses we lived in. They were gladly received... and went from house to house preaching.... When we wanted camp meetings or protracted meetings we would go to some nice grove of trees and if the shade was not sufficient a brush arbor was built, grounds cleared off, seats prepared, and if it was to be a camp meeting camp-houses were built forming a square around the arbor and when the time came for the meeting all hands moved to the grounds with their provisions.... People sometimes come fifty or sixty miles on horseback and in wagons.... All were welcome.... All denominations, preachers, and people would come together to worship.

The first sermon preached in the Three Forks area was by Thomas Brown, an itinerant Methodist minister, who addressed a small group at the home of William Cochran at Farmers Branch in March of 1844. The text used was Romans 1:16. The group, consisting of the Isaac B. Webb, M.F. Fortner, and Cochran families organized the first church in the county, a Methodist church. In the spring of 1846, they built the first church building, a log house 18 x 18 feet, near the Webb residence. The church was named Webb's Chapel and the congregation is still in existence today, although it is housed in a larger building.

The first church service in the village of Dallas is credited to Elder Amon McCommas, who came to Texas from Kentucky and preached in 1845 for a group that organized in 1852 as the Christian Church. This congregation grew rapidly and divided in 1873 into the Pearl and Main Church of Christ and the Central Christian Church.

Even before the early settlers organized churches, they practiced a form of religion described by this excerpt from John Billingsley's journal:

> We were a self-ruling, self-supporting, and self-protecting band.... We had no law but the law given to Moses on Mt. Sinai.... All was peace and quiet everywhere.... We knew everybody in twenty miles and called them neighbors.... A band of brothers and neighbors all along the border line and whenever one cried for help, his cry was heard and responded to, and if a stranger came among us, he was fed, lodged, if sick was nursed without pay.... We needed no law or officers of law to keep the peace.... Our motto was peace, friendship with everybody, and everybody was our friend.

Religious camp meetings, which often lasted two or three weeks, were held in the summer, and were as much social gatherings as church revivals. People came from all over the county, in wagons and on horseback, bringing with them bedclothes, preserves to give to neighbors, and food to cook over the campfires. Preaching was usually in the open or in specially constructed brush arbors (as described above) at midday and by torchlight at night. Community singing, outdoor meals, and friendly gossip made these fellowships very popular and well attended.

Some of the frontier preachers were quite colorful characters, as the one described below by Billingsley:

> The preacher's name was Welch and had but one eye but that was his shooting eye and it was a good one. He was dressed in buckskin and brought his gun with him. We all carried our guns everywhere we went Sunday and every other day, for we never knew when we would need them.

The little band of settlers on the banks of the Trinity faced many hardships, such as crop failure, illness, harsh weather, and fear of Indian attacks. Death was such a common occurrence in their lives that they found much comfort in their belief of an afterlife.

As Dallas grew into a bustling frontier town, it was inevitable that saloons and gambling would come to town, and it wasn't long before Dallas was known far and wide for the drinking, fighting, and gambling that went on there. A hotel proprietor's daughter, Mrs. Kate M. Bryan, wrote:

> Although Dallas was a wild frontier town in the sixties and early seventies, it was in many ways a more moral town than the present great city. There were saloons in plenty, and gambling houses, too, but they felt no need to hide their character.... At all events, they were neither thugs, thieves, nor despoilers of women and children, and lived not by trickery but by matching their skill against that of their opponents.

Even the gamblers adhered to certain moral codes, as Mrs. Bryan relates in the following incident that occurred in 1860. She was practicing her piano in the hotel parlor when a delegation of gamblers came in and asked her to "go for the parson." When the Rev. Silas D. Davenport, a missionary recently arrived from New York, appeared, the gamblers presented the surprised minister with a bag of gold and silver coins, and said:

> Parson, we heard that you was figgerin' on puttin' up a meetin'-house, and we figgered too that you was having an uphill pull, and as you've treated us like we was more or less human we thought we'd help you out a little, so we just passed the bag around among the boys and packed it to you without delay, and we want you to take it and buy lumber and start your meetin'-house.

Section I

The Rev. Davenport used the money to begin construction of the first Episcopal church in Dallas, at the corner of Elm and Lamar streets, one block from the courthouse square. The first Catholic priest came to Dallas in 1859 and held mass in the home of Maxime Guillot. A Catholic parish was organized in 1872.

The first Jewish congregation in Dallas was Emanu-El, organized July 1, 1872, from a Hebrew Benevolent Association. The congregation was chartered as a Reformed Jewish congregation in 1874, and Rabbi A. Suhler of Akron, Ohio, was the first permanent rabbi. The group built a synagogue in 1876 at Commerce and Field streets, and later conducted a school. An Orthodox Jewish congregation, Shearith Israel, was organized in 1884 by J. Emin and M. Wasserman.

According to historical records, early church leaders had to contend with such obstacles as hogs wandering into the services, members spewing tobacco juice on the floor and walls, and "black, waxy, and sticky" Dallas mud that in rainy weather would "pull your shoes off." There were many small frame church buildings in Dallas, among them Baptist, Methodist, Christian, Church of Christ, Presbyterian, Episcopal, and Catholic. One historian described the church buildings as "humble frame buildings, wanting in paint, in comfort, and having but one thing in abundance—religion."

Religion was an integral part of life among Negro residents as well. In the days of slavery, most slaves adopted the Christian religion, which they clung to in the hope of freedom or at least an afterlife. Many old spiritual folk songs, such as "Go Down, Moses," express the slaves' burning desire to be free. The black population, however, brought with them the superstitious beliefs of Africa, and many continued to practice black magic and voodoo (*see Sec. I:3—Deep Ellum*).

In 1846 there were 45 slaves in Dallas County, and by 1860 census records show 8,655 people in the county, 1,074 of whom were slaves. The town of Dallas had an estimated population of 2,000 in 1860. Although the number of slave-holders was small compared to the rest of the Southern states, slavery—as elsewhere in the country—became a heated topic and was the subject of many religious debates.

A number of those advocating abolition were Northern ministers who traveled to Dallas and other areas to preach against slavery. In fact, the devastating city fire of July 8, 1860, was blamed on three slaves who were allegedly stirred to action by two ministers from Iowa. The slaves were hung and the ministers flogged and ordered to leave town (*see Sec. IV:3—The Day Dallas Burned*).

After the Civil War and emancipation, many of the freed slaves remained with their former masters and worked for wages, and some began sharecropping in the vicinity, while others moved to one of the "Freedman's Towns" which sprang up in the late 1800s (*see Sec. IV:4—Freedman's Towns*). Religion continued to be a vital link between the newly freed slaves. One of the first schools for black children was organized in 1878 by the Colored Methodist Episcopal Church (C.M.E.), in a church building at the corner of Boll and Juliette (now Munger) streets. Another early school for black children was begun by Rev. Harris Swann in the church building at the corner of Juliette (Munger) and Burford (Routh) streets.

The church played a significant role in black communities, not only as a refuge from their difficult lives, but also as a social, cultural, and political institution. The 1879 city directory for Dallas listed four "colored churches:" St. Paul Methodist, Free Mission Baptist, Free Will Baptist, and Evening Chapel Church (C.M.E.).

Although first- and second-generation freedmen had little assistance from government sources, they were aided by Christian and Hebrew benevolent groups during this time. The churches, both black and white, were primarily responsible for beginning schools and colleges for the black community. Wiley College, the first black college in Texas, was established in Marshall in 1873 by the Freedmen's Aid Society.

Black preachers were powerful figures, not only in their own communities, but among politicians and city leaders, who often consulted them to get the opinions of the black community. But in the black churches, members still sang, "...my face is black, my heart is strong, my past is a bloody story. Oppression's reign won't be long, mine eyes have seen the glory." Some of the better known preachers were Rev. P. D. Saddler, Rev. T. M. (Bless my Bones) Chambers, Bishop E. M. Page, and Rev. Maynard Jackson, whose son later served as mayor of Atlanta.

In March of 1956 Dr. W. A. Criswell of First Baptist Church of Dallas, preached a fiery sermon denouncing integration at the Annual Statewide Baptist Conference on Evangelism in South Carolina. Dr. Criswell, a long-time Dallas leader and founder of Criswell College, asserted that "integration of the races in the church is a thing of idiocrasy and foolishness." His speech was only the beginning of what was to be a long and arduous battle over civil rights. Although the transition from a totally segregated society to an integrated one was fraught with frustration and limited success, Dallas was spared the extreme violence, looting, and riots that were prevalent during the sixties, thanks to a powerful black and white leadership.

Dallas today has more churches per capita than any other city in America. Fundamentalist Christian groups and mainstream Protestant churches are very strong in Dallas, and there are a growing number of "Bible churches" that for the most part are fundamentalist in philosophy. Going to church is considered not only the proper thing to do in Dallas; it's also good business. If you want to make the right connections, find a job or a date, your best bet is to start attending an adult Sunday School class, where you'll likely encounter friendly, well-educated, bright men and women, who today continue the traditions and beliefs passed down to them from their frontier ancestors.

Uniquely Dallas

A.V. Hester watches Pleasant Mound Methodist Church built in 1873 being torn down. The church stood as a county landmark for 80 years. c. 5-22-53. (From the collections of the Texas/Dallas History and Archives Division, Dallas Public Library.)

Built in 1891 at the corner of Ninth and Patton streets, this Oak Cliff Presbyterian Church building stood until 1923. Dr. A.P. Smith led the meeting on Jan. 26, 1880, that organized the church. (From the collections of the Texas/Dallas History and Archives Division, Dallas Public Library.)

Section I

15.
Wilson Historic District

Just three blocks east of Baylor Medical Center is Swiss Avenue, a historic street that once linked the farm of Jacob Nussbaumer to the town of Dallas. Originally called "Butcher Pen Road," Nussbaumer changed the name to "Swiss Avenue" in honor of his numerous Swiss friends and relatives who purchased homesites in the vicinity.

The Wilson Block covers houses in the 2800 through 3000 block of Swiss Avenue. The district consists of a group of original dwellings that are owned and operated by the Meadows Foundation, which makes the homes available for nonprofit agencies.

Frederick P. Wilson (1863-1923) was an English Canadian who moved to Dallas in 1880 to join his brother John. By 1900 John Wilson had become one of Dallas' wealthiest citizens through real estate, manufacturing, and banking investments. Frederick managed some of his brother's businesses, and in 1894 he married Henrietta Frichot, whose parents and uncle, Jacob Nussbaumer, had moved to the area from Europe in the 1850s as part of the failed La Reunion colony (*see Sec. IV:1*).

Jacob and Dorothea Boll Nussbaumer (sister of Henrietta's mother) sold part of a vacant tract of land on their farm to their niece, Henrietta Frichot Wilson. Frederick Wilson began building homes on the block, which he planned to rent or sell.

He first built a home for his family, at the corner of Swiss and Oak, which was a Queen Anne style house completed in 1899. Members of the Wilson family occupied this home for over 75 years until it was sold in 1977. Wilson also built several other houses similar to his own on the block.

The Queen Anne style was fashionable in America from 1880 to 1910 and featured front porches that wrap around one side of the house. Queen Anne houses are asymmetrical and have patterned wooden shingles decorating the gables and walls. Those built in the Wilson Block have simple classical columns that support the front porch, along with decorative dentils, garlands, and other classical details.

Frederick Wilson's family home has a turret covered with wood shingles cut in a fish-scale pattern. Behind the main home is a carriage house and servants' quarters which are original to the Wilson house but were moved a short distance from their former locations.

In 1981 the Meadows Foundation decided to purchase and renovate a block of Victorian homes in the inner city in order to demonstrate that historic houses could be renovated for office use at around the same cost as new construction. Additionally, the Foundation wished to encourage inner city rehabilitation and revitalization.

The result of the Foundation's efforts is not only the Wilson Block, but adjacent restoration projects, including renovated parks and other Victorian homes in the surrounding area, giving rise the name "Wilson Historic District." The District is unique because it offers rent-free office space to various nonprofit community agencies. The restoration work done on these homes is remarkable and well worth a visit to the area to see how Dallas citizens lived around the turn of the century.

2800-3000 blocks of Swiss Avenue
214-821-3290

16.
Lower Greenville

If you love oyster bars, jazz clubs, Tex-Mex cuisine, and live country bands, then you will enjoy a visit to the Lower Greenville area of Dallas. Located in East Dallas along Greenville Avenue, the neighborhood consists of a long strip of unusual shops, nightclubs, and restaurants.

Back before World War II, this area was considered to be out in the country, but one of the city's most popular nightclubs, LouAnn's, was located at the southeast corner of Lovers Lane and Greenville. There was plenty of afterhours action at LouAnn's, which was run by Lou and Ann Bovis. After the death of Lou in the early '50s, Ann kept the club open during the Big Band era, hosting such guests as Tommy Dorsey, Benny Goodman, Glenn Miller, and Harry James.

Eventually, the club closed, but Greenville Avenue continued the tradition begun by the Bovises, and on any night, you are likely to find hundreds of SMU students, tourists, locals, and conventioneers having dinner and listening to music at a spot along the famous avenue.

Greenville Avenue is also known for being on the nightlife circuit of aspiring models, artists, dancers, writers, and professional athletes, who frequent the area hoping to see or be seen with the right people. Dallas is considered an important fashion center (the Apparel Mart is located here), so the city attracts a large number of beauties hoping to start a career.

In the section of Greenville near Ross Avenue, old storefronts have been renovated to house antique shops and a variety of restaurants and markets. Past Mockingbird Lane, the shops and restaurants are newer and there are many franchise-type eateries. Many restaurants offer outdoor dining. The relaxed crowd that frequents the Lower Greenville area is generally casual and easy-going.

17. Shopping—*The Most Popular Sport in Dallas*

The first store in Dallas was opened in 1842 by John Beeman, one of the earliest settlers in the Three Forks area, who stocked it with gunpowder, lead, tobacco, and whiskey. In 1845 a trading post was established at Cedar Springs, three miles above the little settlement known as Dallas. The primary medium of exchange was buffalo hides, which were traded for ammunition and groceries. "There was nothing else to buy," one patron recorded.

You've come a long way, Dallas. Today, Dallas has more shops per shopper than any other U.S. city, attracting buyers from all over the world. There aren't many things that one cannot find in Dallas.

For the ultimate shopping experience, the Galleria is a must. Two hundred stores, including Macy's, Tiffany's, and Marshall Field's, are housed under a glass barrel vault atrium. The design of the Galleria was inspired by the famous Galleria Vittorio Emanuele in Milan. Galleria shoppers are treated to unique displays, especially at Christmas, when the mall is decorated with an 85-foot Christmas tree, thousands of sparkling lights, and the Galleria Wonderland Express. Plenty of natural light, greenery, and an ice rink give the Galleria its dazzling ambience.

The four-star Westin Hotel, located in the Galleria, makes it possible for patrons to shop without ever leaving the premises—or for husbands to watch television and lounge in the room while their wives explore. For commuters, the shopping center offers valet parking. The Galleria is the Number Two visitor destination in Dallas, with 28 percent of its shoppers from at least 50 miles away. Since the Galleria has an unusually high number of customers from other countries, it offers bilingual employees, foreign currency exchange, and "Texas Tax Back," a sales tax refund for international shoppers.

Built in 1931, the historic Highland Park Village was one of the country's first shopping centers and today is a popular gathering place for affluent Dallas citizens. Such internationally known boutiques as Harold's, Calvin Klein, and Polo/Ralph Lauren share space with the Gap, as well as an assortment of neighborhood shops and eateries. Patrizio's, a fashionable upscale restaurant, offers inexpensive Italian fare and al fresco dining, and the Celebrity Restaurant & Bakery sells pastries that will break the will of any dieter *(see Sec. I:2)*.

A favorite shopping center of North Dallas residents is Prestonwood Town Center, which offers all the usual upscale stores, including Neiman Marcus, Dillard's, Lord & Taylor, and J.C. Penney, but without the usual crowds. Easy to reach via the Dallas North Tollway or Belt Line, Prestonwood has an ice rink, children's play area, and a day care center. Parking is plentiful, and there are over 170 stores and restaurants.

If you're feeling seaworthy, you might enjoy cruising along the shops and restaurants lining Mandalay Canal in Las Colinas. Water taxis transport customers every fifteen minutes year-round at the Las Colinas Canal and Shops, a specialty shopping area patterned after European villages. Additionally, the famous bronze mustang sculpture is located at nearby Williams Square.

Northpark Mall is a popular, centrally located shopping center at Northwest Highway and Central Expressway. Over 150 merchants, including Neiman Marcus, provide a variety of shops. Northpark was built in 1965 and is continually updated to maintain its elegant style.

Valley View Center, opened in 1972, is located in North Dallas and has nearly 200 stores and restaurants, including Dillard's, Foley's, and Sears. It is easily accessible at the intersection of LBJ Freeway (Interstate 635) and Preston Road.

If money is no object, the shops and galleries of the Crescent, at 2215 Cedar Springs Road, offer a distinctive array of merchandise, art, and restaurants. Celebrity Dallas visitors are often spotted shopping at Stanley Korshak, a popular clothing store for the affluent crowd. It is also entertaining to sit in the courtyard and observe fashionable Dallas society ladies coming to have tea and nibble on watercress sandwiches over at the Primrose.

The shopping centers described above are for mainstream shoppers, but Dallas has plenty of great secondhand stores, outlets, antique stores, and unusual shops. For more information on these, see Sections XI:2, XI:3, and XI:4.

Galleria—214-702-7100; Westin Hotel 800-228-3000
Highland Park Village—214-559-2740
Prestonwood Town Center—214-980-4275
Las Colinas Canal and Shops—214-541-2626
Northpark—214-363-7441
Valley View Center—214-661-2424
The Shops and Galleries of the Crescent—214-871-5150

18.
Dallas Culture—Yes, Virginia, there is culture in Dallas

A. Museum Collections

One of the quickest ways to kill a business deal in Dallas is to criticize the arts, particularly if you don't know what you're talking about. Culture in Dallas is deadly serious. Thanks to generous citizens and corporations with plenty of wealth to spread around, Dallas has an impressive, active, and well-established arts district.

Section I

The Dallas Museum of Art is unique because it houses several museums at one location: The Museum of the Americas, the Museum of Europe, the Museum of Contemporary Art, and the Museums of Africa, Asia, and the Pacific. Located in downtown Dallas, the museums of the DMA reflect views that art, until the mid-twentieth century, is best appreciated in its geographical and cultural context, whereas contemporary art is not confined to geographical boundaries.

The Museum of the Americas, the first of its kind to survey art of the Western Hemisphere, opened in 1993 and is housed in the 140,000-square-foot Hamon Building, located at 1717 North Harwood. Nancy (Mrs. Jake) Hamon contributed $20 million to construct this museum, which includes over 6,000 works that tell the story of civilizations in the Western Hemisphere.

The DMA has one of the foremost collections of Pre-Contact art in the U.S., including Olmec and Maya stone sculpture, Chavin and Nasca ceramics, and Paracas and Chimu textiles, as well as collections of Native American art and eighteenth- and nineteenth-century American paintings and decorative arts. Decorative arts include the Wendy Reves collection, consisting of $38 million worth of art donated after Emery Reves, Mrs. Reves' husband, died. Additionally, the museum has built a replica of the Reves' villa in France.

Prominent displays in the Museum of Europe include the collection of Ancient Mediterranean Gold, Renaissance, and Baroque paintings; Rococo silver; and a strong collection of Impressionist and Post-Impressionist works by Monet, Degas, Renoir, Pissaro, Van Gogh, Gauguin, and Toulouse-Lautrec. This museum's layout is chronological and incorporates themes of idealized humanism, religion, and realistic representation found in Greek sculpture and Roman portraiture, to the synthesis of religious imagery and humanist naturalism in Renaissance and Baroque art.

The collections of the Museums of Africa, Asia, and the Pacific are currently being catalogued and arranged for display in the new facility, although some of the art is interspersed among the other groups displayed at the present time.

Included in the Museums of Africa, Asia, and the Pacific are rare collections of Indonesian art and Indonesian textiles, exotic tribal art, and art from New Guinea and the islands of the Pacific. Ancient Egyptian and Nubian art will be displayed with more recent African-American art. Over 400 pieces of Egyptian and Nubian art are on a long-term loan to the DMA from the Museum of Fine Art in Boston. Scheduled openings for the African Art collection is late 1994 and Asian-Pacific in the fall of '95.

The Museum of Contemporary Art displays internationally acclaimed art from 1945 to the present. The J.E.R. Chilton Gallery presents works representing color field painting, minimalism, and conceptualism, and includes the art of Morris Louis, Robert Mangold, Carl Andre, Jennifer Bartlett, and Ellsworth Kelly, to name only a few. Paintings, sculpture, and works on paper are shown from artists Jackson Pollock, Franz Kline, Mark Rothko, Lee Bontecou, and David Smith.

Temporary exhibitions are displayed in the Barrel Vault and Quadrant Galleries and have in the past featured the electronic art of Jenny Holzer, multimedia installations by New York artist Renee Green, and figurative paintings of Texas artist Ray Smith.

Along with its exhibits, the DMA sponsors numerous lectures, concerts, films, and thematic exhibits. A surprisingly popular program is "Arts and Letters Live," a literary series of readings and performances by noted writers and actors. The "Texas Bound" segment of Arts and Letters Live showcases Texas actors reading works of fiction by Texas writers. "Distinguished Writers," also part of the Arts and Letters Live series, features well-known writers reading from their works. Past readers include

Tommy Lee Jones, John Updike, Judith Ivey, Tess Harper, Molly Ivins, and Jim Lehrer. The program runs from the end of February into May and is usually sold out in advance. Saturday concerts given in the Horchow Auditorium are also very popular. If you're in the museum around lunchtime, be sure to dine at the DMA's Gallery Restaurant or the new Atrium Cafe on the ground level. And what would any Dallas institution be without a shop of some sort? According to the Museum Store general manager Ginger Reeder, great care was taken to ensure that the store would not be "aloof" or intimidating, but would reflect the eclecticism of the DMA collection. From artist-inspired throw rugs to a South African oven mitt to art glass by Texas artists, the store is a treasure chest of diverse items in every price range.

People at the Dallas Museum of Art are a mite touchy about a few subjects. For one thing, there is an ongoing rivalry between Dallas and Fort Worth *(see Sec. VIII)* over just about everything, including the arts community. While Fort Worth museums are spectacular, some Dallasites don't consider Fort Worth to be in the same cultural league as they are, although they will concede that when it comes to buffalo art, Fort Worth has them beat hands down. (Re: The "Bison-tennial Salute" to images of the buffalo at the Amon Carter Museum, 1994.)

Another touchy subject involves something that occurred in the past. In the 1950s, the DMA was involved in a controversy regarding art and politics. Works by Picasso, Diego Rivera, and others were removed, and a statement was issued by the museum's directors, "It is not our policy to knowingly acquire or to exhibit the work of a person known by us to be now a Communist or of Communist-front affiliation."

Although the statement was subsequently retracted and a new policy issued that works of art would be considered solely on the basis of artistic merit, the reputation of Dallas suffered. The national media branded the city a center of right-wing extremism, a reputation that exists to this day. Because of Dallas' strong fundamentalist religious roots, it has always been a politically conservative town. While the DMA today chooses art primarily on its artistic merit, the art is carefully selected with huge corporate and private contributors in mind.

Yet one more sensitive point regards the snickers one sometimes hears from hoity-toity artsy people who think "Dallas" and "Art" can never be synonymous. These unbelievers, usually from the New York/East Coast/Europe art world, will tell you that, sure, Dallas money can buy all the art in the world, but real artists wouldn't dream of setting up their easels in this town.

As usual, Dallas has proven them wrong. When it comes to art, Dallas patrons are extremely knowledgeable and conscious of having only the best. And even though money can't buy everything, it can buy lots of art, which attracts lots of artists, art collectors, and art critics, of which Dallas has plenty. If you like art, come to Dallas, and you will be impressed. (And if you happen to *be* one of the unbelievers, come on down to Dallas, have some barbecue, sit a spell, experience our art, and we'll forgive you.)

The newly opened African-American Museum of Art, which houses the largest collection of African-American folk art in the United States, is one of only a handful of U.S. museums dedicated to the preservation and display of African-American artistic, cultural, and historical materials. Constructed in the shape of a cross, the 38,000-square-foot museum is located in Fair Park and contains four vaulted galleries augmented by a research library.

In addition to the DMA and the African-American Museum, the Meadows School of the Arts at Southern Methodist University, privately endowed by the Meadows Foundation, has a very popular museum. This museum is known for its vast collection of fifteenth- through twentieth-century Spanish art, an outdoor sculpture garden, and exhibitions of the works of regional artists.

Dallas Museum of Art
1717 North Harwood
214-922-1200

Meadows Museum of Art
SMU, Owens Fine Art Center
214-692-2727

African-American
Museum
Fair Park (Grand Ave.)
214-565-9026

Artsline—214-522-2659

B. Performing Arts

The history of theater in Dallas, while not exactly noteworthy, is interesting. The first dramatic performances were tent shows that traveled by wagon and were billed as "Queer, quaint, and quizzical." Although the entertainment value is questionable, these early shows after the Civil War provided some comic relief from the tedium of daily life.

"Theaters" during the late 1800s were often houses of ill repute that featured burlesque and crude dramatics. Many townspeople resented these "sporting houses," and one indignant writer of the period proclaimed:

> These places were the resorts of the most depraved characters in the country, whose carryings-on would now and then reach such a scandalous pitch that the better class of people considered it an act of patriotic vandalism to bribe some good man to set fire to the theaters. Such fires usually occurred between 1 and 2 o'clock in the morning.

Needless to say, these fires were bad for business. One notorious theater, the Black Elephant, operated during the late eighties, first at 716 Commerce Street and later at Young Street and Central. This theater was for black patrons and was closed in 1890 when the city council banned all variety theaters.

Fortunately for theater-lovers, things have changed, and Dallas, while it may not be at the cutting edge of great theater, does offers a wide variety of dramatic entertainment and is considered the birthplace of the regional theater movement. The town's first legitimate theater was the Field Opera House, built by Thomas and J.Y. Field in 1873, on the south side of Main Street between Austin and Lamar. It was operated by Misses Jessie and Cecelia Crisp, sisters of Captain William H. Crisp, who leased the facility. Unfortunately, the builders neglected to include a dressing room, so performers were forced to run across the street to the Grand Windsor Hotel to change costumes between acts. Over the years, Field's was host to numerous plays, one-night stands, and even a few operas.

In 1905 theater magnate Karl Hoblitzelle built the Majestic vaudeville house on the corner of Commerce and St. Paul streets, which in 1921 was relocated to a new facility at 1925 Elm Street. The ornate theater was for many years the site of colorful vaudeville acts and Little Theatre plays. It has recently been renovated and is presently used by the Dallas Ballet and the Lyric Opera of Dallas.

The Dallas Opera House, which opened in 1883 at the southwest corner of Commerce and Austin streets, thrived from 1883 to 1901, sponsoring such performers as Edwin Booth, F.S. Chanfrau, C.B. Bishop, John A. Hearne, Sarah Bernhardt, and Lily Langtry. This opera house burned in 1901 and was replaced later that same year by another structure, also known as the Dallas Opera House, at the northeast corner of Main and St. Paul streets. Since 1983, the Lyric Opera has been performing three light operas and musicals each summer.

Another popular place of entertainment during this era was the Craddock Theater, erected in 1879 by L. Craddock. This two-story structure at the northwest corner of Main and Austin streets featured a wholesale liquor establishment on the first floor and a stage on the second floor.

The Dallas Opera Company was created in 1957 by Lawrence Kelly and Nicola Rescigno, who came to Dallas from Chicago's Lyric Theater. In true Dallas style, the two proceeded to jump right in and perform difficult operas, recruiting outstanding European performers, including the world's most exciting—and temperamental—operatic performer, Maria Callas. The Dallas Symphony provided music under the direction of Rescigno.

With such productions as *L'Italiana in Algeri, La Traviata, Medea,* and *Don Giovanni,* the Dallas Opera quickly gained an international reputation, prompting Elsa Maxwell to remark in 1960, "It's really incredible—incredible, the greatest opera in the world in a little town like Dallas."

Today, the Dallas Opera performs at Fair Park Music Hall during November to February. A chartered bus, the Dallas Opera Coach, provides round-trip transportation from three area shopping centers: Highland Park Village, Valley View, and Northpark Mall.

During the 1940s and early '50s, Dallas enjoyed the talents of a lively actress named Margo Jones. Miss Jones, an enthusiastic lover of theater, was very prominent in Dallas theater during this time. As a teenager growing up in nearby Denton, Margo had often traveled the 40 miles to Dallas to see Dallas Little Theatre productions.

After working in Houston, Austin, and Chicago, the vivacious Miss Jones moved to Dallas and raised funds to sponsor a theater. Although her plays were held in the humble Gulf Oil Building in Fair Park and not in a legitimate theater, she managed to adapt to her circumstances and establish a "theater-in-the-round."

Her productions, including classics such as *Hedda Gabler* and *The Sea Gull,* along with works by unknown playwrights Tennessee Williams and William Inge, were widely acclaimed. *Inherit the Wind,* an original production

Uniquely Dallas

Actress and theater magnate Margo Jones arrives in Dallas, 10-07-53. (From the collections of the Texas/Dallas History and Archives Division, Dallas Public Library.)

by Jerome Lawrence and Robert E. Lee, went directly from the Dallas Theatre to Broadway. Unfortunately, Miss Jones died from cancer in 1955, and her theater faded away a few years later.

Today, there are numerous professional and amateur drama groups active in Dallas. The annual "Shakespeare Under the Stars" summer series presented by the Samuell-Grand Park Amphitheater is quite popular and offers a unique way to enjoy Shakespeare. Other theater groups include the Pocket Sandwich Theatre, Pegasus Theatre, Deep Ellum Theatre Garage, Dallas Repertory Theatre, Moonstruck Theatre Company, Dallas Childrens' Theatre, and Actors' Theatre of Dallas.

The Arts District Theater, operated by the Dallas Theater Center, stages many experimental and new productions often written by local playwrights. The Kalita Humphreys Theater, also operated by the DTC, is nearby in the Turtle Creek area and is the only theater designed by Frank Lloyd Wright.

Ballet and dance groups include the Dallas Black Dance Theatre, Ballet Dallas, and Dancers Unlimited. Music lovers will think they're in heaven in the newly constructed Morton H. Meyerson Symphony Hall, home of the Dallas Symphony Orchestra (*see Sec. II:9*). On almost any weekend, one may drop in and listen to performances by musical groups from all over the metroplex. Dallas is also home to the Bach Society, whose annual *Messiah* performance held at the Majestic Theater during the Christmas season draws an SRO crowd.

Fair Park, a 277-acre cultural and entertainment complex, is home to several museums and hosts a number of performances in Dallas. This treasure of Art Deco buildings, recently designated a National Historic Landmark, is bounded by Parry Avenue, Cullum Boulevard, Fitzhugh Avenue, and Washington Street. Host to the annual State Fair of Texas, Fair Park has been the site of state fairs since 1886.

Uniquely Dallas

Today, Fair Park consists of Fair Park Music Hall (home of the Dallas Opera), the Museum of African American Life & Culture, Age of Steam Railroad Museum, Dallas Aquarium, Dallas Museum of Natural History, Starplex Ampitheatre, Science Place I & II, Texas Hall of State, Texas Vietnam Veterans Memorial, and Leonhardt Lagoon. Fair Park Music Hall is host to many Broadway shows and performances, and the Starplex Amphitheatre hosts celebrity entertainers.

Dallas Artsline—214-522-2659—complete listing of arts events.
Dallas Morning News Arts Hotline—214-522-2659

SECTION II
Dallas Places

1.
Adolphus Hotel

The history of the renowned Adolphus Hotel is as rich as the early Flemish tapestries and twin chandeliers that grace its elegant lobby. Opened in 1912, the 21-story hotel was built by and named after beer baron Adolphus Busch. The Adolphus is located in the heart of downtown Dallas at the corner of Commerce and Akard streets, where for many years it was the site of countless social events and debutante balls, as well as host to numerous celebrities and entertainers.

When the Adolphus first opened its doors, Dallas was emerging from the frontier boom town of its past to a leading Southwestern city. The Hotel Adolphus, as it was known, confirmed Dallas' new status, with an architectural splendor and rich decor that caused critics to hail the structure as "the most beautiful building west of Venice." The mansard roof and Beaux Arts styling of the hotel towered above surrounding buildings on Commerce Street. The opulence of the Adolphus, with its gilt, high-arched ceilings, and elaborate murals, was reminiscent of Europe's eighteenth-century palaces and chateaux.

As Dallas grew around it, the Adolphus became famous not only for its impeccable service and grand decor, but for such things as the roof garden, where many dancers welcomed the slightest breeze offered by the hot Texas prairie on a summer night. For decades, the hotel was *the* place in Dallas to lunch, dine, dance, and, if you were really lucky, stay the night.

Celebrity guests who have enjoyed the hospitality of the Adolphus include Presidents Roosevelt, Truman, Carter, Reagan, and Bush and Queen Elizabeth II. Other past notable guests range all the way from Rudolph Valentino and aviators Charles Lindbergh and Amelia Earhart to Bill Cosby and George Strait.

The hotel became known for its fabulous pastry kitchen, incredible ice sculptures, and pulled-sugar works of art created by Chef Patissier Prosper A. Ingels, who was on the staff of the hotel for 48 years. Prosper Ingels' pastry kitchen designed countless confections and pastries, including a candy replica of the *Spirit of St. Louis* for Charles Lindbergh and a sparkling violin of ice and Jello for comedian Jack Benny.

The Century Room was a popular gathering place to showcase entertainers, such as Hildegarde, Edith Piaf, and Tony Bennett, to name but a few. The Ice Revue at the Adolphus was hailed as "the hottest cold show in town." In 1940 the Adolphus became the world's first hotel to be fully air-conditioned, a feature that was to prove invaluable for those living in the Sunbelt.

Today, it is difficult to imagine that the highbrow hotel was for many years the site of the annual Texas-Oklahoma University football feud. Every year in October, the two teams faced off at the Cotton Bowl, during the State Fair of Texas.

In years past, Texas Longhorn fans filled the Baker Hotel across the street (now demolished), while the Oklahoma Sooners took over the Adolphus. On the Friday night before the game, there was a pregame rally and confronta-

Dallas Places

tion on Commerce Street, and on Saturday night after the game, there was a loud celebration by the winners.

In 1958, when Texas beat Oklahoma for the first time in ten years, the rowdiness and revelry got out of hand. Along with the usual fights, windows were broken out and airborne furniture flew to the street below. Even the extra security guards hired by the two hotels failed to stop the wild brawl. Today, the Texas-OU feuding and fighting have moved down the street to the West End area.

Since the balconies of the Adolphus overlook downtown Dallas, the hotel was a favorite site for parade-watching, particularly the Cotton Bowl Parade each New Year's Day. On November 22, 1963, a happy, excited crowd on the Main Street side of the hotel watched President John F. Kennedy and the pink-suited Jacqueline ride toward Houston Street in an open car, with Governor John Connally and his wife Nellie. Some of the historic photos of the Kennedy entourage were taken from a balcony of the hotel.

One eyewitness, Gale Sliger, reported that by the time she ran from the cheerful scene at the Main Street balcony over to the Commerce side of the hotel, a TV screen was already reporting the shooting. Ms. Sliger returned to a meeting of the Advertising League's Board of Directors and directed her food captain to see that anyone on the Board with a heart condition have nitroglycerine in hand. She then announced to the shocked group that President Kennedy had been shot.

"There was quite a contrast to the parade scene by 5:00," she says. "You could have fired a cannon down Main Street and not hit anyone. Downtown Dallas was completely deserted."

After the assassination, the Adolphus went into a period of decline. The sixties decade was not compatible with Old World grandeur. Although the hotel had been in need of renovation for many years, its age really began showing. Several past additions to the Adolphus had left it divided, changed, and redivided, so much so that there were

Section II

boarded-up hallways and stairways leading into blank walls, resulting in a maze of sorts. The famed Century Room closed in 1965.

A loyal staff and clientele kept the hotel going until 1979, when it was shut down. In 1980 the seventy-year-old property was purchased by Westgroup Hotels and Resorts, Inc., and the New England Mutual Life Insurance Company. The new owners began the extraordinary task of turning a rundown hodgepodge structure into a brand new grand old hotel.

Under the new management, the massive renovation was completed, and the new Adolphus opened in November 1981. A four-day celebration took place, with a mile-long parade of bands, drill teams, clowns, floats, antique cars, and even Santa himself. Dallas Mayor Jack Evans cut the spun-sugar ribbon, and a kaleidoscope of balloons floated heavenward past the famous copper roof and bottle-shaped tower.

The hotel shone with the polish, refinement, and splendor of $80 million worth of renovations. The number of rooms had been reduced from 850 to 435 individually decorated suites. Although you could no longer get a room for "$1.50 and up," as you could in 1912, it wasn't long before the Adolphus took its place among world-renowned hotels.

The French Room, the hotel's dining room, has been particularly extolled, with the *New York Times* hailing it as "a Louis XV fantasy on the prairie...indisputably the most striking and sumptuous restaurant in Dallas." For eleven consecutive years, the Adolphus has been awarded the coveted AAA Five Diamond rating.

Today, the Adolphus is a popular gathering place once again for Dallas society, with its acclaimed restaurants, as well as its Grand Ballroom and meeting and banquet facilities. In the European tradition, the Adolphus serves afternoon tea, which is attended by many Dallas society ladies, in the lobby living room. Along with restoring the hotel's old-world ambiance, the new owners have given the Adolphus the grace and opulence that Adolphus Busch envisioned.

1321 Commerce Street
214-742-8200; 800-221-9083

2. Freedman's Cemetery

Thousands of shells, from the Caribbean, the West Coast of Africa, and the Trinity River, arranged in neat ovals and rectangles, mark some of the 9,000 graves of slaves and former slaves buried in a four-acre plot beneath Lemmon Avenue, next to North Central Expressway. The graveyard, known as Freedman's Cemetery, has been lying for decades under concrete and buildings and is now the site of an excavation project begun in 1991 by the Texas Department of Transportation (TxDOT).

According to Dallas County courthouse records, the burial site was originally bought by a group of ex-slaves in 1860 who made payments on the land until 1869, when the last payment was made. Three additional acres were purchased in 1874. Today, all but approximately one acre of the original cemetery is covered with buildings. The burials took place between 1860 and 1911.

As Dallas grew around the old graveyard, the Houston and Texas Central Railroad was built along what used to be a cattle trail and is now North Central Expressway. Black residents of the nearby area, which was one of the Freedman's Towns (*see Sec. IV:4*), were dispersed, and the cemetery fell into disuse and became overgrown with weeds. Eventually, buildings were literally built on top of the graves.

Section II

In 1986 the Texas Department of Transportation, in conjunction with the widening of North Central Expressway, conducted an environmental impact study and came across the cemetery. Project archaeologist Jerry Henderson was contacted by members of Black Dallas Remembered, Inc., who also knew about the old graveyard. After three years of negotiations between the highway engineers, the Black Dallas group members, and living descendants of those interred in the graves, the exhumations began.

As thousands of cars and trucks rush by them, archaeologists and workers carefully remove caskets and human remains, cataloging each find, careful to adhere to health laws and to show respect for the remains. As each grave is uncovered, work is done under a white tent-like structure for privacy and protection from the elements.

It was originally thought that some 1,600 graves existed, and the city of Dallas purchased enough land south of the cemetery to relocate that many graves. As work progressed, it was discovered that boundaries of the original Freedman's Cemetery were much larger than previously thought, and that some 9,000 people were buried there, including many graves with one person buried on top of another one.

Perhaps the most amazing thing about the cemetery is that many of the grave markings were still intact beneath the pavement. Headstones were rare, but diggers found wooden crosses and markers and thousands of shells, including oyster and seashells. Experts at the Museum of Natural History traced the shells to marine species typical of the West Coast of Africa, the Atlantic, and the Caribbean. Only one of the species was found to be from the Trinity River.

Many interesting artifacts have been discovered, including dishes, elaborate wrist bands, and pieces of clothing used for burial and mourning. A total of twelve types of "viewing windows" have been identified. These were built into the wooden coffins and enabled the mourners to view the body. In addition, many unusual pieces of coffin hardware have been salvaged.

The city of Dallas formed the Freedman's Art Council to oversee the preservation and memorial for the cemetery. Thus far, over 800 bodies have been exhumed and prepared for reburial at the adjoining Freedman's Cemetery and Memorial Park.

Freedman's Cemetery has been the subject of a television show, "Feel It In My Bones," produced in 1993 by Sheila Cooper and Channel KERA. The Texas Department of Transportation publishes a quarterly newsletter about progress being made on the excavation.

North Central Expressway at Lemmon Avenue
214-320-4480

Sec. I:3—Deep Ellum
Sec. IV:4—Freedman's Towns

3.
The Old Red Courthouse

No, you haven't walked into the land of Hansel and Gretel, but you are looking at the massive red sandstone building that served as the fifth seat of government in Dallas County. Built in Romanesque Revival style with gigantic rounded arches, this courthouse was designed by Architect M.A. Orlopp and completed in 1892, replacing an earlier structure that burned in 1890.

The courthouse site was designated as public land in the city plat of 1844. Originally, a log structure served as the courthouse when Dallas County was created in 1846, and in 1850 a larger log structure was erected.

In 1856 a two-story brick edifice was completed and then rebuilt in 1860 after a city fire. A fourth courthouse, a two-story granite structure built in 1871, burned in 1890. The Old Red Courthouse, as it is known, was constructed of Arkansas gray granite and Pecos red sandstone. The lower portion is made of blue granite that is also used on window trims, providing a pleasing contrast with the red stone.

The actual design is dominated by eight circular turrets. Notice the acroterium (gargoyle-like figures) on the roof. A clock tower, complete with a 4,500-pound bell, originally topped the building but was removed in 1919. The clock tower bell was so large that it had to be cut into three pieces and lowered to the ground. A few Dallas youngsters particularly felt the loss, because they were accustomed to playing in the tower and causing the clock to ring 13 hours at 1:00.

Many weddings were performed in the halls of the old courthouse and on its stairs. The attic of the building was reached by a narrow iron stairway from the fourth floor. One writer, describing a trip to the attic, wrote, "This dismal maze of passages and supporting arches inhabited by doves and mindful of the old Italian catacombs is spooky enough for a No. 1 mystery thriller."

One of the huge gargoyle-like creatures crashed to the ground during a windstorm in 1933. In 1947 an attempt was made to remove three of the remaining grinning, grotesque ornaments, each of which weighed approximately 350 lbs. After spending one entire day pulling unsuccessfully on one of the humpbacked, grimacing eyesores, workers determined that if they couldn't get them down, the creatures would probably defy another windstorm as well.

Hangings took place at the gallows on the sixth floor of the nearby jailhouse on Houston Street or on the Trinity River banks. Old Red was the site of a lynching in 1910 *(see Sec. IV:6, IV:7).*

As the courthouse continued to age, judges and engineers alike warned of the edifice's danger. During severe

Dallas windstorms, huge chunks of the sandstone would fall to the concrete below. In 1983 State Dist. Judge Theo Bedard walked into her courtroom and found that tiles from the attic had crashed through the ceiling directly over the jurybox. The judge started wearing a personalized hardhat, given to her by her bailiff, to work. In other sections of the structure, gallons of debris would from time to time crash down.

Old Red has undergone several renovations and attempts to turn it into a historical showpiece and tourist attraction. "The Friends of Old Red" and the Dallas County Historical Commission have sponsored Old Red renovations, and efforts continue to restore the building to its original grandeur. The last employees and records finally moved out in the late 1980s.

Dallas County commissioners recently approved a $5.2 million transformation of Old Red. Today, court is held across the street on Commerce, and the Old Red Courthouse is closed to the public. Do take time to peer in the windows and imagine the deteriorating halls of justice as they once were, particularly on the Commerce Street side, where you can see the old pews still in place from earlier trials. (Note: Beware of pigeons.)

West End Historic District, Main and Houston streets

Sec. IV:6—Clock Tower Atop the Old Red Courthouse
Sec. IV:7—Elks' Arch

Section II

4.
Log Cabin *(and a little pioneer history)*

This log cabin is often credited as being John Neely Bryan's original dwelling that he constructed in 1842 on the east bank of the Trinity River. However, that structure was destroyed by flood, and the one on display was given to Dallas County by the Buckner Orphans Home and restored in 1935.

Built of cedar logs before 1850, this one-room cabin is typical of the early settler period. It is believed to have been built by Gideon Pemberton, a settler from Kentucky, and was moved from its original site (7.5 miles east) in 1926 and rebuilt at several locations, ending up across from the Old Red Courthouse.

Most of the early pioneers settled in the "Three Forks" area of the Trinity River, as it was known. People came to this area from Arkansas, Illinois, Kentucky, Missouri, and Tennessee, bringing with them a tradition of building log cabins.

First known as the "Peters Colony," the region was abundant in oak, juniper (or cedar), walnut, ash, bois d'arc, and elm trees. Settlers who agreed to work at least 15 acres and erect a "good and comfortable" cabin were granted title to the land. Milled lumber made its appearance in Dallas by 1849, and bricks became available by 1860. Most of the town's original log cabins were destroyed by a city fire during that same year.

Peek in and try to visualize your typical modern American family making do in this structure. Parents, be sure to carry on the tradition of telling your kids how hard it used to be and how easy they have it now.

West End Historic District, Elm Street, between Market and Record streets

5.
Southfork Ranch

The world's most famous ranch, Southfork was the home of the Ewing family of the popular CBS television series, "Dallas," that ran from 1978 to 1990 and continues today in syndication and even first-runs around the world. Located just north of Dallas in Parker, the ranch was built in 1970 by a Dallas businessman and is today maintained as a working ranch, although it is devoted to "Dallas" fans.

Get a taste of luxurious Texas ranch life and watch longhorns and American paint horses graze peacefully on the plains as you ride the tram through 41 acres of fields, barns, and ballrooms, and walk through the mansion itself. Bought in 1992 by Rex Maughan, an Arizona businessman, Southfork is open to the public and has undergone a massive renovation that includes a "Dallas" memorabilia exhibit, Oil Baron's Ballroom, conference facilities, rodeo arena, a unique gift shop, Miss Ellie's Deli, and a western clothing store.

Visitors are free to walk around the grounds and take photographs. The mansion itself has been extensively redecorated as well, in a style described as "American Elegance with Texas Arrogance." The hospitable guides are very friendly and eagerly answer questions and point out places where filming occurred, such as the kitchen and out by the pool. Be sure to look out from the balcony of J.R.'s bedroom and note the spectacular view of the sprawling ranch.

Since the show is in first-run status in many foreign countries, Southfork attracts a large number of international tourists. Visitors come from as far away as Denmark and Bangladesh to see where the Ewings lived, and on any given day, you are likely to run into several excited fans from other countries.

Section II

Although most of the actual filming of "Dallas" was done on Hollywood sets, Southfork has been restored to appear much as it did during the "Dallas" episodes. Southfork also offers full service event planning and catering and has become a popular place for corporate and private parties.

For the truly decadent and adventurous, Southfork offers a unique bed-and-breakfast experience for $3,500 that includes accommodations for up to eight people, full and complete use of the mansion and pool, a personal wait and bar staff for the evening, an elegant, Texas-sized dinner, and a full Southern breakfast the next morning, plus Southfork glasses and monogrammed robes for guests to take home.

The rest of us will have to settle for a tram tour of the mansion and grounds.

Southfork Ranch—Take Highway 75 north (Central Expressway) to Exit 30 (Parker Road); go east 6.5 miles, turn right on FM 2551 (Hogge Road). Southfork is immediately on the left. Open daily, year-round. Hours vary by season; call 214-442-7800.
Cost of tram tour (includes mansion): $4 adult; $2 children; parking $2.

6.
The Sixth Floor: John F. Kennedy and the Memory of a Nation

As the twentieth century recedes into history, Dallas, for all its sparkle and glamour, may unfortunately be most remembered as the site of the "shots that shook the world."

When, on November 22, 1963, a world leader in his prime was viciously killed, part of America's naiveté died with him.

Try as it might, Dallas was unable to ignore or deny its place in one of the darker days of history. After decades of attempting to bury the whole affair, the city leaders realized that public curiosity and historical significance demanded an accounting.

The result is the Sixth Floor Museum, opened in 1989, which houses an impressive collection of photos and rare newsreels from that fateful day. Located on the actual sixth floor of the old Texas School Book Depository (now the Dallas County Administration Building), the museum is the site where Lee Harvey Oswald fired his fatal shots.

Regardless of your political affiliation, you will not leave the Sixth Floor unmoved. It is difficult, if not impossible, to walk through the poster-size photos of the life of John F. Kennedy, listening to the actual recordings of the police, newscasters, and eyewitnesses, without beginning to believe that you are in downtown Dallas on November 22, 1963.

Recently declared a National Historic Landmark, the Sixth Floor hosts some three to four hundred thousand visitors per year, many of them international citizens. Even children will be fascinated by the tour, which includes a photo maze of the Kennedy family and presidency, as well as continuous videos that show original home-camera and television broadcast footage of the event.

It is chilling to watch the unsuspecting Jack and Jackie descend from the steps of Air Force One at Dallas' Love Field, where, only two and one-half hours later, the President's mangled body would be returned. The arrangement of the Sixth Floor is such that it allows visitors to peruse leisurely while listening to the audio (available for an extra $2 and strongly recommended). As you gaze over Elm Street, watching the cars proceeding west toward Dealey

Section II

Plaza, you will relive that infamous day—a day that no one can forget.

Perhaps Nellie Connally, wife of Texas Governor John Connally, who, with her husband, was in the limousine with the Kennedys, expressed the shock of tragedy best when she stated, "There was no screaming in that horrible car. It was just a silent, terrible drive."

Dallas County Administration Building
(former Texas School Book Depository)
411 Elm St., Dallas 75202

Sun.-Fri. 10:00 a.m.-6:00 p.m.
Admission $4 adults, $3 senior citizens, $2 children 6-18
Parking available
214-653-6659

Number One Visitor Destination in Dallas—1992

7.
Dealey Plaza/Grassy Knoll

After touring the museum, it is possible to visit Dealey Plaza and the "grassy knoll" that overlook Elm Street, where the presidential motorcade was traveling at the time of the shots. This area looks much as it did in 1963, and on any given day, one will usually see a dozen or more visitors milling about, pointing to the actual site of the shooting, taking photographs, or discussing assassination theories with one of the vendors who peddle maps and souvenirs.

Named after civic leader and newspaper publisher George Bannerman Dealey, Dealey Plaza is the site of a high bluff overlooking a shallow ford of the Trinity River, where a trading post in 1839.

At the time, the limestone pathway was a natural crossing point of the Trinity River (see *following section*). During the 1840s, the Republic of Texas designated this crossing point as a "national road" to the U.S. border and began offering liberal land grants to anyone who settled here.

Dealey Plaza and the high bluff referred to as the "grassy knoll" figure prominently in the Kennedy assassination and is where the famed Abraham Zapruder film of the assassination was taken. It is this site, west of the Depository Building on the north side of Elm Street, where eyewitnesses to the shooting dropped to the ground, believing they were in the line of fire.

Immediately following the gunfire, dozens of people ran up the grassy incline toward the railyards, which were located over a stockade fence that separated the incline from the tracks. Hundreds of onlookers in Dealey Plaza witnessed the assassination, two dozen of whom recorded it on film. A number of these witnesses claimed they saw a puff of smoke from the trees near the fence and suspicious-looking cars and men, thus giving rise to many of the conspiracy theories.

Some of the claims may have been due to echo patterns in Dealey Plaza itself. Several of these witnesses actually reported seeing the rifle from the School Book Depository, which led police almost immediately to a search of the building, where investigators found a barricade of boxes on the sixth floor, three spent bullet cartridges, and a rifle.

The Warren Commission, headed by Supreme Court Chief Justice Earl Warren, concluded in its report issued September 24, 1964, that Lee Harvey Oswald, acting alone, had killed the President. A separate report, later disputed, issued January 2, 1979, from the House of Representatives' Select Committee on Assassinations stated a "95% probability" that there had been a second gunman firing at the motorcade from behind the stockade fence. The Kennedy assassination continues to be a source of enigma and controversy today.

8.
The Trinity River: Where is It?

When John Neely Bryan first stood on the high bluff that overlooked an area known as "Three Forks" of the Trinity River, he envisioned a great navigable highway that would be the foundation of a bustling port city. Unfortunately, the Trinity refused to cooperate. Its flow was an erratic one, and depending on the weather, the Trinity was at times nothing more than a narrow, crooked channel blocked by debris and driftwood, while during rainy seasons, it became a swollen waterway that overflowed its banks.

Early settlers ridiculed Bryan's plan to navigate the river, but Bryan nonetheless continued to pursue his dream, once even setting fire to the main log jam near Dallas, hoping that rising waters would carry the debris away. The blaze failed to clear the logjam, but the undaunted Bryan began operating a ferry across the uncooperative river.

The lower regions of the Trinity were by this time being navigated by steamboats and flatboats, and Bryan hoped that the natural river crossing where he had staked his claim would be the main point for river traffic. There is evidence that a steamer named the *Scioto Belle* had indeed traveled from the lower regions of the Trinity to the Three Forks area in the late 1830s.

In 1848 Bryan, along with some other Dallasites, represented the town at a conference held in Huntsville on navigating the Trinity River. Steamboats operating on the lower reaches to the Gulf of Mexico reminded Bryan of how close his dream was. According to a U.S. Army engineer, the Trinity was the "deepest and least obstructed river in the state of Texas."

John Neely Bryan's dream of a river port city was never realized, but the aggressive pioneer was successful in persuading Houston and Texas Central Railroad officials to alter a proposed route so that it came through Dallas. Once the railroad came to town, the city began its remarkable growth.

The Trinity River, however, continued to be a source of problems and controversy. Following the Civil War, new efforts were made to tame the Trinity. In 1867 a prize of $15,000 was offered to a riverboat captain if he would pilot a boat from Galveston Bay to Dallas.

Captain James H. McGarvey left Galveston in May 1867 on a steamboat named *Job Boat No. 1*, arriving "within shouting distance of the Dallas Courthouse" exactly one year and four days later. This laborious voyage inspired a group of Dallas businessmen to build their own steamboat, the *Sallie Haynes*, which ran into a number of obstacles and eventually sank.

In 1872 an iron toll bridge was completed across the river, and in 1892 a group of Dallas businessmen formed the Trinity River Navigation Company. They sent both a rowboat and a "snag-puller" down the uncooperative waterway in an attempt to clear obstructions, and in 1893 succeeded in navigating the river from Galveston to Dallas in a steamboat called the *Harvey*. The boat was greeted with great fanfare when it arrived at Dallas.

For the next several years, there was river traffic along the upper Trinity, thanks in part to a temporary dam built at McCommas Bluff, just below Dallas. Seven locks and dams were built within 50 miles downstream of the city, and by 1909 the Trinity River Navigation Company had spent $165,000 on river improvements, while the federal government by 1915 had allocated a total of $2.1 million dollars on various river projects.

Section II

A major turning point in the history of the temperamental Trinity came in May 1908, when the river waters, swollen by days of rain, flooded the city of Dallas. Although other floods had occurred over the years, this was by far the worst. For three days, Dallas was in complete darkness, without drinking water or fire protection. Telephone lines were down, and rail service was suspended. There was great loss of property, including livestock, whose decaying bodies were found lodged in trees when the water subsided. Months and years of debate among city officials resulted in the ambitious Kessler Plan, developed by planning engineer George E. Kessler and released in 1911. The basis of the plan was to divert the Trinity into an artificial channel between two levees, remove the T&P Railroad lines, and unify the railroad depots into a single terminal.

Triple underpass and Dealey Plaza (note courthouse), c. 1959. (From the collections of the Texas/Dallas History and Archives, Dallas Public Library.)

Texas and Pacific bridge as it crosses the Trinity River. West approach washed away during the flood of 1908. (Note crowds on riverbank.) (From the collections of the Texas/Dallas History and Archives, Dallas Public Library.)

The buildings and land for the triple underpass and Dealey Plaza were cleared away in 1934 (note the courthouse), c. 1935. (From the collections of the Texas/Dallas History and Archives, Dallas Public Library.)

Section II

The Kessler Plan was met with disapproval, and it would be years before it was reconsidered and finally implemented. By the 1920s, the river was described by one citizen as a "slow-moving, black stagnant, stinking liquid, giving off great quantities of sulfurous acid gas." It was polluted and poisoned by sewage in the stream.

Between 1928 and 1932, Kessler and the city of Dallas straightened the Trinity River, moving the Elm Fork three-and-a-half miles northwest and channeling it between levees to control flooding. This massive undertaking was one-twelfth the size of the Panama Canal project, moving some 21 million cubic yards of earth and building two levees, 30 feet high and 2,000 feet apart.

By the end of the 1930s, the Trinity River had been contained. One of the greatest consequences of the Kessler Plan was that over 10,000 acres of level land was reclaimed and developed as the Trinity Industrial District, one of the oldest planned industrial sites in the country. Few Dallas citizens today realize that until the 1930s, the waters of the Trinity flowed at the edge of downtown. Probably the best view one can get of the Trinity now is from the Reunion Tower observatory on the 50th floor.

And that's what happened to the Trinity River.

See Section II:7—Dealey Plaza

9.
Morton H. Meyerson Symphony Center

What does a very successful Dallas businessman do when he desires to pay homage to his best buddy and business partner? Why, build an $81.5-million building in his honor, of course. Although H. Ross Perot did not contribute the entire amount, his $17-million contribution came with two conditions: that the hall be named after Mort Meyerson and that only Perot and Meyerson could approve changes in the design.

The architect of the world-class hall, I.M. Pei, had a history of cost overruns, and by the time the center opened in 1989, the project had gone from an estimated cost of $50 million to $81.5 million, earning architect Pei a new nickname, "You Will Pay." Other large contributors included Mrs. Eugene McDermott, Louise Kahn, Exxon Corporation, J.C. Penney, and Texas Instruments.

The concert facility is considered among the finest in the world and features one of the largest mechanical-action organs ever built for a concert hall, the Herman W. Lay Family Fisk Organ. Each Fisk organ is handmade for its particular location, and the Dallas instrument has 4,535 operating pipes, creating seven organ sound divisions: La Resonance, Great Positive, Swell, Pedal, Solo, and Pedal

Morton H. Meyerson Symphony Center. A "symphony of style and function" describes the home of the Dallas Symphony Orchestra. Designed by architect I.M. Pei and opened in 1989. (Courtesy of the Dallas Convention & Visitors Bureau.)

Solo. Each pipe was installed and voiced in a dust-free environment. Built by C.B. Fisk Inc. of Gloucester, Massachusetts, this particular organ was the last one that Charles B. Fisk personally worked on before his death in 1983.

Angled on the downtown site of 2301 Flora Street, the Morton H. Meyerson Hall is a basic "shoe box" design wrapped in a swirling wall of glass, which contributes to its bold architectural statement. It's pretty hard to miss if you're wandering around in the vicinity. The central part of the facility is the Eugene McDermott Concert Hall, designed by acoustician Russell Johnson and featuring a ceiling canopy and adjustable sound chambers.

Mort Meyerson, for whom the hall is named, is a descendant of Russian emigres. He studied philosophy and art at the University of Texas, where he was also a member of the U.S. Army Reserve Officer Training Corps. Meyerson was employed at the Bell Helicopter Plant in Fort Worth when Perot recruited him in the early days of EDS. Along with his colorful boss, Meyerson helped build EDS into a billion-dollar empire, eventually serving as president of the huge company.

Meyerson, a lover of classical music who travels to Vienna and Amsterdam to attend his favorite concert halls, had the third story of his home remodeled into a private concert hall, complete with adjustable sound baffles and six-foot stereo speakers. Reports are, however, that one is as likely to hear Joni Mitchell coming from the Meyerson home as Beethoven or Rachmaninoff.

The center is the permanent home of the Dallas Symphony Orchestra and hosts many other performing arts groups. An outdoor plaza and stage is the site for numerous festivals and concerts. Current plans are for the parking lot between the Dallas Museum of Art and the symphony hall to be developed for art studios, a restaurant, galleries, and underground parking.

2301 Flora St.—214-670-3600

10.
Frontiers of Flight Museum

Aviation buffs aren't the only ones who will appreciate the remarkable display of airflight history at the Frontiers of Flight Museum. Located at Dallas' Love Field, the display is housed just above the main terminal lobby and includes such items as giant propellers from transoceanic airships, a piece of the original fabric from the Wright Flyer, charred remnants of the Hindenburg, as well the radio operator's chair from the doomed airship.

The museum collection was begun in 1963, when George Haddaway, aviation historian and publisher of *Flight* magazine, donated his collection of aviation artifacts and archives to the University of Texas at Austin. The collection grew and became second only to the National Air and Space Museum in archival research.

The memorabilia and artifacts were moved to the University of Texas in Dallas in 1978, when the collection outgrew its Austin quarters, and G. Edward Rice, another collector, became curator. Rice brought additional items to the collection, including the million-item Admiral C.E. Rosendahl lighter-than-air collection, known as the finest such collection in the world.

The History of Aviation Collection, as it was called, again outgrew its space and was moved to the Love Field location, where the museum officially opened in 1990. Visitors can wind their way through aviation history, feeling the triumphs, as well as the tragedies, of man's quest for flight, reflected in notes, photographs, and rare memorabilia.

Exhibits include the first ideas of flight in the 1500s, the military's role in aviation, Hollywood's interest in airflight, the race to fly to the North Pole, development of zeppelins and blimps, women in aviation, growth of commercial airlines, and space exploration. Special displays abound, such as Women Airforce Service Pilots (WASPs) of World War II, which shows life-size figures wearing the WASP uniform and chronicles the activities of these distinguished pilots. Many other displays chronicle air combat in World War II.

The history of Love Field as a World War I and II training base is chronicled as well. Offering an ideal location for the aviation collection, Love Field was utilized primarily as a military base during the two world wars, eventually becoming a commercial airline airport. Be sure to see the photo of Mr. and Mrs. Troy Vencil, who lived on Love Field. "Ma and Pa" Vencil, as they were affectionately known, helped out in the early days of aviation. Pa Vencil became a master of flying maintenance disciplines, while Ma Vencil, known as the "Mother of Love Field," fed many a hungry pilot with her pots of chili.

The Frontiers of Flight Museum has become a popular classroom outing, offering inspiration and career motivation for school children with its video presentations and hands-on displays. There is a small gift shop in the museum that sells many scale models and replicas of airplanes and other aviation artifacts.

Perhaps the greatest treasure in the Frontiers of Flight Museum, however, is not on display, but may be found in the guides themselves, most of whom are retired aviation industry workers. These enthusiastic volunteers, some of them World War II veterans, are anxious to share with visitors their own memories of the fascinating history of airflight and offer a rare first-hand glimpse into thrilling adventures in the air.

Love Field Terminal—214-350-3600

11.
Southern Methodist University

Southern Methodist University is perhaps the only institution of higher learning in the country to take cotton in lieu of cash for pledges. Shortly after pledges for the new institution were taken, beginning in 1911, some would-be contributors who were also cotton farmers fell on hard times. President Robert Stewart Hyer and his bursar, Frank Reedy, came up with a plan to take cotton instead of money, crediting donors with 10 cents per pound toward their pledges. The school's first crop was stored on the ground floor of newly constructed Dallas Hall, where it remained until it was sold before classes began at the new school.

Working out of offices of the Methodist Publishing House on Commerce Street, Dr. Hyer raised funds, recruited a faculty, helped with architectural plans, started a library, developed a curriculum, and acquired laboratory equipment. The same firm that designed Stanford University also worked on SMU. It is difficult to imagine now, but the tree-lined esplanades, neat flower beds and shrubbery, and classical buildings that make up the campus are on a site that was a bare, treeless expanse of prairie, without a single building, at the turn of the century.

Dallas Hall, a classic domed structure with Greek columns, was the first building and remains the architectural center of the campus today. It was so named because funds for the construction were donated solely by the citizens of Dallas, among them William W. Caruth and Mrs. John S. Armstrong, who both donated a great deal of land and money for the school.

There was some controversy over naming the new school. President Hyer believed that the word "Southern" would be a handicap to the institution. Originally, the name was "Texas Wesleyan," but founders feared that the school's initials, "T.W.," would be referred to as "Tight Wad," so they changed it to "Southern Methodist University."

One early visitor, touring Dallas Hall with the school president, said, "The Methodists in Dallas should be very proud of what they have done in contributing the money for this building."

Dr. Hyer quickly corrected him. "The Methodists cannot take all the credit for this. Just as much Jewish money has gone into this building as Methodist. In fact, I believe almost all denominations have contributed to this edifice."

The school opened September 23, 1915, with 456 students. The students elected Umphrey Lee, who later would become president of SMU, as student-body president. Following true Texas tradition, the school had a football team that first fall, although they were soundly defeated by Texas Christian University of Fort Worth in the first game, 43-0.

In 1916 the faculty of SMU voted to organize a university church, to be located on the southwest corner of the campus. Although the University Church later became the Highland Park Methodist Church, independent of SMU, it still occupies the same prominent location on the campus.

Today, SMU serves around 10,000 students and offers a wide variety of undergraduate, master's, doctoral, and professional degree programs. The divisions of the university are Dedman College of Humanities and Sciences, Meadows School of the Arts, the School of Engineering and Applied Science, Edwin L. Cox School of Business, Perkins School of Theology, and SMU School of Law.

SMU's campus in New Mexico, SMU-in-Taos, draws upon the area's natural resources to offer summer courses in the humanities, sciences, and performing arts, including the excavation of a thirteenth-century Indian pueblo. The university houses more than two-and-a-half million volumes in its eight libraries. The Meadows School of the Arts is considered one of the nation's strongest and most selective schools in the performing arts, and the Meadows Museum has one of the largest collections of Spanish art

Dallas Places

outside Spain, as well as local art and an outdoor sculpture garden. SMU has grown into one of the major Southwest universities and has become a valuable resource of cultural activity for the city of Dallas.

6425 Boaz Lane
214-768-2000

12.
First Baptist Hard Rock Cafe

Located at the corner of McKinney Avenue and Routh Street in the heart of downtown Dallas, this majestic white building was for many years a prestigious Baptist church. The stately two-story landmark was built in 1904 and features Corinthian columns and three giant stained-glass windows. The recently restored McKinney trolley runs in front of the restaurant, which offers a spectacular view of downtown Dallas from its terrace.

As in other Hard Rock Cafes, there is an abundance of rock 'n' roll memorabilia, including guitars from Stevie Ray Vaughan (who was from Oak Cliff) and ZZ Top. Over 1,000 items are housed in the Dallas location alone. The cafe serves American fare such as hamburgers and barbecue and features a guitar-shaped bar, dance floor, and rock 'n' roll walk of fame outside the building. One can only hope, however, that the Lord is as much a fan of rock 'n' roll as Steve Routhier, the curator of Hard Rock. The building is a registered historical landmark.

2601 McKinney Ave.
214-855-0007

Section II

13.
Pioneer Plaza

Try not to screech to a halt when you first spot Pioneer Plaza in downtown Dallas by the Dallas Convention Center, as motorists tend to do. This dramatic traffic-stopping sculpture of 70 longhorn steers being driven across a stream by three cowboys is Dallas' latest memorial to the pioneers who founded the city.

The Plaza is a 4.2-acre open space, adjacent to Pioneer Cemetery, where a natural setting of native Texan plants, with a flowing stream and waterfall, all combine to memorialize the hundreds of cattle drives that took place at this junction. Early pioneers followed this north-south Indian Trail, variously called the Shawnee Cattle Trail, Coffee's Bend Road, and Preston Bend Trail. The trail is today Preston Road, one of the main thoroughfares in Dallas.

Beginning in 1849, hundreds of gold-seekers passed through Dallas on their way west, taking a route still known today as "California Crossing" (off Northwest Highway). The Shawnee Trail was used by pioneers moving west and by cowboys herding hundreds of thousands of beef cattle from the areas along the Colorado and Brazos rivers (in southeast Texas) north to the Missouri and Illinois markets. They crossed the Trinity at a rock bottom ford near what is today the Hyatt Regency Hotel, then climbed a small bluff and made their way to the Red River, across Indian territory, heading north. The original Shawnee Trail came across the bluff where Reunion Arena is now located.

Nationally renowned Texas artist Robert Summers was selected by the Dallas Parks Foundation, in conjunction with the Dallas Convention and Visitors Bureau, to create the cattle drive monument. Dallas historian A.C. Greene researched the historical data for the project. Sculpted in bronze, the memorial consists of seventy longhorn steers, each over 6 feet tall, and three cowboys on horses. Incorpo-

Dallas Places

rated into the design are learning areas that tell the story of roads and trails and the pioneers who traveled them.

The first bronze longhorn was unveiled September 21, 1993, along with the trail boss and his horse. The entire project was completed in 1994. With the striking Dallas skyline as its background, Pioneer Plaza promises to be the new landmark in Dallas.

And Fort Worth says there aren't any steers in Dallas.

S.E. corner of Young St. and Griffin St.
214-977-6653

Sec. II:4—Log Cabin (and a little pioneer history)
Sec. II:8—Trinity River—Where is it?
Sec. III:2—John Neely Bryan

Old Red Courthouse erected in 1892; historical log cabin built in the early settler period. (From the collections of the Texas/Dallas History and Archives Division, Dallas Public Library.)

Section II

Pioneer Plaza. (Photo by Michael S. Kendall - KENDALL - Landscape Architecture.)

SECTION III

Dallas Legends— Ordinary Folks Who Made Good

1.

H. Ross Perot—*The Best Little Billionaire in Texas*

It is summer 1992, a June day in Dallas when the heat just won't quit. On the sixth floor of 6606 LBJ Freeway, at Perot Headquarters, cheerful volunteers answer phones, open mail, and relate their latest amazing phone call, all under the watchful eye of jovial director Bob Wolfson. In the spacious breakroom, volunteers mingle with reporters, watch CNN, eat popcorn, and drink free soft drinks. One volunteer is studying the glassed-wall display of Perot memorabilia, including a life-size cutout of 5-foot-6-inch Ross himself, along with the most elaborate and creative banners, signs, caps, and souvenirs culled from the hundreds that arrive daily in the mailroom.

But across the hall, in a secured set of offices, something else is going on. Quietly, with the stealth of a twenty-first-century military jet, other troops have gathered. These handpicked troops are not like the laughing volunteers.

They are sedate and quiet as they move in efficient, confident motions to set up cubicles, computers, and telephones. Elaborate login codes and strict instructions for secret passwords are given out.

The men, mostly young, wear ties and white shirts, and the women are in business suits and heels. Security is astounding, and coded passes must be used to access any room, including the bathrooms.

There are few smiles, for everyone is focused on the mission, which is never impossible: To turn a coalition of loosely knit enthusiastic recruits from all over the country into a single-minded combat unit with one goal: the Presidency of the United States. Welcome to the Nation of Perot.

Henry Ross Perot was born Henry Ray Perot in Texarkana, Texas, on June 27, 1930, to Gabriel Ross and Lulu May Perot. When young Perot entered the fifth grade, his parents changed his name to "Henry Ross," so that the elder Perot would have a namesake. An older child, Gabriel Ross, Jr., had died of meningitis at the age of three.

Perot's background was that of a Norman Rockwell world; solid small-town America, where parents worked hard and raised their children by the traditional work ethic, God and country were sacred, and sins were dishonesty, drinking, and debt. Young Ross impressed teachers and community members by attaining the rank of Eagle Scout at the age of 13, only 16 months after joining the Boy Scouts.

Perot was also known for his business acumen, striking a deal with the publisher of the *Texarkana Gazette* to double his commission for papers delivered in a ghetto area. In an eerily prophetic statement, the young Boy Scout dumbfounded his scout leader by suggesting a way to become a member of General Motors' board of directors: getting proxies from thousands of minority stockholders.

Perot attended Texarkana Junior College in 1947, where he restarted the school yearbook and was elected president of the student council. In 1949 his compulsive badgering of Senator W. Lee O'Daniel landed Perot an appointment with the United States Naval Academy in Annapolis. A few people were amused at this little dustdevil from Texarkana, Texas. The rigors and disciplined lifestyle of the Naval Academy suited Perot, who had never seen the ocean before. He was elected class president and head of the honor committee, and his grades were respectable, though only slightly above average. Perot graduated in 1953 and served his obligatory four years. He married Margot Birmingham from Greenberg, Pennsylvania, in 1956, after meeting her on a blind date.

By 1957 Perot knew that the navy was too confining for his maverick ways. When his tour of duty was up, he interviewed with IBM at the suggestion of a naval reserve officer who was an IBM executive, and in 1957 he began work in their Dallas office.

It didn't take long for executives at IBM to realize that they had a serious whirlwind in their midst. The aggressive, compulsive Perot quickly reached sales quotas and asked for more challenging assignments. Not content to remain in the company maze, Perot came up with new ways of doing business.

What if, he proposed, we sell a larger-than-needed computer to a company and then allow other companies to access time on this computer, maximizing use of the machine and making a profit for all concerned? Executives at IBM laughed and agreed it was a whole new concept, but not one they were interested in.

Much to the dismay of his employers, the relentless Perot continued to pursue the concept of time-sharing and turnkey systems, where complete computer services, including skilled operators, were provided. When he saw that IBM was not going to cooperate, he knew that the only way to realize his goal was to go it alone. On June 27, 1962, his 32nd birthday, Perot launched Electronic Data Systems Corporation with a starting capital of one thousand dollars.

Section III

In the coming years, Perot would continue to make momentous decisions and announcements on June 27th.

For the first time in his life, Ross Perot was in total control, and total control was what it took to succeed. His method was simple: Hire only top people, focus completely on your goal, and guarantee employees a stake in the outcome. The little dustdevil from Texarkana was whipping up into a full-fledged storm.

In 1964 EDS had only fifteen employees with stars in their eyes. But in 1965 Congress passed legislation that entitled some 30 to 50 million Americans to medical benefits—Medicare. Fortunately for Perot's EDS, an unprecedented amount of red tape accumulated almost overnight. This was the Big One, and EDS lost no time getting its shiny black wingtips in the door. Profits soared, and competition was practically nonexistent.

Initially, EDS was patterned somewhat after IBM, with employees adhering to strict dress codes and standards of behavior—only the standards at EDS were even stricter and higher. In the beginning, the chosen few who made up the company worked day and night to secure contracts and process raw data. Every night at dusk, Perot's stable of systems analysts and engineers fanned out in offices all over Dallas to gather and process data.

There was no hurdle too high, no corporate data too complex for the superteams of EDS. Corporate executives learned that when EDS came on board, things happened. Suddenly, with the ferocity of a Texas thunderstorm, companies found their intricate problems analyzed and categorized, their tasks streamlined. Never mind the chaos and destruction left in their path. EDS delivered. And at the helm of it all was their fearless leader, riding his herd of superwizards into unchartered high-tech territory and a rightful place in computer lore.

On September 12, 1968, Electronic Data Systems Corporation went public, offering its stock for $16.50 per share. The stock closed at $22.00 per share by the end of the day, and its founder, at the age of 38, was a multimillionaire and soon to be a billionaire. In March of 1970, the stock was selling for $160 per share.

Back in Dallas, H. Ross Perot was quickly becoming a legend. His fanatical devotion to faithful employees became well known. Perot spread his wealth freely around the community, giving millions of dollars to charities and often helping individuals anonymously.

Perot lived on a highly guarded north Dallas estate with his wife, Margot, and their five children (one son and four daughters). The Perot household was run like the Perot business: everything on time, ship-shape, in top form—military style. Perot's influence was being felt outside the business world as well. Like any great leader, Ross Perot was not content to merely oversee his domain. All around him, he saw things that needed to be done, and Dallas civic leaders in the know knew one thing: If you want something done, tell Perot he can't do it. There might be debris and destruction when he finished, but the Texas Tornado could get things done.

In 1969 Perot made national headlines when he attempted to deliver two planeloads of food, medical supplies, and Christmas gifts to POWs in North Vietnam. Although North Vietnamese officials refused to accept the gifts, Perot's momentous effort did not go unnoticed. Conditions and medical treatment for prisoners began to improve, and Perot continued to be their advocate, harassing the State Department on the prisoners' (and MIAs') behalf and financing his own rescue missions.

Perot's most famous rescue attempt was a successful one, and it occurred in January 1979, when ex-Green Beret Bull Simons led a group of EDS executives into Iran to free EDS Manager Paul Chiapparone and his assistant, Bill Gaylord, who were being held in an Iranian prison. When Perot saw that the State Department would not be able to free his men, acting on the advice of his dying mother, he arranged the mission himself.

Section III

Perot visited the two jailed executives prior to the mission and then hired Bull Simons to free them. As it turned out, an EDS employee who happened to be an Iranian national organized a mob that broke into the prison and released all the prisoners, including Chiapparone and Gaylord. The daring rescue prompted Perot to hire British author Ken Follett, who immortalized the incident in his book *On Wings of Eagles*, later adapted as a television miniseries.

In Dallas, Perot himself was making headlines—and enemies—with his education reform proposals. The corporate crusader, asked to look into education problems in Texas schools, flew into action by studying the issue, devising a plan, and successfully lobbying for school reform legislation, including literacy testing for teachers, $3 billion in new spending, and the infamous "No Pass, No Play" rule that required sports participants to maintain passing grades or get benched. This particular piece of legislation made Perot the target of threats from angry coaches and sports lovers.

Meanwhile, an ill-fated merger was in the works between Perot's EDS and one of the country's most powerful institutions—the General Motors Corporation. In 1984 Perot was approached by a representative of Salomon Brothers with General Motors' offer to buy EDS. Accompanied by Mort Meyerson, CEO of EDS, Perot went to visit GM's Detroit facilities. They met with Roger Smith, Chairman of GM, who explained that GM needed the technical expertise of EDS to streamline operations, update communications, and make things more efficient.

This marriage made on Wall Street was a turbulent one. General Motors thought they were getting not only EDS, but Perot's expertise as well—and did they ever. The Dallas billionaire vilified everything from an elitist bureaucracy to the "frozen middle" management and mistreatment of workers at the Goliath auto company. Perot saw himself as the savior of the American auto industry, but this was one mountain even he couldn't conquer. In one of the costlier corporate divorces on record, GM finally rid themselves of the Texas Tornado by paying Perot $700 million dollars to go away.

    H. Ross Perot's main legacy is likely to be in politics. When Perot started speaking out against government policies, he struck a chord with disenchanted voters. Whether it was education, crime, welfare, or drugs, Perot had an opinion—and a straightforward solution to the problem.

    You want to get rid of drugs? Okay, cordon off a section of the neighborhood, call in the National Guard, and go house-to-house. Apply the rules of war. It might not be pretty, but we can do it. You want to end welfare? No work—no check. It's that simple. Tired of gridlock in Congress? Well, the constitution *could* be revised, you know. We're operating under a 200-year-old system here. Germany and Japan wrote new constitutions. Why can't we?

    Whoa! What was that, Ross? Naw, not really. Just something to dangle in front of those fellas up on Capitol Hill to get them off their fannies. It's *your* country! You are the owners. Take it back!

    Americans liked what they heard. Finally, somebody with business sense *and* common sense, speaking the truth. They flocked to Perot by the thousands and millions, begging to place his name on the 1992 Presidential ballot.

    In Washington, scared politicians ran for cover and hoped this was one tornado that would blow over. But they underestimated the man from Texas. He was not a fly-by-night or flash-in-the-pan politician, but a full-fledged norther sweeping the fruited plains of America, a folk hero and man of the people who represented a new breed of politician, attracting Democrats, Republicans, liberals, conservatives, and plain old apathetic voters who hadn't been so stirred up in decades.

    The ideas being spouted by Perot were new and innovative, such as electronic town halls, a drastic deficit-reduction plan, and elimination of Political Action Committees (PACs). Plus, Perot could always be counted on for great quotes. With his amazing blend of business acumen, horse sense, and folksy humor, Perot shot to the heart of the issue with quick-witted, piercing arrows.

On the national debt:
The debt is like a crazy aunt we keep down in the basement. All the neighbors know she's there, but nobody wants to talk about her.... We have to face up to our debt. We have to do it now.

On Congress:
They enjoy the same perks, PAC payouts, bounced checks, fawning staffs, and personal exemptions from the laws they pass.

On drugs:
Drugs are the source of many of our rising crime statistics. The drug problem at its core is a reflection of our social decay, resulting from the dissolution of the family structure, lack of economic opportunity, and the decline of individual responsibility.

On abortion:
I support a woman's right to have an abortion. It is the woman's choice.

On the environment:
Certainly I am an environmentalist, and any thinking, reasoning person is an environmentalist.

On workers:
We need an environment where top to bottom—I'd like to just eliminate the word "management"—top to bottom, we're all labor. We work night and day to win.

The grass-roots petition drive quickly mushroomed into a national movement. President George Bush and Governor Bill Clinton, the Republican and Democratic contenders, now had a new worry: Candidate Perot. But Perot was more than just a contender; he was leading a phenomenal movement that would change the American political structure. At the peak of his campaign, in June 1992, polls showed that Perot had gained the support of an astounding 37 percent of American voters.

Perotistas, as his followers were called, were a rabid group. At rallies all over the country, inspired converts waved flags and shouted slogans, while bands played "Crazy," Perot's theme song.

Candidate Perot shocked and angered his faithful ranks by abruptly withdrawing from the presidential campaign on July 16, 1992, accusing the Republicans of spying and alluding to vague threats to ruin his daughter's August wedding. Thousands of hardworking volunteers were stunned that their fearless leader had left them. Perot was crucified by the media, who accused him of being a quitter.

In Washington, there was good news and bad news. The good news was Perot had quit, but the bad news was that his followers wouldn't. Although some of their movement's momentum was gone, Perotistas had started something that gave no indication of subsiding—getting involved in your government and fighting city hall. Desperate fans pleaded with Perot to change his mind, and in Dallas, hundreds of mirrors arrived in the mail, sent by volunteers who admonished Perot to "look in the mirror," for the solution, as he had often told them to do.

Dismayed by the reaction to his withdrawal, Perot promised to help the movement from the sidelines. He continued to fund volunteer groups, but his presence was primarily felt by candidates Bush and Clinton, as Perot seized every opportunity to criticize government practices. George Bush and Bill Clinton learned what Roger Smith and hundreds of other people knew a long time ago: Ross Perot was tough, radical, intimidating, and controversial, but he was usually right.

The clamor for Perot to return to the race was so great that in October, with the election only a few weeks away, he jumped back in. The "October Surprise," as newspapers billed him, bought prime television time for his thirty-minute "infomercials," during which he used graphs and flow charts to show how government spending was wildly out of control and to recruit members for his new political watchdog group, "United We Stand America."

Although he garnered only 19 percent of the popular vote and failed to carry a single state, his influence on the race and forthcoming policies was incalculable. Perot continued to offer constructive criticism, give speeches, and appear before congressional committees. His vocal opposition to NAFTA (North American Free Trade Agreement) led to a televised debate with Vice President Al Gore. Gore won, and NAFTA passed, but Perot pressed on.

Today, Ross Perot lives in Dallas with his wife and, along with Mort Meyerson, heads Perot Systems Corporation, a computer-services company. He continues to support United We Stand America and offer his unique brand of succinct wisdom to those who will listen, and the nation's politicians, as well as business leaders, continue to fear an encounter with the Texas Tornado.

2.
John Neely Bryan (1810-1877)

John Neely Bryan, a Tennessee lawyer and adventurer, arrived in the area now known as Dallas in 1841, after hearing about the "Three Forks" area of the Trinity River from Indians and other travelers. Although Bryan is credited with founding and developing the city that is today

Dallas, he was given little credit for this accomplishment during his lifetime.

Upon reaching the high bluff of the Three Forks (now Dealey Plaza), Bryan built a camp using poles, brush, and dirt and staked his claim there. At that time, the bluff was overlooking the Trinity River, which was later straightened and moved away from town.

Relatively little is known about Bryan's activities, because he was too busy building, farming, negotiating with Indians, and planning a town to leave written records. His actions are visible, though, in the carefully chosen site, which was a natural river crossing point, and which Bryan hoped would be a major navigable port someday.

John Neely Bryan, founder of Dallas, and his wife, Margaret Beeman Bryan. (From the collections of the Texas/Dallas History and Archives Division, Dallas Public Library.)

Section III

By August of 1842, Bryan had registered his town and named it Dallas. During that first winter, supplies ran low, weather was harsh, and attacks by hostile Indians occurred in the area. But Bryan, alone on the bluff, persevered, with help from settlers at nearby Bird's Fort. Travelers to the area reported that the enthusiastic Bryan would dash out of his cabin and practically pull them off their horses, offering free meals, whiskey, and honey—even free land, if they would only stay (although Bryan himself did not have legal title to the land yet).

The land of the entire upper Trinity area was at the time under the management of the Texas Emigration and Land Company, and was known as "Peters Colony." Along with the settlers at Bird's Fort, Bryan was considered a squatter, and only he was able to negotiate a legitimate claim to the land with the Peters Colony agent. Bryan convinced the Bird's Fort settlers to move down to his bluff.

In the meantime, land developers from Peters Colony were conducting an extensive advertising campaign in the United States and Europe to lure settlers to Texas. Apparently, the Texas art of boasting had already begun by this time.

A man passing through the area, John B. Billingsley, who later settled in the area, wrote:

> We had heard a great deal about the Three Forks of the Trinity and the town of Dallas.... We heard of it often, yes, the place, but the town where was it? Two small log cabins, the logs just as nature found them, the walls just high enough for the door boards and the covering of clapboards, held to their place with poles, chimneys made of sticks and mud and old mother earth serving as floors; a shelter made of four sticks for a smith shop, a garden fenced in with brush, and mortar in which they beat their corn into meal. This was the town of Dallas and two families, ten or twelve souls were its population ... One deep,

narrow and crooked channel was all we could see of the far famed Trinity River.

Indian attacks continued, and in an attempt to alleviate the problem, Sam Houston, who was president of the Republic of Texas, invited nine tribal chiefs to meet with him in August of 1883 at Grapevine Springs (now Coppell). On his way to the meeting, Houston stopped at Dallas to visit John Neely Bryan and his new bride, Margaret Beeman.

According to E. Parkinson, an Englishman who accompanied Houston, Bryan was a "hardy backwoodsman, and a sensible, industrious, ingenious and hospitable man," but Parkinson expressed skepticism about Bryan's vision of river navigation. Eventually, Sam Houston was successful in negotiating a treaty with the nine tribes, and the threat of warfare soon ended.

Bryan's dream of a navigable river was never realized, but the town known as Dallas continued to grow, thanks to his foresight. In 1844 surveyor J.P. Dumas laid the original town square, including the block marked for a courthouse, which is the site of the Old Red Courthouse today. Bryan deeded this land to Dumas and eventually it was given to Dallas County.

A church and school were begun, and other settlers began to move to the area. The town's first established business was a tent saloon, and Bryan continued to oversee the settlement, farm his land, and greet newcomers, wearing his usual attire of buckskin leggings, moccasins, and a plaid blanket coat.

For a short time, Bryan left Dallas, joining the many others searching for riches in California. He soon returned to Dallas, however, to live with his wife and young son, John Neely Bryan, Jr. He secured Dallas' position in the territory by promising to donate the courthouse square if Dallas was chosen as the county seat.

Section III

This accomplished, Bryan entered a period of depression and heavy drinking. At 39 years of age, he had given away or sold much of his property, failed to bring navigation to the Trinity, and returned from California without finding gold. Eventually, after wounding a man in a brawl, Bryan left for the Oklahoma Territory in disgrace.

Bryan returned to Dallas in 1861 so "haggard and worn" that his own children did not recognize him. At the age of 51, he enlisted as a volunteer in the Confederate forces and was discharged in 1862, when he returned to Dallas and built a house at Big Springs on White Rock Creek.

Along with others, Bryan succeeded in persuading the officials of Houston and Texas Central Railroad to change their proposed route so that it passed directly through Dallas. This feat was secured amidst much celebration and feasting on July 16, 1872.

Bryan continued to live at Big Springs until February 1877, when his family committed him to the state mental hospital in Austin. His death at the hospital on September 14, 1877, went unrecorded in the local newspaper, and he was buried in the institution's graveyard, leaving his indomitable pioneer spirit as legacy to his beloved city.

Sec. II:4—Log Cabin (and a little pioneer history)
Sec. II:8:—Trinity River—Where is it?
Sec. II:13—Pioneer Plaza
Sec. III:10—George Mifflin Who?

3.
The Hunt Family—*Silver, Scandal, and Texas Tea*

Long before there was Ross Perot, long before there was J.R. Ewing, there was Haroldson Lafayette Hunt. And if you think you have troubles, imagine how Mrs. Lyda Bunker Hunt felt when her husband, H.L., informed her that he had sired two other families in order to spread around his "genius genes," as he called them.

H.L. Hunt, Jr. was the last of eight children born to Haroldson Lafayette "Hash" Hunt and Ella Rose Myers Hunt, who lived on a farm near Vandalia, Illinois. He was born February 17, 1889, and was named after his father, but everyone called him "June," shortened from "Junior."

June Hunt was an early reader whose father took pride in having the little boy read livestock reports out loud to visitors. He was, however, very much a "mama's boy," who wore baby dresses until the age of three and was permitted to nurse his mother's breast until he was seven years of age, when his father caught him standing on a crate in the kitchen nursing and put a stop to the activity.

In 1905, at the age of 16, June, with not one cent to his name, boarded a freight train bound for Kansas. He did, however, have a pack of cards with him, and he worked along the way as a dishwasher, sheepherder, and mule-driver. For a short time, he stayed in San Francisco, departing the city only a few days before the devastating 1906 earthquake.

Hunt wandered back to Texas and spent the next several years working odd jobs with his brother Leonard. He developed a talent as a "card locator," a player who memorizes the sequence of cards played in one hand. This ability earned the young Hunt a great deal of money and the nickname "Arizona Slim." Most of Hunt's games were played with strangers in railroad yards and logging camps.

121

After spending around six years on the road, Hunt settled in Lake Village, Arkansas, where he bought 960 acres and planted cotton. His entire crop was wiped out when the Mississippi River flooded. June continued his card-playing, however, often ferrying across the river to Greenville, where he would stay up all night playing cards.

In 1914 June met Lyda Bunker, a 25-year-old schoolteacher from Jonesboro, Arkansas, who offered him the emotional security he apparently sought after the death of his mother that same year. They married on November 26, 1914, in the Lake Village home of Lyda's parents. Their first child, Margaret, was born in 1915, and in 1917 a son, Haroldson Lafayette, Jr., later called "Hassie," was born. Note that H.L. gave the boy his own name, rather than naming him H.L. Hunt III. Lyda gave birth to a third child, Caroline Rose, in 1923.

Hunt continued his poker-playing and was by this time a professional gambler. Soon, he decided to try his gambling methods on another commodity: land. At first, he did quite well, but in 1921 he lost everything by selling short on cotton futures.

The story is told in the Hunt family that H.L., with the last $100 in his pocket, took his daughter to New Orleans to have her tonsils examined by a doctor there. While in New Orleans, he went to the Grunewald Hotel and got into a poker game with Jinks Miller, White Top, Indian Jack, and John Crow, high-powered players whose names were well known in the region. When Arizona Slim left the table that night in New Orleans, he had turned his $100 into $10,000, which he quickly spent on land deals. Lyda Hunt was not thrilled with her husband's card-playing and land speculation deals and had returned to teaching school in order to make ends meet.

In 1921 Hunt heard about an oil boom going on over in El Dorado, Arkansas, and decided to see what the fuss was all about. It was in El Dorado that Hunt first leased property, borrowed and bought old drilling equipment, and struck oil drilling his first well. It was the beginning of what came to be known as "Hunt luck."

By acting on hunches and staying one step ahead of the oil-thirsty crowd, Hunt bought up leases and quickly learned what worked and what didn't in the oil business. He became known as one driller who was honest and would always see that his men were paid. Lyda Hunt learned to manage without her husband and became known in El Dorado as a friendly, unassuming, religious woman who ran a strict household and never put on airs.

Tragedy came to the Hunt family on March 20, 1925, when their one-month-old daughter died after breathing gas fumes. H.L. took his distraught wife to New York City in an attempt to console her, and she became pregnant once again. In the summer of that same year, Hunt informed his wife that he was going to Florida to check out the oil business there.

Somewhat of a loner, H.L. Hunt was gone from home most of the time and had few close friends, but he did enjoy charming the ladies. While in Tampa, Florida, Hunt met 21-year-old Frania Tye, a beauty who was selling real estate. She was charmed by the dashing 36-year-old Hunt, who continued commuting back and forth from El Dorado.

According to later testimony by Frania, Hunt, whom she knew as "Franklin Hunt," asked her to marry him, and they were married in November 1925. Later, she claimed she had no idea he was already married, and H.L. privately denied that the two were ever formally married. He did not, however, deny that he fathered her four children: Howard (1926), Haroldina (1928), Helen (1930), and Hugh (1934).

On February 20, 1926, Lyda gave birth to Nelson Bunker Hunt in El Dorado. During that same year, Hunt moved Frania to Shreveport, Louisiana, and she had her first child, Howard, followed by a daughter, Haroldina, in 1928. In 1929, Lyda gave birth to another son, William Herbert, followed in 1932 by Lamar.

Meanwhile, the busy father was shuttling back and forth between El Dorado and Shreveport, spending the majority of his time in the oil fields. He incorporated his first company, H.L. Hunt, Inc. The oilman found that the black, sticky goo, although difficult to remove, softened skin texture, so he arranged to market some of his oil for cosmetic use. Most of the money Hunt made was put back into wildcatting ventures.

In 1930 Hunt moved Frania and her children to the prestigious Dallas neighborhood Highland Park, and she gave birth to a third child, Helen. Hunt heard about an East Texas wildcatter named C.M. "Dad" Joiner. The two men met on September 5, 1930, at the site of the infamous Daisy Bradford No. 3 well. On the day Hunt met Joiner, a drill stem test had just indicated that, after fifteen months of drilling on this well, they had tapped into the first major oil field discovered in Texas.

The Daisy Bradford well was to become the largest pool of oil ever tapped into at that time, and H.L. Hunt had to have a piece of it. Unfortunately, when news of the big discovery reached investors, they claimed to have been defrauded by Joiner, who holed up in the Hotel Adolphus in Dallas in an attempt to avoid being served with court papers.

Hunt, desperate for a piece of the action, convinced Joiner to sell his leases to him, in exchange for $1.335 million—$30,000 in cash and the rest in future oil payments. Hunt also inherited Joiner's legal problems, which were manifold. The legendary deal was made on November 25 and 26, 1930, in Suite 1553 of the old Baker Hotel in Dallas.

Leases from the Joiner deal, according to Harry Hurt III, in his book *Texas Rich*, were the foundation of the Hunt fortune, paying an estimated $100,000,000 over the next fifteen years. Hunt Oil Company was officially founded in Tyler, Texas, in 1934, and eventually became one of the world's largest independent oil companies.

The Dad Joiner leases were drilled under Panola Pipeline Company, so named after the county where the land was located. H.L. decided that six-letter words beginning with P were lucky, and he proceeded to name more than a dozen ventures with six-letter "P" words: Parade Co., Penrod Drilling, Parade Press, Patron Properties, Penrod International Drilling, Petrol Marine, Placer Properties, Placid Oil, Planet Investments, Portal Boat Co., Primal Boat Co., Profit Island, Profit Investments, and Pursue Energy.

In 1934 Hunt's extramarital activities caught up with him in Dallas, when a friend of Frania told her that her husband "Franklin" had another wife and family. The guilty party was called on the carpet, and Hunt's response was to attempt to convert Frania to Mormonism, because "having two or three wives was normal in that religion." Frania refused his offer to fly to Utah and become a Mormon, and eventually Hunt moved her and the four children to a house he purchased in Great Neck, New York.

In 1938 Hunt moved Lyda and their six surviving children to Mount Vernon, a Dallas estate that is a replica of George Washington's home of the same name. The famous house on the northwest shore of White Rock Lake has been used as a backdrop for most of the documentaries done on the Hunt family.

The oldest Hunt son, "Hassie," who looked eerily like his father, had become partners with H.L. in drilling ventures and had evidently inherited his father's knack for oil. Unfortunately, the young man developed severe mental problems that eventually resulted in a lobotomy being performed on him in the 1940s, a tragedy that would continue to haunt the family.

Sometime around 1942, Hunt began a relationship with a Hunt Oil secretary, Ruth Eileen Ray, and it was not long before she was pregnant with her first child. Ruth, her fellow employees reported, was a religious woman who read the Bible every day and kept a can on her desk for tithing.

Section III

Hunt confided to Ruth and others that he believed he had special powers and carried a "genius gene" and was doing the world a great service by fathering many children.

Apparently, she succumbed to Hunt's "genius gene" theory, for although he moved her to New York and provided her with a cover story during her pregnancy, she made no secret of the 1943 birth of Ray Lee Wright, declaring to one person that he was destined to be president of the United States. Ruth, who had assumed the surname "Wright," and her son were set up in a house on White Rock Lake, less than two minutes from Mount Vernon. Hunt and Ruth had three more children, all girls: Ruth June (1944), Helen LaKelley (1949), and Swanee Grace (1950).

Hunt continued to live in Dallas, building his fortune in relative obscurity until 1948, when *Life* magazine ran a photo of him with the caption, "Is this the richest man in the U.S.?" Suddenly, the Hunts were thrust into national spotlight, and, although it was debatable whether or not Hunt was the richest man in the U.S. at that time, his myth began to grow, fueled by the national image of wealthy Texas oilmen.

Hunt seemed to relish the attention and used the opportunity to begin promoting his ultraconservative political views, primarily through Facts Forum, a group organized by Hunt to broadcast a radio show and publish a newsletter. During the anticommunism wave of the 1950s, Facts Forum was well received by a number of Americans who feared the growing communist assault. Hunt's political views, however, would come back to haunt him in 1963.

Lyda Hunt, a deeply religious woman, continued to raise her children and grandchildren and work in the Highland Park Presbyterian Church in her unassuming manner. Frania, the mother of Hunt's second family, even reported being introduced to Lyda at a meeting arranged by H.L. in a Dallas hotel room in 1940, and she concluded that, "Mrs. Hunt was the finest woman I ever met."

The first Mrs. Hunt did not have an easy life. Saddened by the mental breakdown of her oldest son, Hassie, and continually hurt by Hunt's infidelities, she at one point broke down and cried in front of one of her husband's secretaries. Shocked by this unaccustomed outburst, the secretary asked her why she did not divorce Hunt. Mrs. Hunt replied, "Because I have children to be considered, and as long as I live, I'm going to protect them from what's going to happen when I'm gone."

In 1955 Lyda suffered a serious stroke and was flown to the Mayo Clinic, accompanied by H.L. and five of her children. On May 6, 1955, at the age of sixty-six, Lyda Bunker Hunt died. Although Hunt never memorialized his wife, her children gave a large donation to a college and a church in her name. H.L. did suffer with his wife's loss, according to those who knew him well.

In the fall of 1957, Hunt married Ruth Wright after Ray, their son, paid Hunt a visit and demanded that he marry his mother, who was, according to Ray, "a good, religious person." Hunt's first family knew nothing about their father's marriage until they saw newspaper headlines the next day.

Dallas tongues were wagging, especially after Hunt announced that he was "adopting" Ruth's four children and changing their last name to Hunt. H.L. Hunt might be the richest man in the U.S., but as far as Dallas was concerned, he was an embarrassment to the city.

Ruth began working on reforming her husband. One of her first accomplishments was getting him to give up gambling, a "hobby" that he had continued to pursue with vigor, wagering enormous sums of money. Ruth, a Baptist, engaged the powerful Dr. W.A. Criswell of the huge First Baptist Church in Dallas to convert her sinful husband.

Hunt resurrected his defunct Facts Forum group as "LIFE LINE" and promoted it as a quasireligious and political organization. By this time, Hunt had branched into the food business. HLH Products, a subsidiary of Hunt Oil, had food-processing plants in seven states and eventually produced 1,340 items, many of them touted as "health foods."

H.L. became involved in the 1960 presidential campaign by paying for the distribution of 200,000 copies of an anti-Catholic sermon aimed at John Kennedy preached by Dr. Criswell. Hunt's scheme backfired when the Criswell leaflet became the subject of a Senate investigation, because the sermon leaflets did not state who paid for the printing and mailing, a violation of federal election laws.

Hunt and one of his aides went into hiding in West Texas, prompting a search played out in newspapers across the country. One Texas paper printed the taunting headline, "Come Out, Big Daddy, Wherever You Are." Hunt surfaced in the fall of 1960 and faced the public, admitting his role in the leaflet. Although he had not technically violated the law, Hunt was the target of moral outrage. Surprisingly, four days before the election, Hunt announced his support of the JFK-Lyndon Johnson ticket.

In spite of Hunt's enormous wealth, he led a routine life. Ruth packed his lunch in a brown paper sack each morning, and he drove downtown in his Chevrolet Impala to the First National Bank building, where Hunt enterprises occupied several floors.

As H.L. pursued his health food business and political interests, he began leaving the oil business to his sons Bunker and Herbert. In November 1963, Bunker, along with other Dallas businessmen, contributed several hundred dollars to run an ad in the *Dallas Morning News*. The full-page black-bordered ad, consisting of inflammatory questions regarding President Kennedy's stance on U.S. foreign policy and communism, appeared in the morning paper November 22. In bold letters, the ad proclaimed, "WELCOME, MR. KENNEDY, TO DALLAS."

The presidential motorcade passed right below the Hunt offices on Main Street. Moments later, in the midst of the noisy, cheering crowd, President Kennedy was shot and killed. Pandemonium swept through Dallas. Acting on the advice of the FBI, Hunt and his wife left town under assumed names. People in Dallas knew Hunt and his sons were outspoken critics of the President, and it was feared they would be the object of death threats.

Threatening phone calls and letters were sent to the Hunts, and there were even gunshots fired at Mount Vernon. A widespread boycott of HLH products began. After spending two weeks in Washington, H.L. and Ruth returned to Dallas. Although H.L. insisted he was in no danger, Ruth and the family convinced him to allow police protection of the family.

The FBI and later the Warren Commission investigators found several connections between the Hunts and those known to be involved in the Kennedy assassination. Lamar Hunt's name appeared in a notebook of Jack Ruby's, the Dallas nightclub owner who shot and killed Kennedy's assassin, Lee Harvey Oswald. Apparently, a girlfriend of Ruby's had interviewed for a job with Lamar.

Police also found LIFE LINE literature in Ruby's pockets when he was arrested. Curiously, a few weeks before the assassination, Ruby had thrown a temper tantrum when he came across some LIFE LINE political literature at the Dallas Exhibit Hall. Grabbing up a handful of leaflets, Ruby declared, "No one should be able to talk that way about the government." FBI investigators also found Ruby and the Hunt family (daughter Caroline Hunt Sands) shared a domestic worker. No evidence uncovered anything more than coincidental links between Hunt and those involved in the Kennedy assassination, but the family members were dogged with continual questions.

In 1965 a giant oil discovery in south-central Louisiana, the Black Lake Field, made the Hunts bona fide billionaires for the first time. Discovered by Placid Oil, the Black Lake Field brought with it new problems, because Placid was not owned by H.L. himself, but by the trusts of the six children from the first family.

Section III

H.L. Hunt in front of Mount Vernon, his White Rock estate. (From the collections of the Texas/Dallas History and Archives Division, Dallas Public Library.)

In the meantime, HLH Products, Hunt's food division, was rapidly gobbling up H.L.'s fortune. Since the mid-1960s, HLH Products, which supported both LIFE LINE and the food division, had been losing $1 million annually, a loss that was absorbed by Hunt Oil. The first family, fearing that their father was losing everything, tried to take matters into their hands, which resulted in their estrangement from H.L., who refused to believe that HLH Products was bleeding him dry. Eventually, Bunker and Herbert, who apparently inherited H.L.'s paranoia, set up an elaborate wiretapping scheme to find out where all the money was going, a move that would cost them in the future.

The Hunt children continue to leave their marks on the city of Dallas. In 1960 sports-loving Lamar founded the American Football League after the NFL rejected his Dallas Texans, who became the Kansas City Chiefs in 1963. After several years of struggle, the AFL began to gain respect in the clubby world of pro football, particularly after the Super Bowl games began. Eventually, the NFL and AFL merged. Mild-mannered and soft-spoken, Lamar is often compared to Clark Kent. He is a member of the Pro Football Hall of Fame and the National Soccer Hall of Fame. Lamar has also been very active in tennis, and his Dallas-based World Championship Tennis revolutionized the game.

Norma Hunt, Lamar's second wife, is given credit for bringing class and style to the Hunt family. A Richardson schoolteacher and great football fan, Norma married Lamar in 1964. She changed her hair to blonde and began wearing designer clothes and appearing at social events with her husband, breaking the Hunt tradition of shunning high society. In 1979 Lamar and Norma stunned the Dallas arts community by donating the Frederic Church painting "Icebergs," which they had acquired for $2.5 million, to the Dallas Museum of Art. It was a record price for an American painting. Happy curators at the DMA knew better than to ask questions, but word around town was that the couple, after purchasing the painting, got home and found that the thing was too large to fit in their house. Norma and Lamar live in a palatial estate on ten acres in North Dallas.

Bunker Hunt, who is perhaps best recognized as the heavier Hunt, is married to Caroline (not to be confused with Hunt's sister Caroline) and lives on Lakeside Drive in Highland Park. Herbert, married to Nancy (not to be confused with Ray's wife Nancy), lives in University Park.

The two "boys," internationally known wheeler-dealers, have gotten into a number of high-stakes scrapes. The first was being indicted in 1973 for wiretapping, when the two were investigating alleged thefts involving their father's food company and three of his closest business associates. Bunker and Herbert were accused of illegally tapping the home phones of four of their father's aides, a nephew, and a secretary in 1969 and 1970, in order to expose an embezzlement scheme.

In the midst of family legal troubles, H.L. Hunt died in 1974 at the age of eighty-five. When his will was filed for probate on December 3, 1974, it was a "stunner," according to *People* magazine. Hunt left his Mount Vernon home and all of his stock in Hunt Oil Company to Ruth, his second wife, and named Ray, Ruth's thirty-one-year-old son, sole executor of the estate. The Louisiana oil leases were divided between the children of the three families.

Naming Ray as executor of the estate was a slap in the face to Bunker and Herbert, who had long been running things at Hunt Oil, which they considered to be rightfully their company. Now it was clear their father had passed his mantle of leadership to Ray. Technically and legally, Ray was now in charge.

At first, the brothers refused to relinquish any control to him or even talk to him, despite repeated attempts by Ray, who is known as "the nice Hunt," to contact the two. A showdown was imminent. Lamar and the sisters were not directly involved in Hunt Oil, so the battle was primarily between Ray, Bunker, and Herbert.

Although Ray's business experience up to this point was mostly in real estate, he was elected president of the Dallas Petroleum Club in February 1975, less than three months after his father's death. This prestigious honor was bestowed on him by oilmen who saw him as the up-and-coming leader of Dallas.

Meanwhile, Bunker and Herbert were too busy forming their new company, Hunt Energy Corporation, to siphon away as much of Hunt Oil as they could legally, and too busy preparing for their upcoming wiretapping trial to worry about talking to Ray Hunt. The desperate Ray finally got through to the hardheaded boys almost three months after H.L.'s death, and they agreed on a temporary truce, in which Bunker and Herbert would move all the first family's companies, trusts, and accounts out from under Hunt Oil and reorganize them under Hunt Energy. The two would retain seats on the Hunt Oil board of directors, however, because the first family still held 18½ percent of Hunt Oil stock. Ray Hunt, who now controlled 80 percent of Hunt Oil, would assume the title of president.

Meanwhile, there was a trial coming up in Lubbock, and in July of 1975, about two months before the scheduled trial, the Hunt brothers were indicted by a federal grand jury for obstruction of justice in connection with the wiretapping. Things didn't look so good for the Hunt boys. Their attorney, Phil Hirschkop, planned a "good ole boy" defense that would portray his clients as a couple of well-meaning businessmen looking out for the best interests of their family. The trouble was that Bunker and Herbert came across to the public as anything but good ole boys. That problem was remedied by the hiring of a public relations man who taught the two to loosen up in front of cameras, beam to reporters, and at least act like they were big buddies with the second family.

At the drop of the gavel, the secretive, private Hunt families decided that there really was no family feud over that fortune. More than a dozen Hunt family members, including second wife Ruth, attended the trial to show their support of the "boys." Newspapers around the state carried photos of a jousting Bunker, who, although he might look like he hadn't cracked a smile in a decade, sure was having a jolly old time now. Photogenic Norma (Mrs. Lamar), Nancy (Mrs. Herbert), and Caroline appeared with Ruth, their stepmother, looking as though they were at a Dallas high-society tea. Herbert, with tears in his eyes, testified that he and his brother tapped phones because they could not walk away from their father's financial troubles. Bunker and Herbert were shown on the news chit-chatting with reporters, with Ruth, slapping backs and joshing with the public.

"We've determined to help show we're a family that sticks together," Norma Hunt told a reporter.

The strategy worked. After all these years of privacy, the public finally got a good view of the Hunt family, and they liked what they saw. Bunker and Herbert were acquitted of the wiretapping charges, although they still had to face obstruction of justice charges. Two HLH employees, John W. Currington and John H. Brown, were found guilty in 1975 of defrauding HLH Products by setting up a dummy corporation to rake off brokerage charges on the sales of HLH Products. Each was sentenced to three years' probation, a $1,000 fine, and forced to pay $2,501.40 in restitution. In 1976 the government dropped its charges against Herbert, and Bunker entered a plea of nolo contendere and was fined $1,000.

But the boys' troubles were only beginning. Bunker had long been investing in a wide variety of things. His stable of racehorses was unmatched in the world, and he had extensive holdings in Libyan oil fields before they were nationalized in 1973. Bunker and Herbert were also in the sugar business and somehow managed to throw the entire Colorado beet farming business into chaos. The infamous duo had a run-in with soybean farmers when they accumulated millions and millions of bushels of soybeans before the feds caught up with them and determined that the brothers' interest in soybeans was "disruptive and in violation of laws preventing manipulations." It seemed the brothers, once they determined to buy something, wanted *all* of it.

But sometime in 1973, Bunker and his little brother quietly began buying silver. A lot of silver. A whole lot of silver. More silver than anyone else they knew. As a matter of fact, more silver than anyone on the planet, maybe even more than King Solomon himself. Coins, bars, bullion, silver futures, anything sterling they could get their hands on. Also, the boys were doing something extremely rare—they were not only buying all the silver futures they could, they were actually taking delivery of the silver! This was not as simple as one might think it would be. The two had to lease 747s that flew in and out of New York, filled with the precious metal that was transported to old underground bomb shelters of friends, vaults in Switzerland, and other hiding places. Not only that, these 747s were manned by trained Texas gunmen who guarded the costly cargo.

While all this was going on, Ray Hunt stayed busy running Hunt Oil and planning his Reunion development. In 1973 Ray, who was known for being fair and civic-minded, undertook a project that would leave a permanent mark on Dallas: the development of the old Union Terminal area. When Ray purchased twenty acres of land on a decaying urban tract, he hired urban planners who drew and redrew parks, streets, and sports arenas. He met with Dallas city manager George Schrader and convinced him that it might be worthwhile for Dallas to enter a partnership with him to develop not only the original twenty acres, but also nearby parcels owned by the city. Although it was a novel approach to involve the city with private property owners, Ray convinced Schrader that what was good for business in Dallas was usually good for Dallas as well.

Ray gave his project, which was to include a large sports arena, hotel, and office towers, the name "Reunion." This name was seen as a particularly appropriate choice for several reasons. Since the project was being built in the old Union Terminal area, it meant remaking or renovating the Union Terminal. Also, the unprecedented partnership between private and public enterprise was a "reunion" of sorts.

But most significantly, Reunion was named in honor of the "La Reunion" colony, a group of French and Swiss utopians who established a colony in Dallas in the mid-1800s. Although the social experiment failed, many of the colonists remained in Dallas, giving the growing city an international flavor (*see Sec. IV:1*). Ray, a businessman, decided to honor their vision and pioneer spirit with the name "Reunion."

Reunion Tower, lighted at night as a sphere and described as "a giant dandelion," quickly became the new symbol of Dallas. *D, the Magazine of Dallas*, which was published from 1974 through 1993, was another project of Ray Hunt.

While their half-brother was busy with development projects, Herbert and Bunker carried on business as usual, or so it was thought, until 1979, when rumors that somebody was trying to corner the silver market heated up, and the big escapade was on. Silver shot from $9 an ounce in September to $20 in December, $35 in January 1980, and $50 on January 18.

Comex (Commodity Exchange) announced that effective February 18, traders would be limited to no more than 10 million ounces' worth of futures contracts. Bunker was furious and accused the exchanges and government of destroying the silver market by changing rules in the middle of the game. "The market will move to Europe," Bunker stated. "The silver market in this country is a thing of the past."

On January 17, 1980, the Hunts had silver-bullion worth almost $4.5 billion. Incredibly, the Hunts kept on buying, insisting that they were not trying to corner the market and telling the Commodity Futures Trading

Commission (CFTC) officials they were moving all their silver to Europe, because they feared the U.S. government might expropriate silver from citizens as they had done with gold in the 1930s. Although nobody was really sure what the Hunt boys were up to, everybody was anxious to get a piece of the action.

The silver world was in a panic, as rumors swirled around the globe. Swiss bankers were allegedly involved. The royal family of Saudi Arabia was allegedly involved. Grandmothers and eager granddaughters started melting down the family silver and cashing in. Silver stealing became a widespread problem, and many families hid their sterling flatware in attics or vaults.

In 1975, while all this was going on, Frania Tye Lee, Hunt's former mistress/wife, along with her children, filed suit against the estate, Frania claiming that H.L. promised to include her in his will. Although Hunt had provided for Frania's children in his will as part of the "Reliance Trusts," he never mentioned them by name nor did he refer to this family in his autobiography.

Frania's suit against the estate demanded that she be declared the putative (common-law) wife of H.L. Once again it was decreed, this time by Ray, that the two families pull together and put up their best front. In a long and drawn-out affair, the two other families agreed to pay Mrs. Lee and her heirs $7.5 million dollars.

Meanwhile, on the international front, the Great Silver Caper was still going on. On January 21, Commodity Exchange officials, who had decided the two Hunts were up to something, announced that trading would be limited to liquidation orders only—no more futures buying. Silver prices started to drop. Bunker began rolling his futures forward, as the price of silver fell to $35.20 an ounce on March 3, $21 on March 14. Bunker, convinced that the price would rise, refused to sell out.

On March 25, 1980, a tense Bunker, realizing they were unable to meet their margin calls, sent a three-word message to Herbert and Lamar (who had joined the silver jubilee), "Shut it down." The brothers were forced to pledge everything they owned, right down to Bunker's Rolex watch, to obtain a $1.1 billion loan to cover their silver debts.

Being Hunts, the brothers would not admit defeat easily. Bunker showed up in Paris on March 26 and released a statement to the press that he and four Arab partners had acquired "more than 200,000,000 ounces of silver" and were putting up this silver to back the sale of silver bonds, which would be distributed through "big European banks." Now, it seemed to the rest of the world that the Hunt brothers were attempting to create their own economy.

On Thursday, March 27, the silver market collapsed, with the price of silver falling from $15.80 at opening to $10.80 an ounce at the close of the day. Rumors and shock waves caused the Dow Jones average to drop 25.43 points on that same day. "Silver Thursday," as the day was known, caused panic around the world, but it was short-lived panic. The price of silver rallied the next day to $12 an ounce, and while small investors and those who had gone short on silver made money, the Hunt brothers, and those who had been following their lead, lost billions.

The recovering, but shaken, finance world could now sit back and enjoy watching the Dallas billionaires squirm. Bunker and Herbert's silver bullion alone had depreciated by nearly $4 billion since January, one of the biggest losses in U.S. financial history. When confronted with his loss of billions, the jet-setting, exhausted Bunker, arriving in Dallas from Saudi Arabia, merely stated that "a billion dollars isn't what it used to be."

The Hunts negotiated several deals with their creditors, and Federal Reserve Board Chairman Paul Volcker, fearing repercussions throughout the nation's financial system, agreed to a plan to bail the brothers out. Bunker, Herbert, and Lamar were forced to mortgage practically all of their companies' oil and gas leases, as well as many of their personal possessions.

Finally, observers noted, the brash Hunts were getting their comeuppance, and not only that, but the curious public was getting a chance to see what treasures the family had been hoarding. Personal items put up for collateral included sixteenth-century antiques, thousands of ancient coins from the third century B.C., Greek and Roman statuettes of bronze and silver, American landscape paintings, over four million acres of oil and gas leases, coal leases, real estate, lawn mowers, water coolers, and 500 race horses, with rather intriguing names: Extravagant, Overdrawn, and Trillionaire. There was not, however, a racehorse named "Overextended."

Bunker and Herbert's high-profile problems prompted Ray to issue a press release stating that Hunt Oil and Hunt Energy were "entirely separate organizations" and that "Hunt Oil never speculated in the silver market." The Securities & Exchange Commission, the CFTC, and two congressional committees began investigating the Texas brothers, who were portrayed by the media as greedy and mean, two real-life J.R. Ewings, referring to the villain of the popular television series "Dallas."

Photographs of the robust Bunker and slightly robust Herbert were run in papers all over the country, Bunker's picture even making the cover of *Newsweek*. The astounding wealth and art and coin collections of the Hunt brothers impressed even jaded Dallasites.

After ignoring one congressional subpoena and being cited for contempt, the two boys showed up in Washington in 1980 to testify before the House Subcommittee on Commerce, Consumer, and Monetary Affairs. Although the two had been depicted for weeks in the press as greedy villains, they managed to awe the lawmakers with their upfront, downhome style.

When asked how much the Hunts were worth, a straight-faced Bunker replied, "I don't have the figures in my head. People who know how much they're worth usually aren't worth that much."

Banks and the U.S. government weren't the only ones to call Bunker and Herbert on the carpet. Sister Margaret, who never approved of their wheeling and dealing to begin with, demanded to know what exactly was going on. The eldest of the Hunt children, Margaret Hunt Hill usually stayed on the sidelines, but some said she was the real chairman of the board in the family, and when Margaret spoke at family meetings, even Bunker and Herbert heeded what she had to say. Some Hunt employees referred to Margaret as "the big boss."

In the end, the Hunt women fared far better than the men, since they stayed out of the wheelings and dealings that almost destroyed their brothers. Margaret recently completed a biography of the Hunt family, and Caroline Rose Hunt has become one of the world's richest and most powerful women (*see following section*).

The Hunts managed to weather the silver storm with typical Hunt resilience. Although they lost billions on paper and their reputations had been soiled, they continued to battle on, restructuring debts and enduring their new notoriety. Followed everywhere by photographers and the press, the money-conscious Bunker noted, "At least I know they're using a little bit of silver every time they take my picture."

Well, boys, nobody can say it's easy being a billionaire.

Sec. I:5—That Famous Skyline
Sec. III:4—Caroline Rose Hunt
Sec. IV:10—D Magazine

4.
Caroline Rose Hunt—*A Class of Her Own*

Caroline Rose Hunt is now considered the wealthiest and classiest member of the Hunt family, although she would never want to be described as such. The third child of H.L. and Lyda Hunt, Caroline was born in 1923. She grew up surrounded by wealth, but like the rest of her family, led a low-key life for many years.

Caroline once compared her philandering father to King ibn-Saud of Arabia, who reputedly fathered some 300 children, saying, "He just likes children, until they get to be about six or seven years old. Then he isn't interested anymore." She went to college at the University of Texas, where she met Loyd Sands, who married her and went to work for Hunt Oil. After Caroline married and began having children, she led such a typical upper-middle-class life in Dallas that most people did not realize she was a Hunt. Like her mother before her, the shy and unassuming woman was content to stay busy raising her five children and volunteering for church work.

When H.L. Hunt died in 1974, Caroline inherited a sizable estate and interests in Placid Oil and other Hunt enterprises. Most of her money was in the Caroline Hunt Sands Trust Estate, and she was content to leave it alone and let it multiply, unlike her brothers Bunker, Herbert, and Lamar, who risked almost everything on wild deals— and managed to lose a great deal of it.

In 1973 Caroline and Loyd Sands divorced, and Caroline eventually married sportsman Hugo "Buddy" Schoellkopf, a member of an old Dallas family. Although Caroline was still relatively low-key, she remained a member of the Board of Directors of Hunt Energy and continued to oversee her vast estate, which emerged practically unscathed from Nelson and Bunker's misfortunes in the silver market (*see Sec. III:3*).

After raising her five children and being, in her words, a "homebody," for most of her life, Caroline started to blossom. She and her husband formed several corporations in the seventies, among them a "country" airline, called "Pumpkin Air," because the first cargo it carried was pumpkins. Caroline formed a hotel corporation, the Rosewood Hotel Group, which has become one of the world's top hospitality companies.

The heiress is credited with bringing a new level of taste and sophistication to Dallas, with the opening of her restaurant and hotel, The Mansion on Turtle Creek, and her multi-use Crescent complex. The Mansion, the only Mobil Five Star hotel in Texas, offers some of the most luxurious accommodations in Dallas. Originally built in 1925, the trilevel home was completely restored and converted in 1980 to the Mansion Restaurant. The hotel, an adjoining nine-story tower, was opened in 1981. Suites are furnished with fine furniture and linens and include fresh flowers, magazines, and 24-hour room and concierge service.

The Crescent Complex, opened in 1985, consists of the Crescent Court Hotel and a collection of fine shops, galleries, and restaurants. The hotel offers guests such luxuries as works of art, fresh flowers, down pillows, and woodburning fireplaces. Beau Nash, a restaurant in the complex, is a popular Dallas nightspot for jazz lovers.

Caroline has long been in love with the English countryside and antiques. Her love of all things English is best displayed in Lady Primrose's Shopping the English Countryside, an antique store located in the Crescent that offers afternoon tea in the English tradition.

Mrs. Hunt has succeeded in bringing a taste of England to Dallas with Lady Primrose's, where the antiques are placed as they would be in an English home. There is one exception, however. Due to popular demand, Lady Primrose's set aside a corner of the shop for Texas antiques and memorabilia, because so many English customers were shopping for Texas items (*see Sec. VIII*). The Thatched

Cottage Pantry, located on the upper floor of Lady Primrose's, serves cottage lunches and cream teas in the fine English tradition and is quite popular among Dallas ladies.

In 1987 Caroline divorced Buddy Schoellkopf and returned to her maiden name, Caroline Rose Hunt. In November of 1990, she was named one of the 50 most powerful women in America by *Ladies' Home Journal*. Much to her chagrin, Mrs. Hunt has been labeled the richest woman in America, with a fortune estimated at $900 million by *Forbes* (1988).

Mrs. Hunt is well known in Dallas for her generous charitable contributions. When she isn't shopping the world for antiques, she is busy promoting her luxury hotel business. Additionally, Caroline Hunt is active in AIDS fund-raising and is a sought-after guest on the international party circuit. She lives in a suite at the Crescent Court.

5. Mary Kay Ash

When in Dallas, you may notice a large number of women driving around town in pink Cadillacs. This is because pink Cadillacs are one of the many perks offered to outstanding beauty consultants at Mary Kay Cosmetics. Founded in 1963 with $5,000 and a dream, Mary Kay Cosmetics has become something of a phenomenon in the Dallas area, particularly when 30,000 beauty consultants descend on the city for Mary Kay's annual seminar.

The founder of the company, Mary Kay Ash, was sitting at her kitchen table one day when she wrote down a list of improvements she thought would help the direct sales business, her line of work for many years. She decided she had some pretty good ideas of her own, so Mary Kay purchased the formulas for skin care products that she had been using.

Aside from making a profit, Mary Kay's goals were twofold: to provide women with unlimited opportunity for success and to build an organization where the Golden Rule was the guiding philosophy. Together with her son, Richard Rogers, Mary Kay went to work.

The basic product lines were improved and expanded, and marketing seminars were begun for the "beauty consultants," who were told that their priorities should be "God, family, and career." In an age before big business became socially conscious, Mary Kay's emphasis on family values, integrity, and the Golden Rule were provocative and unusual.

Mary Kay's theories proved correct. With her unique approach and creative rewards, she was able to attract homemakers and businesswomen, sending them into homes all over America armed with cosmetic showcases. Soon, millions of women had purchased beauty products from Mary Kay, and many had become consultants as well. The company became known nationwide for its unusual compensation and recognition plans, such as the pink Cadillacs, diamond jewelry, and vacations.

Today, Mary Kay Cosmetics has over 200 personal care products, distributed by some 300,000 consultants in 19 countries. The products are still produced in Dallas at the company's manufacturing facility. Certainly, the story of Mary Kay is proof that determination, perseverance, and originality really do pay off. (Note: If you don't want a pink Cadillac, the company also offers pink Grand Prixes and red Grand AMs.)

6.
Anderson Bonner—(c 1835-1920)

One of the more remarkable success stories of early Dallas residents is that of Anderson Bonner, a former slave who had extensive land holdings north of Dallas along White Rock Creek and Cottonwood Branch. Bonner came from Alabama with his brother and sister to settle and farm land in the area north of White Rock Creek.

Although he signed his name with an "X" on deeds, Bonner purchased hundreds of acres of land with profits from his farm produce and that of sharecroppers who leased from him. His business acumen was evident in the variety of legal transactions handled by Bonner. The earliest recorded deed for Bonner's land purchases was filed in Dallas County August 10, 1874. Married to Eliza Bonner, who preceded him in death, Anderson had nine children and later married Lucinda from Waxahachie, Texas.

The first school for black children in the area was named for Anderson Bonner (formerly Vickory and Hillcrest School). Today, in Anderson Bonner Park, bicycle riders cruise along trails that were once part of the Bonner farmland.

7.
Barney the Dinosaur

Long, long ago, in another time, giant reptiles ruled the earth. Dinosaurs, as they were called, were the largest living creatures ever created. For reasons unknown, they all died off and became extinct.

All, that is, but one.

Section III

In the year 1987, a dinosaur appeared—perhaps resurrected—on the plains of Allen, a small town twenty miles north of Dallas. The dinosaur was conjured up by Sheryl Leach, a former schoolteacher who was staying home with her small son.

But this was no lumbering, selfish monster that Sheryl Leach discovered. Her dinosaur was not only all positive and refined—he was politically correct as well. The talking tyrannosaur was very friendly, nonaggressive, and liked to sing ancient children's play tunes, such as "This Old Man," with new lyrics.

I love you
You love me
We're a happy family...

The creature's name was "Barney."

Mrs. Leach got together with Kathy Parker, who, like herself, was experienced in marketing and education, and Dennis DeShazer, an SMU graduate from nearby Richardson who produced educational videos.

Phase 1—Barney was hatched.

The trio produced three videos, featuring Sandy Duncan, Barney, and a group of singing children. Barney was stiff and formal, and there were no elaborate sets or fancy music. It was not a slick production.

The producers noted that child viewers lost interest whenever adults were on-screen. They decided to nix the adults and further refine Barney, so that he was softer, looser, and more approachable. His color was changed from a cool bluish purple to a warmer reddish purple. They retained the simple sets and childish music.

The producers then began aggressively marketing their *Barney and Friends* videos, which featured the huge purple dino on playgrounds and in backyards, singing his message of love, hugs, and self-esteem. In 1991 the producers introduced Barney's sidekick, Baby Bop, a spotted pink and green dinosaur who carried a security blanket.

During that same year (1991), Barney's big break finally came. An executive with Connecticut Public Television was so impressed when his young daughter insisted on watching her Barney video over and over that he obtained $2 million in grants from PBS to produce thirty Barney shows.

In the spring of 1992, after only six weeks, executives at PBS attempted to cancel the show and were deluged with mail and calls from hysterical parents. May ratings came in, and "Barney and Friends" was the highest-rated children's program on the network—surpassing even "Sesame Street."

Phase 2—Barneymania began.

Even Barney's creators were astounded at the Barney phenomenon. It seemed that American children just couldn't get enough of the Purple One and his backyard gang. Barney seemed to represent all that is associated with an idyllic childhood: constant love, swings, lots of friends, coziness, and safety. Simple songs, simple ideas.

Viewership at PBS soared, along with sales of videos and Barney and Baby Bop plush toys and merchandise. Barney was named one of *People* Magazine's Most Intriguing People of 1992 and even floated in Bill Clinton's inaugural parade. Throughout it all, Barney continued preaching his happy message.

But, unbeknownst to the lovable purple dinosaur, something sinister was going on. Parents were tiring of Barney. Even those who liked him at first became weary of Barney's sappy songs, his goofy looks, and his syrupy messages. They couldn't understand why their toddlers sat for hours on end, eyes glazed and jaws slacked, in front of the television, transfixed by Barney. Any attempt to take the Barney videos away resulted in hysteria on the part of the child. Millions of children all over the country were addicted to Barney. A monster had been created.

Phase 3—Barney bashing, soon followed.

Barney's critics were many, ranging from disc jockeys who came up with lists, such as "Ten Things Barney Did in

Section III

the 1970s" (followed the Grateful Dead around) to Jay Leno of the "Tonight Show" remarking that the IRS was auditing Barney's tax returns for the last 64 million years.

There were articles by parents who claimed Barney was not only nauseating, but anatomically incorrect (in the place of teeth, Barney has two smooth strips of white shirt cardboard). Barney was called a "talking eggplant" by *The New York Times* and "a newt with dentures" by *The Washington Post*. One Barney critic, John Kelly of the *Post*, decried Barney's childish music as "Chinese water torture." Barney was hailed as the "Mister Rogers of *Jurassic Park*," and one distraught father began publishing the "I Hate Barney Secret Society Newsletter."

Barney songs were parodied:
I hate you
You hate me
We're a dysfunctional family....

On college campuses, Barneybashing became a favorite pastime, with students gathering to rip apart stuffed Barneys and Barney pinatas. It wasn't long before the worst criticism of all surfaced: Barney was not only a politically correct liberal, but he was connected with the occult. This cry came primarily from the Rev. Joseph R. Chambers, a minister operating a radio ministry based in Charlotte, North Carolina. His booklet *Barney the Purple Messiah* explained it all. According to the Rev. Chambers, Barney was a "conjurer" who gave children a hypnotic feeling and "leads kids into a world of miracles and fantasy."

Barney's publicist and his friends at The Lyons Group in Richardson who handled these matters, were undaunted. They refuted claims that Barney was related to the occult and stated that Barney was not designed to appeal to adults, but to children.

"There is no subliminal or subversive message or intent behind the character," stated Barney's spokesperson. "...Barney is a reassuring presence that is important in children's lives, particularly in this day and age." And so, in spite of vicious attacks by parents, the media, and one clergyman, the gentle purple creature continues his reign in the hearts of children everywhere.

8.
Alexander and Sarah Horton Cockrell

If you know anything about Alexander and Sarah Horton Cockrell, you know that contemporary husband-wife corporate teams have nothing on these two. Dallas' first entrepreneurial couple were responsible for many of the struggling town's early ventures and successes. Alexander Cockrell, a Kentuckian, moved to Dallas County around 1850 and was described by one contemporary as "a man of tireless energy." Cockrell was also a man of the wilderness and had at one point during his life left civilization to live with the Indians, as had John Neely Bryan, founder of Dallas.

Shortly after moving to Dallas County, Cockrell met and married Sarah Horton, a native Texan whose parents had settled at nearby Hord's Ridge. In 1853, for $7,000, Cockrell contracted for the purchase the entire holdings of John Neely Bryan, including Bryan's cabin on Commerce Street, about one-third of downtown Dallas, and Bryan's ferry rights. Since he and Bryan were friends, Cockrell allowed Bryan to continue living in the cabin.

Cockrell began right away to develop his land. First, he formed the Dallas Bridge & Causeway Company and in 1854 constructed a red cedar log bridge across the Trinity River in an attempt to unite the East and West Dallas residents. The steam-powered sawmill built by Cockrell to cut the logs for the bridge was opened to the public once the bridge was completed. A ford and ferry Cockrell established at the sawmill were responsible for Dallas' first building boom. Now that Dallas had a sawmill, bridge, and ferry, the city attracted architects, carpenters, contractors, mechanics, and brick masons, who had easy access to building materials.

On April 3, 1858, Alexander Cockrell was shot to death by Dallas City Marshal Andrew M. Moore at Cockrell's home on Commerce Street. The circumstances of his death remain unclear, but the marshal apparently was attempting to arrest Mr. Cockrell for violating a city ordinance. Cockrell was shot eight times in the abdomen.

A sensational trial took place in the Dallas Courthouse when Marshal Moore was tried for the murder of one of the town's most prominent citizens. The three-day jury trial resulted in a verdict of not guilty. Cockrell's widow, Sarah, was a 38-year-old frontier housewife with four small children.

Immediately following her husband's untimely death, Mrs. Cockrell assumed control of his businesses and land holdings and eventually became Dallas' leading entrepreneur. In 1859 Sarah opened the St. Nicholas Hotel, which quickly gained a reputation as the town's finest inn. Although the hotel was destroyed by the devastating fire of 1860, it was rebuilt.

Sarah Cockrell secured a charter from the state of Texas to form the Dallas Bridge Company and proceeded with plans to construct a new bridge over the Trinity. Unfortunately, the Civil War intervened and her plans were put on hold. After the war, Mrs. Cockrell established the Dallas Wire Suspension Bridge Company and erected an iron toll bridge that opened March 2, 1872. The bridge was built at the foot of Commerce Street and served Dallas until it was replaced in the 1890s.

Another of Mrs. Cockrell's enterprises was the city's first commercial flour mill, which she owned and operated with a partner. During the 1850s and through 1870s, wheat was one of the major crops in Dallas County, and the *Dallas*

Herald reported in 1858, "Dallas flour is beginning to be known and appreciated in every section of our state, and wherever used, has invariably, we believe, been preferred to the best Western flour."

When Sarah Cockrell died in 1892, she owned approximately one-fourth of downtown Dallas, along with other property, and the city directory in that year listed her occupation as "capitalist." Alexander and Sarah's son, Frank M. Cockrell, wrote a recollection of early Dallas life that has proved invaluable to historians.

9.
Henry Keller (1817-1911)

One of the major black landowners in the early days of Dallas County was an emancipated slave named Henry Keller. Born on a plantation in Greenville, Tennessee, in 1817, Keller married Mary Jane Reed, who grew up on the same plantation. As freed slaves, they migrated to Collin County, Texas (just north of Dallas), where they lived in a house with a dirt floor and worked the land for several years before amassing enough money to purchase their own farm.

The Kellers then settled in Addison (far North Dallas), where they continued to farm and eventually acquired several parcels of land in the upper White Rock area. A spring on the Keller property supplied water for the entire region, thus giving rise to Keller Springs Road, a major artery in North Dallas named in honor of Henry Keller.

The Kellers continued to farm and raise their ten children, eventually acquiring 640 acres of land. A devout Christian, Mr. Keller was one of the founders of Christian Chapel CME Church, which is now located on Montfort Drive and Spring Valley Road. Preceded in death by his wife in 1898, Henry Keller died in 1911 at the age of 94.

10.
George Mifflin Who?

There are those historians who will tell you that John Neely Bryan named Dallas for his "friend," George Mifflin Dallas (1792-1864), a Pennsylvania lawyer and diplomat who was elected Vice President of the United States in 1844. Bryan's own son said so, they will tell you.

Then there are the historians who point out there is no evidence Bryan ever met the aristocratic lawyer from Philadelphia and that Bryan was calling his town "Dallas" as early as 1842, two years before George became Vice President under James K. Polk. Besides, they say, there is nothing in the voluminous genealogy of the Dallas family that would even *suggest* the heady clan ever heard of a settlement of forty souls on the Trinity River.

Okay, say the George guys, but Polk and Dallas were elected on a pro-Texas annexation platform. So, say the detractors, hardly anyone knew about their views until well after the election. They didn't have CNN back then, you may recall. John Neely Bryan probably never heard of George Mifflin Dallas until at least 1845. Confused yet?

In his 1874 book *History of Texas*, Colonel J.M. Morphis states that Dallas was named for George's *brother*, Commodore Alexander James Dallas. It seems the Commodore, a member of the U.S. Navy, was stationed for a while in the Gulf of Mexico, where he combatted piracy. But wait, there's more.

Have you heard of one Walter R. Dallas, who fought at San Jacinto and had a brother, James L. Dallas, who was a Texas Ranger? Seems these boys settled at Washington-on-the-Brazos with their family in the early 1800s. Both of the young men received land grants in Texas after their father, James L. Dallas, died.

To top it off, there was Joseph Dallas, who showed up at Cedar Springs—near Bryan's little village—in 1843, from

Arkansas. It's entirely possible, although not provable, that Joseph Dallas knew John Neely Bryan from their Arkansas days.

Still others come up with more theories. John Neely Bryan grew up in Tennessee, attended a military academy, and aspired to a career in politics. It is reported that in 1826, when Bryan was a mere fifteen years of age, he went to a dinner where the famous General Andrew Jackson, a fellow Tennessean, was present.

Later, it is noted, George Mifflin Dallas was a staunch Jacksonian, as was Martin Van Buren, Jackson's Vice President, who eventually became President. Van Buren, Arkansas, was named for Martin Van Buren, and John Neely Bryan has always received partial credit for founding the Arkansas town, as well as Dallas. Maybe he decided to give George his due, since George, too, was a Jacksonian. Besides, there were already too many "Jacksons" and "Jacksonvilles."

Hey, the official Texas Highway Department historical marker in the courthouse square, dated 1936, says Dallas was named for George Mifflin Dallas. So that settles it. You have to admit it's better than Polkville or Georgetown. And at least John Neely Bryan didn't name his new town after himself.

But what...or how about...maybe.... What if he just liked the name?

SECTION IV
Dallas Remembers

1.
La Reunion Colony

Although most Dallasites are familiar with Reunion Tower, Reunion Arena, and Reunion Boulevard, few know the reason behind the name "Reunion." In 1852 a Frenchman, Victor Considerant, visited the Dallas area, accompanied by Albert Brisbane, an American. The two men were proponents of Fourierism, a socialist philosophy espoused by Charles Fourier, that called for the reorganization of society into cooperative communities.

Impressed by the Texas countryside, Considerant returned to France and wrote *Au Texas*, a book that promoted Texas as the site for a planned community based on Fourierism. Considerant arranged to start his utopia, which he named "La Reunion," where he hoped genius, harmony, and love would flourish.

In 1855 the first group of French and French-speaking Swiss and Belgians arrived—200 people in all—equaling half the population of Dallas at the time. The site chosen

Section IV

La Reunion Colony settlers (left to right) Mrs. Louie Maas, Annie Gramatky, Paul Hartman, and Elizabeth (Lizzie) Gramatky. Shady View Park, May 12, 1896. (From the collections of the Texas/Dallas History and Archives Division, Dallas Public Library.)

was 2,000 wilderness acres in limestone hills three miles west of Dallas, overlooking a valley of the Trinity River. Considerant said the chalky limestone bluffs reminded him of his native Burgundy.

The original plan was for the colonists to navigate the Trinity River from Houston to Dallas, but a severe drought had left the riverbed dry, so settlers were forced to either walk the entire distance or travel by oxcarts. One group who walked all the way brought with them thirteen trunks, for which they paid three cents per pound for hauling.

On June 16, 1855, after 26 days of travel from Houston, the first group of weary settlers arrived in Dallas. There were 200 men, women, and children, who entered Dallas dressed "in foreign garb, the clatter of their wooden sabots on the boardwalks followed by slowly moving ox-carts laden with implements and household goods." The entire town, which had declared a holiday, turned out to greet the newcomers from Belgium, France, and Switzerland.

The new settlers cleared land, erected houses of stone or wood, and built a common storehouse, dining hall, and brewery (the first in the county). Hopeful Europeans continued arriving for the next year and a half, bringing with them an organ, piano, flutes, and violins. Although members of the group were artists, musicians, jewelers, weavers, and shoemakers, few knew much about farming.

By April 1856 the colonists had established a phalanstery (the name given to a Fourierist communal city), including a president's office, a soap and candle-making building, a kitchen, grocery store, beehives, laundry, and smokehouse. The group's fund was $600,000, and they cultivated 430 acres of land, purchased 500 head of cattle, and planted a large formal European garden.

The colony was well received by nearby Dallas residents, one of whom wrote:

> We are indebted to the courteous and gentlemanly proprietors of the Reunion store for a lot of choice cigars and a jar of delicious brandy pears. They have at Reunion a well-selected stock of new and fashionable goods, which they are prepared to sell at unreasonably low prices.

Some of the Dallas residents were concerned over the Sunday evening parties at La Reunion that included dancing, which was forbidden on the Sabbath. The colonists heatedly defended their parties, saying that in Europe, Sunday was both a day of worship and pleasure, while in America, Saturday was the day of pleasure. It wasn't long before some of the young people of Dallas began attending the lively gatherings.

One La Reunion leader, Dr. Eugene Savardan, wrote extensively about plant and animal life in the region; some of his work was later published in scholarly French journals. In particular, Dr. Savardan wrote of the multitude of grasshoppers, which the older people ate with gusty appetites, often concocting various sauces using them.

Section IV

All was not well at La Reunion, however. The artisans were ill-prepared for the rigors of pioneer life and cold Texas northers. An unusually harsh winter in 1856 caused the Trinity to freeze over. The limestone proved resistant to planting of any sort, and in fact the site was later used for a cement plant.

By 1858 the utopian community of La Reunion was disintegrating. Considerant was among the first to depart, pronouncing the experiment a failure. His bookkeeping, or lack of it, was incomprehensible to the colonists, and there were allegations of misuse of funds.

Some Reunion settlers returned to Europe, and others moved elsewhere, but many remained and introduced their distinct culture into the Dallas community. One of the original colonists, Swiss-born Ben Long (anglicized from Lang), later served as mayor of Dallas. Others, such as Jacob Nussbaumer, a Swiss colonist, became civic leaders and extensive land holders *(see Sec. I:15)*.

Although the La Reunion social experiment failed, Dallas was able to boast of having the culture of Europeans in its otherwise primitive midst. Dr. Eugene Savardan later wrote an account of the adventure, *Naufrage au Texas (Shipwreck in Texas)*.

The last remaining original La Reunion colonist, Emmanuel Santerre, who immigrated from France at the age of five, died in 1939. In the 1970s, Dallas developer Ray Hunt decided to name his new Reunion Arena Complex in honor of the utopian pioneers.

All that remains today of the original colony are a few woodworking tools, salvaged by the Dallas Historical Society, and Fishtrap Cemetery (located one half mile off Singleton Road on Fishtrap Lane) in West Dallas, where the colonists were buried. The cemetery is now in the middle of a government housing project and is secured by a locked chainlink fence.

2.
Dallas Times Herald

There are those who believe that when the *Dallas Times Herald* died, part of Dallas went with it. Certainly, when the city's oldest newspaper celebrated a century of service to Dallas in 1979, no one would have predicted that a mere fourteen years later, the newspaper would have ceased publication and its downtown building be nothing but debris.

"GOODBYE DALLAS" was the headline on Monday, December 9, 1991, the final edition of the 112-year-old paper, which traced its roots to 1879, when Colonel James Alonzo Adams began publishing the *Dallas Daily Times*. The unexpected news put 900 people out of work, sending a shudder through the newspaper industry and leaving Dallas with only one major daily paper, the *Dallas Morning News*.

For 21 years the *Herald* had been engaged in a battle with the *Morning News* that ended when the *News* bought the *Times Herald's* assets for $55 million dollars in December 1991 and proceeded to lock up the plant. Although many people blamed the *News* for the *Herald's* demise, the passing of the newspaper was a reflection of what continues to take place all over the country as major newspapers see profits dwindle and advertisers go out of business while they are forced to compete with computers, on-line news, and CNN.

The word spread quickly across Dallas that fateful Sunday, December 8, among reporters, plant workers, and editors as they settled down to watch the Cowboys game on television. The new owners removed what printing equipment they could use and then auctioned the remaining equipment and memorabilia.

Section IV

The *Times Herald's* 64-year-old building at Pacific Avenue and Griffin Street was bought by a Cincinnati real estate developer from the A.H. Belo Corporation, parent company of the *Dallas Morning News*. The building was demolished in June 1993 and replaced by a parking lot.

3.
The Day Dallas Burned

It was a Sunday, one of those blinding white hot Dallas afternoons, July 8, 1860. The temperature had climbed to 105°F, and there was almost no activity around the sleepy courthouse square.

In front of W.W. Peak & Brothers Drug Store, on the east side of the courthouse, a box of wood shavings mysteriously ignited. Within five minutes, Peaks' was swallowed by flames, and in only two hours, the savage fire had consumed some 25 business establishments, including every store, the *Herald*, the post office, both hotels, and almost the entire business district.

Dr. Charles R. Pryor, editor of the *Dallas Herald*, reported the disaster in a letter printed in the *Houston Telegraph*:

> A terrible disaster has befallen our once flourishing little city. Dallas is in ruins—burned to the ground—not a business house left standing, hotel, shop, printing office, or anything...

The *Telegraph* offered its "heartfelt sympathies" to their Dallas friends and noted that, "They are all men of pluck[,] however, and such men as nothing can ruin."

The people of Dallas wasted no time rebuilding their city, and by October, when the *Herald* was able to resume publication, it noted:

[T]he sound of the hammer is heard from morn till night, and scores of industrious, active and competent mechanics are busy in forwarding on the work.

Once again, Dallasites were pulling themselves up by their own bootstraps.

The fire of 1860 had other implications as well. On the same day as the Dallas fire, there were mysterious fires in Denton, Pilot Point, Milford, Austin, and several other towns. Houses in the area were torched during the week following the fire.

The general consensus in the community was that the fires were deliberately set by slaves plotting to overthrow their masters. Abolitionist preachers had been in Texas for several years, encouraging insurrection among the slave population. Vigilante groups determined that the preachers had planned to devastate North Texas with fire and then, with assistance from the Indian population, begin a general war in August.

Three black males were identified as the ringleaders of the rebellion: Patrick Smith, who allegedly ignited the trash, Sam Smith, and "Cato." These three were hung on July 24, only two and one-half weeks after the fire, before a large crowd gathered on the banks of the Trinity River. Two preachers from Iowa were jailed, publicly whipped, and ordered to leave.

Contemporary historians have been reluctant to believe that there actually was such a plot, but those who have studied the facts in great detail concluded that the attempted insurrection was genuine. In any case, the devastating fire fueled racial strife in Dallas that continues to the present day.

See following section.

Section IV

4.
Freedman's Towns

One of the unique aspects of early Dallas life involves blacks who settled in the area. Although slavery was not particularly important economically in Dallas, as it was in the rest of the South, it was common, and most of the early black pioneers who came to Texas were either slaves or former slaves.

Prior to the Civil War, there were 1,074 slaves in the community, comprising 12 percent of the population. During and following the war, the black population in Dallas increased considerably as slave-owners and newly freed slaves moved to the area. The "freedmen," as they were called, found many opportunities in the sparsely populated region, particularly when the railroad came to Dallas.

Old family Bibles passed down through generations, along with oral histories, photographs, and written records, are slowly allowing historians to reconstruct life in two areas of Dallas known as "freedman's towns." After the war, the emancipated slaves settled in two freedman's towns: one located on the eastern section of Elm Street at Central Avenue (now Deep Ellum), and the other in the region of Hall, State, and Thomas streets. Other smaller regions developed also, with names like "Stringtown" and "Little Egypt," and eventually, there were some thirty segregated enclaves in the Dallas area.

In spite of the unprecedented opportunities offered in Texas, prejudice and hardship define this era. Although racial discrimination was widespread throughout the South, it was fueled in Dallas by the city fire that occurred on July 8, 1860, destroying virtually the entire business district of Dallas. Most residents and city officials believed that the fire was set by three Negroes, with the help of Northern abolitionists, as part of an insurrection plot to free slaves.

Even though the evidence was mostly circumstantial, historians have since concluded that a group plotting to overthrow their masters were likely responsible for the fire. Whether they were or not, this event contributed greatly to racial problems in the Dallas area. The Ku Klux Klan began harassing black settlers by 1868, and lynchings and beatings were not uncommon, although the KKK was not particularly strong in this area until the 1920s.

A number of blacks came to Dallas to work laying railroad tracks and by 1880, blacks composed approximately 18.6 percent of the town's population. Many of the settlers began farming, either on their own land obtained through land grants or as sharecropper tenants.

Through amazing diligence, these men and women toiled and worked the land to produce the crops that provided their meager living, and in some cases, hope for a better future. Slowly and in spite of many obstacles, self-contained communities were established, complete with churches, schools, grocery stores, barber shops, and medical clinics. Many settlers, among them Dock and Nannie Terry, Paul and Sallie Smith, and Jeff and Hannah Hill, owned and operated successful businesses in the communities.

With little or no education, other pioneers such as Noah and Ida Penn, Taylor and Mary Jane Tarpley, James H. and Mamie Abernathy, and Allen C. and Beulah Smart, to name only a few, tilled the ground, planted seeds, harvested wheat, laid tracks, nailed boards, and in general provided much of the labor that made Dallas what it is today.

Following World War I, the Klan reemerged with great prominence, and it was estimated that some 13,000 Dallas citizens were Klan members. On a dark night in 1921, the streets of Dallas became pathways of terror as city streetlights were extinguished and hundreds of Klan members, dressed in full white regalia, marched behind an American flag and a burning cross. Dallas Klansmen, among them local law enforcement officials, were credited with flogging 68 people in the spring of 1922, including at least one Jewish victim, Philip Rothblum, who later identified one of his attackers as a Dallas police officer.

A "Klan Day" held at the State Fair in 1923 was attended by some 75,000 citizens. Writings from this period reflect the persecution endured by black pioneers. In 1923 the *Daily Times Herald* reported an incident in which "Alex Johnson, negro bell boy[,] was flogged until blood flowed from his lacerated back" and "branded on the forehead with the letters, 'K.K.K.'" Allegedly, Mr. Johnson had consorted with a white woman in the hotel where he had once been employed.

Dallas County Sheriff Dan Harston was quoted as saying, "If they were good citizens who attacked him, and I believe they were, or they wouldn't have avenged the negro's act, I am satisfied with this treatment of him. He no doubt deserved it." This particular deed, observed by a *Times Herald* reporter who had been "invited" to witness it, was written about in newspapers across the nation.

Eventually, the Klan began declining, and the vigilante spirit was replaced by law and order. Nonetheless, racial strife was prevalent in Dallas and despite many advances, continues today in various forms.

Freedman's towns and other black neighborhoods provided relatively safe refuges for blacks during these years. Family, community, and religion played key roles in the lives of the residents. Belief in God inspired many settlers such as Elija Davis and Taylor Anderson to establish churches, primarily Methodist Episcopal, African Methodist Episcopal, and Baptist. Pastors were usually highly respected leaders in the communities and played important roles in lives of their church members, often assisting in the establishment of schools.

Church activities provided the social life for many citizens, and weekends were often busy with Saturday night fish fries, Heaven and Hell parties, summer revivals,

Sunday School, choir practice, and elaborate Sunday dinners.

Gospel music wasn't the only music heard in black communities during this time. The area of Dallas known as "Deep Ellum," was attracting nationwide attention as the birthplace of jazz and blues artists. During the Great Depression, jobs became scarce as many businesses failed. The black worker was often the "last hired and the first fired." Many people, both black and white, worked for food and lodging, but there were still long food lines downtown. The black citizens who worked as domestics seemed to fare better than the average black citizen.

Domestic workers averaged $7.00 a week, plus streetcar fare, for six days' work. Some of these workers—maids, chauffeurs, and gardeners—lived with their employers in servants' quarters and were provided with food and clothing. The area known as "Deep Ellum" came alive, particularly on Thursday nights, which was traditionally the night off for maids and chauffeurs. Dance halls and cafes were crowded with housekeepers dressed up in hand-me-down dresses from their employers, and Deep Ellum's streets were congested with chauffeurs driving their bosses' cars.

Since financial help from banks was out of the question for most black Americans, the domestic often turned to his or her employer for assistance in financial emergencies. Unemployed black men who courted domestic workers were referred to in the black community as "hot pan men," because they were often treated to meals by the employing family. When odd jobs needed to be done, the "hot pan man" was usually offered the job.

Integration brought about many changes in the black communities, and freedman's towns were soon swallowed up by the growing city. Today many volunteers continue to gather information about the history of black Dallas residents. Dallas remains segregated to a large extent and is often a hotbed of hatred, prejudice, and strain. Although

Section IV

civic leaders on both sides strive to unite citizens and work together to solve such problems as crime, drug use, poverty, and prejudice, racial strife is an ongoing problem in Dallas.

Contact: Black Dallas Remembered, Inc.
             P.O. Box 398334
             Dallas, TX 75339-0334; 214-376-3424

Sec. I:3—Deep Ellum
Sec. II:2—Freedman's Cemetery
Sec. III:6—Anderson Bonner
Sec. III:9—Henry Keller, Sr.
Sec. IV:3—The Day Dallas Burned
Sec. IV:5—Dallas Express

African-American Merchants, c. 1890. (From the collections of the Dallas Historical Society.)

5.
Dallas Express

One of the oldest black newspapers in Texas was the *Dallas Express*, a paper printed by and for members of the Dallas black community. The *Express* was founded in 1892 as the *Dallas Bee* by William Elisha King, a former Mississippi schoolteacher. It first appeared on newsstands as the *Dallas Express* in late 1893.

King was born in Macon, Mississippi, in 1866, to Richard and Marguerite King, former slaves. As a youth, King was very studious and received a good education in Mississippi public schools. A moderate and a Republican, King took care that his paper was never radical, stating that he was "for the principles and policies that would advance the race along these lines."

The *Express* gives a rare firsthand look at daily life in the freedman's towns, early African-American communities that sprang up in Dallas after emancipation. The paper's offices were first located at Jackson Street, then moved in 1900 to 361 Commerce Street, in 1909 to 383 Jackson, and in 1919 to 2600 Swiss Avenue.

Along with local news, the newspaper printed society news, including weddings and debutante parties, obituary notices, editorials on politics, a gossip column, and occasional cartoons. Furniture stores, clothing stores, dentists, attorneys, railroads, blacksmiths, hotels, laundries, and cure-alls were some of the advertisers in the *Express*. One unique feature was the "Lost Friends Found" section, which requested the whereabouts of friends and relatives.

The following quotes from the December 31, 1898, issue of the *Express* are attributed to W.E. King:

> A great many people are talking foolishly about the Negro staying out of politics. So long as the Negro helps to support the government, so should he contend for his rights.

The *Paul Quinn Express Weekly* stands with the *Express* against Bishop Turner's African scheme. Let the Negro quit thinking of Africa and demean himself like a man, and he need not despair.

This is what Mr. King thought of Booker T. Washington and "Christian" preachers:

The *Galveston New Idea* after throwing a bouquet at us for pulling the long feather out of Booker T. Washington's tail for that Fort Worth speech, grows intelligible on lots of matters. We scraped up the following lines which will interest a dead beat anywhere on earth, especially if he has pulpit inclinations.

This year will wind up with six loud mouths, pulpit robbers, sister hunting, Christ disgracing "preachers," leaving us in the hole $23.00. This is a class of religious suckers which are low-rating the pulpits and retrograding the progress of Christianity....

Unfortunately, editor King met an early death when he was shot on August 22, 1919, by Miss Hattie C. Burleson, his former secretary and landlady, after a quarrel. He lived only minutes after being shot in the upper right chest.

Other early associates and editors of the paper include politician Melvin Wade, Lee Burl Fuqua, J.R. Jordan, John W. Rice, J.P. Starks, and Henry "Pop" Strickland, who was said to be the "wealthiest Negro in Dallas in the 1930s."

During the 1920s, lynching was one of the biggest concerns in the black communities, and the *Express* printed many editorials condemning these acts of violence and urging passage of an antilynching law. Other editorials urged residents in the black community to patronize black-owned businesses.

The *Dallas Express* survived two world wars, the Great Depression, harassment by the Ku Klux Klan, and integra-

Dallas Remembers

tion. After King's death, wealthy black leaders of Dallas kept the paper alive until 1940, when Houston attorney Carter Wesley gained control of it. The paper was beset by financial problems throughout its existence and changed hands several times before being discontinued in 1971.

Surviving issues of the *Dallas Express* are on microfilm in the Texas Archives Department of the Dallas Public Library.

6.
Clock Tower Atop the Old Red Courthouse

For many years, the bell of the massive clock tower on the top of the old red courthouse chimed out the hour to Dallas citizens. It is possible to find a few old-timers who recall the unusual resonance of the old courthouse bell, that so shook and vibrated the tower it was believed the bell itself caused the structural damage that eventually necessitated its removal.

In 1919 the clock stopped, and repairmen brought to Dallas all the way from St. Louis found the mechanisms uneven and cracks in the tower itself. It was determined that the courthouse was no longer safe for habitation, and the tower, including the 4,500-pound bell, should be removed. Citizens also were concerned because during severe windstorms, which Dallas is famous for, chunks of sandstone would fall from the tower to the ground below. In fact, during a storm in 1933, one of the huge gargoyle-type creatures on top of the structure became airborne.

The tower, however, held a piece of history that most Dallas residents would prefer to forget. On a muggy March 3, 1910, a prisoner, Allen Brooks, who was being held in the courthouse (Old Red) for assaulting a girl in nearby

169

Sherman, was attacked by a mob that broke through a cordon of deputies and charged up the stairs.

Dallas County Sheriff A.A. Ledbetter had moved Brooks from the jail to a room upstairs for his own protection. There was a great deal of racial tension in Dallas during that time, and the alleged incident had been the cause of a vigilante mob several days earlier.

Sheriff Ledbetter and his deputies, who had subdued the previous mob, were unable to control a large group that broke through a cordon of deputies and city police officers to gain entry to the upstairs room where Brooks was being held.

Brooks' fiance, who carried proof that he was innocent, watched in horror as the enraged group fought officers blocking their way, seized the prisoner, tied a rope around his neck, and hurled him head-first out the second-story window to a murderous mob awaiting him below. The fiance, who was never identified, ran in terror up the winding steps of the belltower of the courthouse. As the victim was thrown down to the maddened multitude, the courthouse bell began to peal.

The vigilante mob below the window took Brooks' battered body by the hanging rope, dragging it down Main Street, where he was hoisted to hang from a telephone pole at the ornate Elks' Arch (Main and Akard). It was not known whether Brooks was killed by the fall or died later. The crowd, estimated between 2,000 and 3,000, cheered and tore Brooks' clothes from his body to keep as souvenirs.

Judge R.H. Seay later ordered the Dallas County grand jury to investigate the lynching, but no subsequent report was issued. Law enforcement officials who witnessed the event stated that they did not recognize any members of the mob. The Elks' Arch was dismantled soon after the lynching.

Nearly a decade later, when the clock tower was dismantled, workers found a weatherbeaten wallet wedged in the workings of the bell that contained Allen Brooks' pay stub for work he'd been doing in Gainesville the day the crime was committed.

Some old-timers who remember the bell claim the real reason it was removed was its eerie tendency to ring on muggy afternoons for no apparent reason, right after muffled sounds of a sobbing woman were heard.

See following section.

The lynching of Allen Brooks near the Elks' Arch at Main and Akard, c. 1910. (From the collections of the Texas/Dallas History and Archives Division, Dallas Public Library.)

Section IV

7.
Elks' Arch

In 1908 the city of Dallas was host to the national convention of the Elks' Club, and in honor of the event, a massive arch was constructed at a cost of $25,000. The huge sign, a steel arch blazing with purple and white electric lights and crowned with a great white elk, covered the intersection of Main Street at Akard. "WELCOME ELKDOM" was printed across the arch. In honor of the event, downtown Dallas streets were lavishly decorated, lamp posts were erected near the arch, and fountains at the base of the arch's four columns spouted jets of multicolored water.

A welcoming parade, attended by a crowd estimated at 100,000, took place on July 16. Because of the novelty of the Elks' Arch, it was left in place until 1910, when it was the site of a grim incident *(see preceding section)*.

Sec. II:3—Old Red Courthouse
Sec. IV:6—Clock Tower Atop the Old Red Courthouse

8.
Braniff's Colorful Jets

For a while in the late 1960s and early '70s, Dallas skies were ablaze with vibrant colors, such as pumpkin, lavender, and lime green. This was due to the fleet of colored jets flown by Braniff Airlines. In 1965 Mary Wells, wife of Harding Lawrence, chief executive officer of the Dallas-based airline, came up with the concept of "flying colors."

The idea actually originated from the varied paint schemes used in the 1930s for the Braniff Lockheed Vegas. Beginning in 1931, the airline had each of its Lockheed Vega fuselages painted a solid color different from any other. Braniff flew nine Vegas with plywood, fabric-covered fuselages and three, built by Detroit Lockheed, with metal monocoque fuselages. Several Vegas remained in Braniff's fleet until 1937.

In the fall of 1965, Braniff introduced its new colored fleet that included 56 colors, such as aqua blue, lavender, brown, yellow, red, sky blue, and its first colored model, a DC-6 painted half-blue and half-red. There were even four "Calder models" that were designed by the renowned artist of the same name. These flying works of art were described disparagingly by some as looking like "splotches and splashes of paint such as a child might make." A Calder model is on display at the Frontiers of Flight Museum at Dallas' Love Field.

Thanks to Mary Wells and Braniff Airlines, Dallas citizens were treated for several years to sights such as the Boeing 747-227B "great pumpkin" soaring from Love Field, along with other multihued Braniff flying machines.

9.
Routh Street Cafe

On January 6, 1993, Dallas diners and food critics across the country were shocked when the renowned Routh Street Cafe unexpectedly closed its doors. Opened in November 1983, the Routh Street Cafe was located in the Oak Lawn District in an elegant old blue house at 3005 Routh Street. The restaurant quickly gained a loyal following and national attention with its unique American Southwest cuisine.

Section IV

Restaurateur John Dayton and co-owner chef Stephan Pyles made names for themselves in the gourmet dining world. The month before it closed, their restaurant became one of only 18 restaurants in the country to receive a Five Diamond Award from the American Automobile Association. In June 1992, *Food & Wine* magazine had named Routh Street Cafe as one of the nation's best 25 restaurants.

Pioneering such palate-pleasers as grilled catfish with smoked peppers, free-range chicken with black bean sauce, and avocado-tomatillo relish, the restaurant enjoyed nine years in Dallas. Its demise was blamed on the sluggish economy, a kitchen renovation, and the wallet-conscious diners of the nineties, who had changed their free-spending eighties ways.

Rather than lower their standards of excellence, Stephan Pyles and John Dayton chose to close the restaurant, leaving many disappointed fans. The two partners did open "Baby Routh" in 1986 down the street, featuring less expensive and more casual dining, but the restaurant closed in 1994 and Dallas gourmet diners continue to remember and pine for the old R.S. Cafe.

10.
D Magazine

For nineteen years, *D, the Magazine of Dallas*, gave the city of Dallas a journalistic boost with provocative exposés, a glimpse into Dallas social life, "Best and Worst" lists, local tidbits, and much more. Whether you wanted to read about the latest political casualty, sensational murder, or merely find a new restaurant, *D* delivered the goods. In the interest of the common good, *D* Magazine even profiled the Fort Worth Ballet (maybe that's where it went wrong).

Launched by developer Ray Hunt in 1974 under Southwest Media Corporation, the magazine gained a monthly circulation of over 60,000 readers who represented the highest-income and highest-spending groups in Dallas. The magazine targeted North Dallas and Park Cities residents. For a while, under editor Wick Allison's oversight, *D* was one of the most prosperous city magazines in the country, with advertising and circulation revenues reaching $3 million per year.

Although the slickly designed magazine refrained from in-depth writing about the Hunts or their business interests, in general, its founder exercised little influence on editorial subjects, although he did insist that the magazine not use "four-letter words." The magazine saw its share of controversy before its demise, however. Former Dallas mayor Wes Wise filed a $1.55-million lawsuit against the publication over an article entitled, "The Unauthorized Biography of Wes Wise." The article criticized the mayor's political style at a crucial time: right before the election. Although Wise won reelection, he charged *D* with libel, but the lawsuit was dismissed in 1979.

The magazine of distinction was purchased by the American Express Corporation in 1990, which marked the beginning of *D's* collapse. Controversial pieces, such as the one on Dallas County Commissioner John Wiley Price that ran in March 1991, didn't go over too well with the new owners. Provocative stories sent corporate censors into convulsions, and the Magazine of Dallas began its decline.

The corporate control of *D* was reflected in its newly subdued editorial content that was accompanied by a slump in retail advertising. Although no particular reason was given, American Express Publishing Corporation suspended publication of *D* Magazine on May 25, 1993.

Note: A 28-year-old real estate investor, Glenn Soloman, bought *D* Magazine in the spring of 1994. The first issue of the revamped *D* came out in October.

SECTION V

The Sports Page

1.
Da Boyz—*Those Incredible Dallas Cowboys*

On March 29, 1994, when Dallas Cowboys owner Jerry Jones announced the unexpected departure of Supercoach Jimmy Johnson, it was said that Mr. Jones dare not walk the streets of Dallas for a long, long time. Whatever happened to cause the two former college roommates and best buddies to part ways, they will still go down in the annals of sports history.

The Dallas Cowboys were formed in 1960 in response to Dallasite Lamar Hunt's attempt to compete with the National Football League. The son of legendary oilman H.L. Hunt, Lamar formed a football club in 1952 called the "Dallas Texans." Seeking to obtain an NFL franchise in the late 1950s, Hunt was rebuffed by the league, so he promptly turned around and formed his own professional football league, the American Football League (AFL). Of course, the Dallas Texans was one of the franchises in Hunt's league.

The NFL responded to Hunt's action by expanding their league and starting the Dallas Cowboys to compete in Dallas with Hunt's Texans. In 1962 Hunt's team won the championship of the AFL in an overtime play with the Houston

Oilers. Hunt moved the Texans to Kansas City in 1963, renaming them the "Kansas City Chiefs." It wasn't long before the two feuding leagues ended their rivalry by merging and establishing the "Super Bowl."

The new Dallas Cowboys franchise was owned by Dallas oilman Clint Murchison, Jr. and Bedford Wynne. Tom Landry began coaching the Cowboys in 1960. The first league game for the newly organized team was on September 24, 1960, against the Pittsburgh Steelers. The Steelers won, 35-28. On September 17, 1961, the Dallas team won its first league victory, scoring ten points in the final 56 seconds over the Pittsburgh Steelers; final score, 27-24.

Although their first few seasons were difficult, by 1966 the Cowboys were consistently winning and finished that year with an impressive 10-3-1 record, losing the NFL championship title to the Green Bay Packers, 34-27. In 1967 the team easily won the Eastern Conference championship but lost a second bid for the NFL title to the Green Bay Packers, 21-17.

In 1968 the Cowboys won the Capitol Division but lost the Eastern Championship to Cleveland, 31-20. Dallas won the Runner-up Bowl over Minnesota that same season, 17-13. Original Cowboys players "Dandy" Don Meredith (quarterback) and rushing great Don Perkins announced their retirement from the ball club in 1969, ending the first era of Cowboys' football.

The team in 1970 won its last five games to finish 10-4, claiming the Eastern Division championship and making the playoffs for the fifth year in a row. On January 3, 1971, the Cowboys defeated the San Francisco 49ers, 17-10, giving Dallas the coveted NFC crown for the first time in its history. In January's Super Bowl, the Dallas team lost to Baltimore, 16-13.

Cowboys home games were played in the Cotton Bowl in Fair Park until 1971, when Texas Stadium, a plush, semi-covered football stadium in Irving, opened. On opening day, October 24, 1971, the Cowboys scored a 44-21 victory over the New England Patriots. Duane Thomas scored the first touchdown in the new facility, a 56-yard run just two minutes and sixteen seconds after the kickoff. Some 65,708 fans attended the event.

The Cowboys won their first world championship during the 1971-72 season, defeating the Miami Dolphins, 24-3, in New Orleans on January 16 in Super Bowl VI. Roger Staubach, who passed for two touchdowns, was named Most Valuable Player.

The year 1972 saw Calvin Hill become the first Dallas player to rush for 1,000 yards, and the Cowboys qualified for the NFL playoffs for a record seventh consecutive year. On New Year's Eve in Washington, in a play for the NFL title, Dallas was downed by the Redskins, 26-3. Coach Tom Landry and his Cowboys celebrated their 100th victory on September 24, 1973, after a 40-3 win over the New Orleans Saints. Once again, the Texas team became NFC Eastern Division champs but fell in the second round to Central Division winner Minnesota, 27-10.

The Cowboys, for the first time in their history, had first choice in the NFL college draft in 1974. Their No. 1 pick was Ed "Too Tall" Jones from Tennessee State. However, the team failed to qualify for the playoff games with an 8-6 season, ending the record-breaking string of eight years in the NFL playoffs.

In 1975 the team went once again to the playoffs after finishing the season with a 10-4 record, earning the Dallas team the NFC Wild Card berth. The first playoff game was against Minnesota, and Roger Staubach's fifty-yard Hail Mary pass to Drew Pearson clinched the first round for Dallas. The Cowboys then traveled to Los Angeles for the big showdown, which Dallas won 37-7, after Staubach threw four touchdown passes, three of them to Preston Pearson. Once again, the team had a shot at the Super Bowl but lost to Pittsburgh on January 18 in Miami, 21-17.

"Mr. Cowboy," player Bob Lilly, was honored during the '75 season at Bob Lilly Day on November 23, 1975, at Texas

Stadium, the first such honor bestowed on a Cowboy. Lilly, the first college player drafted by the team, played from 1961 until he retired in 1974, playing in the Pro Bowl seven times and never missing a game in fourteen years with the team.

The 1976 season saw the team winning the NFC Eastern Division title with an 11-3 record but losing to Los Angeles in the first playoff round, 14-12. Football greats Don Meredith and Don Perkins joined Bob Lilly in the Cowboys "Ring of Honor" during halftime ceremonies at the New York Giants game on November 7.

The Dallas Cowboys were on a roll in 1977, completing their season with a 12-2 record and defeating the Chicago Bears at Texas Stadium, 37-7, in the first round of playoff games. Former All-Pro linebacker Chuck Howley, a player from 1961 to 1973, became the fourth member of the Ring of Honor. The Cowboys next crushed the Minnesota Vikings 23-6, winning their fourth National Conference crown and paving the way for Super Bowl XII against the Denver Broncos.

On January 15, 1978, in New Orleans, the Cowboys halted Denver 27-10, winning their second world championship. Defensive linemen Harvey Martin and Randy White were named co-Most Valuable Players in the game.

Quickly dubbed "America's Team" (much to the consternation of other pro teams), Dallas enjoyed the spotlight, and football fans everywhere tuned in to watch the Cowboys in their blue, white, and gray uniforms. (Okay, and to watch the cheerleaders in their uniforms.)

After a less than spectacular 6-4 start, the team finished the 1978 season with an impressive 12-4 record, marking the Cowboys' thirteenth consecutive winning season. Dallas beat Atlanta in the divisional playoff at Texas Stadium, 27-20, and went to its seventh NFC championship game in Los Angeles. The Rams were overpowered by the Dallas team 28-0, sending Tom Landry's Cowboys to the Super Bowl a record fifth time, where they were defeated by the

Pittsburgh Steelers 35-31 on January 21 in Miami. The Dallas Cowboys celebrated their 20th anniversary on October 21, 1979, with a halftime ceremony that honored Coach Tom Landry and outstanding players from each past season. The '79 season was marked by a slump during the first half, but the team rallied and won the last three games, finishing with an 11-5 record and a fourth NFC East title. A divisional playoff against Los Angeles took place in Texas Stadium, with Dallas losing 21-19.

On March 31, 1980, quarterback Roger Staubach announced his retirement after eleven record-breaking years with the Cowboys. Staubach was the all-time leading NFL passer and held all major Cowboys passing records. Bob Lilly became the first Cowboy to be inducted in the Pro Football Hall of Fame. The team rolled through its fifteenth straight winning season in 1980 behind starting quarterback Danny White, finishing with a 12-4 record that tied the Cowboys with Philadelphia and Atlanta for best in the league.

On December 28, 1980, Coach Tom Landry celebrated his 200th victory when the Cowboys beat Los Angeles 34-13, raising Landry's record to 200-119-6, counting regular season and playoff games. The Cowboys lost the NFC East title to Philadelphia but entered the playoffs as a wild card team. They beat Los Angeles 34-13 in the NFC Wild Card Game at Texas Stadium, then went on to conquer the Atlanta Falcons 30-27. They were stopped by Philadelphia 20-7 in their bid for a sixth Super Bowl appearance.

The Dallas team regained the NFC Eastern Division Championship during the 1981-82 season with a 12-4 record. Former All-Pro defensive back Mel Renfro, the team's all-time leading pass interceptor, became the fifth Cowboy to enter the Ring of Honor at the Cowboys-Miami Dolphins game at Texas Stadium on October 25.

The Cowboys entered playoff games, advancing to the NFC Championship by stomping Tampa Bay 38-0. A last-minute touchdown by the San Francisco 49ers at

Candlestick Park raised the score to 28-27 and cost the Cowboys their chance to enter the Super Bowl.

Dallas finished the strike-shortened 1982 season with a 6-3 record, giving the team an NFL record of seventeen consecutive winning seasons. For the sixteenth time in seventeen years, the Cowboys advanced to the playoffs, beating Tampa Bay 30-17 and Green Bay 37-26. At the NFC Championship game, they were stopped by Washington, 31-17.

The year 1983 was marked by the Cowboys' record eighteenth straight winning season, as they finished 12-4. Roger Staubach, the quarterback who led the Cowboys to four Super Bowls, became the sixth member of the Ring of Honor during halftime ceremonies at the Dallas-Tampa game on October 9. Work was begun on a new headquarters and training facility at Valley Ranch in Irving, northwest Dallas County. Qualifying as a wild card entry, the team entered the playoffs against the Los Angeles Rams on December 26 at Texas Stadium. They were defeated with a 24-17 upset.

A record of nine wins and seven losses marked the 1984 "Silver Season," so named in observation of the Dallas Cowboys' twenty-fifth anniversary. The Clint Murchison family sold the team to an eleven-member limited partnership headed by Dallas businessman H.R. "Bum" Bright. The sale was approved by NFL owners on March 19 and completed on May 18. For the first time in ten years, the team did not go to the playoffs.

The last half of the 1980s was marked by a declining number of victories. After dominance in pro football for over a decade, the Cowboys found themselves on the other end of the spectrum.

In 1985 the "Comeback Kid," Roger Staubach, was inducted into the Pro Football Hall of Fame. The same year, the new and improved Texas Stadium became the first such facility to have two DiamondVision color scoreboards and 296 private Crown Suites.

On August 27 the players and coaches reported to the newly opened Cowboys' ranch at Cowboys' Center in Valley Ranch. Dallas player Tony Dorsett became the sixth player in NFL history to rush for 10,000 yards when he made a 19-yard sweep to give the Cowboys a 27-13 victory over Pittsburgh on October 13. The Cowboys finished their regular season with a 10-6 record. For the first time since 1981, the team captured the NFC Eastern Division championship but was stopped by the Rams 20-0 in Anaheim Stadium on January 4.

The 1986 football season opened for the Cowboys at a preseason game against the Chicago Bears that took place August 3 at London's Wembley Stadium, marking the team's first trip to a foreign country. Although the Dallas Cowboys celebrated their 100th win at Texas Stadium against St. Louis, 37-6, October 26, their streak of twenty consecutive winning seasons came to a halt, and they finished with a 7-9 record.

On March 30, 1987, Cowboys' founder and former owner Clint Murchison, Jr. died after a long illness. Murchison had hired Coach Tom Landry and general manager Tex Schramm back in 1960 and was instrumental in the building of Texas Stadium.

Tony Dorsett became the fourth rusher in NFL history to gain more than 12,000 yards when he made 52 yards against the Rams on December 21, giving Dorsett a career total of 12,036. The Cowboys finished the 1987 season with a 7-8 record.

The 1988 season was not memorable for many things, but Coach Tom Landry tied an NFL record held by Curly Lambeau by coaching twenty-nine consecutive seasons with the same team. The 1988 season ended with a 3-13 record.

Plenty of changes took place in Dallas in 1989. On February 25, Dallas businessman Jerry Jones purchased the Cowboys and the lease to manage Texas Stadium from H.R. Bright. The former co-captain of the University of Arkansas football team chose his old buddy and roommate, University of Miami Coach Jimmy Johnson, to come to Dallas and coach the team. Coach Tom Landry was fired, a move that was widely criticized by Cowboys fans and brought the new owner some bad publicity.

What followed was a shakeup that rivaled any in NFL history. Manager Tex Schramm resigned and took a position as president of the new World League of American Football. The Cowboys held the No. 1 NFL draft pick, for only the second time in their history, and on April 20, 1989, they announced the signing of a promising young quarterback from UCLA, Troy Aikman.

On October 12, 1989, Cowboy Herschel Walker was traded to Minnesota for five players, six conditional draft choices, and a 1992 first-round draft choice. A total of eight players, including Emmitt Smith and Russell Maryland, eventually became Cowboys as a result of this trade. On October 29, 1989, Lee Roy Jordan was inducted into the Cowboys' Ring of Honor.

In moves that proved popular with fans, new owner Jerry Jones announced he was reducing ticket prices at Texas Stadium and moving the Cowboys' training camp from Thousand Oaks, California, to Austin, Texas, their first in-state training camp. It was good that there were lots of things going on with the 'Boys besides football games, because they ended 1989 with a dismal 1-15 record, their worst so far. Dallas fans were not happy.

On March 29, 1990, Dallas signed an NFL-high sixteen Plan B free agents, including 1992 starters Jay Novacek, Vinson Smith, and James Washington. Nearly 100,000 die-hard fans visited the training camp at St. Edward's University in Austin.

Tom Landry, who coached the Cowboys for twenty consecutive seasons and led them to five Super Bowls, was inducted into the Pro Football Hall of Fame on August 4, 1990, at Canton, Ohio. The team posted a 7-9 record, missing the playoffs by one game in a dramatic turnaround season. Coach Jimmy Johnson was named NFL Coach of the

Year by the Associated Press, and running back Emmitt Smith, who led all NFL rookie running backs in rushing yardage and touchdowns, was named the AP's NFC Offensive Rookie of the year. Things were looking up.

In 1991 the Cowboys started the season by using the No. 1 overall selection in the NFL draft to pick Outland Trophy winner Russell Maryland and sixteen other choices, setting a club record for most selections in a twelve-round draft. Tex Schramm, who served as president and general manager of the Cowboys from 1960 until 1989, was inducted into the Pro Football Hall of Fame on July 27, 1991.

Dallas finished the year with an 11-5 record, winning the final five games of the season and advancing to the playoffs as NFC's No. 2 wild card entry. The Cowboys traveled to Chicago and defeated the Bears 17-13. At Detroit the following week, the 'Boys were stopped by the Lions 38-6.

During 1991, wide receiver Michael Irvin and running back Emmitt Smith became the first two players from the same team to lead the NFL in rushing yardage and receiving yardage the same season. Smith had 1,563 yards rushing, and Irvin made single season records for receptions (93) and receiving yardage (1,523). Along with tight end Jay Novacek and quarterback Troy Aikman, Irvin and Smith were named to the NFC Pro Bowl squad.

The first regular season game of 1992 was September 7, when Dallas, with the youngest roster in the NFL, met the defending world champion Washington Redskins at Texas Stadium. Washington wasn't prepared for Dallas' aggressive puncturing of their offense. A pair of spectacular passes and scores by Troy Aikman to wide receiver Alvin Harper and a 79-yard run by wide receiver Kelvin Martin clenched the Cowboys' victory, and the game ended 23-10.

Dallas went on to defeat the New York Giants (34-28) and the Phoenix Cardinals (31-20) before being stopped by Philadelphia on October 5, losing 31-7. The brash young Dallas team conquered the Seattle Seahawks on October 11,

27-0, and the Kansas City Chiefs October 18, scoring a 17-10 victory.

On October 25, 1992, at the Los Angeles Coliseum, the largest crowd to ever witness a Cowboys regular season game saw the Cowboys defeat the Raiders, 28-13. The 'Boys were on a roll.

The following week, on November 8, Dallas whipped Detroit 37-3 with the help of Aikman and Michael "The Playmaker" Irvin. On November 15, the Cowboys were stopped in Texas Stadium by the Los Angeles Rams, 27-3. They came back to beat the Cardinals 16-10 on November 22 in Phoenix.

November 26 marked the Cowboys' 300th win, as they conquered the New York Giants at Texas Stadium. In a pressure-packed game on December 6, the 'Boys came through with a close 31-27 score. However, the Redskins halted the roll on December 13, winning 20-17. Dallas beat Atlanta on December 21, 41-17, and claimed the NFC Eastern Division Championship.

The Chicago Bears had a losing meeting with Dallas at Texas Stadium on December 27, 27-14. Emmitt Smith finished the season with 1,713 rushing yards, becoming the first player to win back-to-back NFL rushing titles since Eric Dickerson. Six Cowboys were selected to play in the Pro Bowl: Emmitt Smith, Jay Novacek, Troy Aikman, Michael Irvin, Nate Newton, and Mark Stepnoski.

Dallas completed the regular season with a 13-3 record and defeated Philadelphia in the divisional playoff on January 10, 34-10. Dallas fans loved it and clamored for more.

The NFC Championship game was held in Candlestick Park in San Francisco on January 17. Record rainfall in San Francisco turned the playing field into a "field of streams," and crews worked feverishly to siphon off as much water as they could. Thanks to fullback Daryl Johnston's blocking, wide receiver Alvin Harper's leaps, and Aikman's passing, the Cowboys splashed their way to a 30-20 victory. The Dallas Cowboys were on their way to Super Bowl XXVII.

The showdown in Pasadena took place January 31 against the Buffalo Bills, in front of 98,374 fans, and featured spectacular plays by Aikman, Irvin, and Harper. Fifty-nine plays, 29 runs, and 30 passes later, Dallas won the title 52-17.

"Da Boyz," as they were affectionately known, were back, and Dallas went wild. The entire metroplex was alive with blue and silver banners, signs, souvenirs, ribbons, and such excitement as hadn't been seen in Dallas in a long, long time. One could not go anywhere in the city without seeing exuberant fans, balloons, proud t-shirts proclaiming victory, and signs of congratulation. "Marry Me, Troy" was written on many a young woman's automobile.

"How 'bout them Cowboys?!!"—words spoken by Coach Jimmy Johnson after winning a playoff game, were plastered all over the city. Dallas loved their Cowboys.

The triumphant team returned to their city and thousands of adoring fans. The Super Bowl victory parade, after much controversy (most of the dispute involved whether or not to hold it on a school day) was held on February 9, 1993, a school day, and unfortunately turned into a riotous affair. Security was lax, and the 300,000-400,000 turnout was much larger than expected.

Quarterback Troy Aikman's convertible was buried in confetti and actually brought to a halt. Police saw the situation getting out of control as fights broke out and looting and vandalism began. To their credit, the players were gracious about the few hysterical fans who grabbed them. None of the players was hurt, but a number of fans suffered cuts and other injuries.

The year 1993 was another super year for Dallas, and Jimmy Johnson entered his fourth season as head coach. Dallas started the season 0-2 without powerhouse Emmitt Smith, who was holding out. After some hand-wringing negotiations, Smith was signed to play again with the Dallas team.

Section V

Dallas Cowboys' Superbowl victory parade, February, 1993. (Courtesy of the Dallas Convention & Visitors Bureau.)

In the last regular season game, January 2, 1994, the Cowboys took the New York Giants at Giants Stadium, 16-13, winning in overtime. Spectacular rushing and plays by injured heavyweight Emmitt Smith clenched the victory. In spite of his painful right shoulder separation, Smith ran for 168 yards on 32 carries and gained 61 yards on 10 pass receptions.

The 'Boys finished the 1993-94 season with an impressive 12-4 record and 15-4 record overall. In the playoffs, the Dallas team defeated the Green Bay Packers 27-17. Then it was back to Dallas to meet San Francisco for the NFC Championship.

Coach Jimmy Johnson angered San Francisco fans when he called a radio show before the game and predicted, "We will win the game. You can put it in three-inch headlines."

His arrogance was typical of those Dallas people, '49ers fans complained. But it worked.

In the NFC game with the '49ers, Smith showed his talent once again, and the Cowboys won 38-21. Quarterback Troy Aikman suffered a head injury in the third quarter and was briefly hospitalized and treated for a concussion. This unexpected blow caused the team much anxiety, but Aikman managed to convince everyone that, aside from being a little dizzy, he was up for the big game. The showdown was set against the Buffalo Bills for Sunday, January 30, 1994, Super Bowl XXVIII.

The battle took place at the Georgia Dome in Atlanta. After a few fumbles and costly errors, James Washington ran 46 yards for a touchdown that enabled Dallas to tie the score 13-13 in the third quarter. This play gave Dallas the momentum it needed to beat Buffalo, 30-13, Dallas' second straight Super Bowl win. Emmitt Smith was named MVP after 30 carries for 132 yards, including two touchdowns.

But all good things must come to an end. Insiders knew that, behind the smiles and hugs of owner Jerry Jones and Head Coach Jimmy Johnson, the two men were involved in a bitter power play, which came to a head in March 1994 and ended with Johnson being "released" for a reported two million dollars.

Football fans were shocked and angered, and Jones actually received death threats. The Cowboys were winners, and winners are good for image and business, two things that are vital to the city. Johnson's replacement was Barry Switzer, a former college coach who led Oklahoma University to three national championships but who had never coached in the pros.

Along with the fans, Dallas team members were visibly upset, realizing that when you're at the peak, there's only one way to go. Well, some fans said, look at the bright side. They were glory days, and there will be more to come. And at least the new coach's initials aren't "J.J." And it was nice while it lasted.

2.
Those Equally Incredible Dallas Cowboys Cheerleaders

There will be times you will remember being uncomfortable. At times, the heat is almost unbearable. You might throw up at rehearsals, thinking you couldn't dance another step as you get severe cramps in your legs, feet, and arms. You will recall dancing in the rain having hairspray drip stinging and burning into your eyes. But, you will also remember it was worth every minute of discomfort. DCC will help you make it through the rough times. It will give you a new respect for yourself.

Still wanna be a Dallas Cowboys Cheerleader? The long hours, incredible effort required, and the mere pittance received ($15.00 each home game) does not seem to deter the approximately 1,000 young women who show up every April at Texas Stadium for preliminary tryouts.

Although the Dallas Cowboys have always had sideline cheerleaders, the phenomenon as it is today began in 1976. In the 1960s, the Cowboys cheerleaders were high school girls from the D/FW metroplex. But in 1976, when Dallas went to Miami for Super Bowl X, the dancing, cheering squad got their chance for national fame. Although the Pittsburgh Steelers defeated Dallas 21-17, TV cameras seemed to be continually rotating to the sidelines, where 36 beautiful young women in dazzling costumes, were dancing and tossing their luxurious manes of hair.

America (and a few cameramen) was captivated by these charming girls, who seemed to embody everything good and wholesome about football—healthy, lively young women, cheering their team. They were dubbed "America's Sweethearts" for America's Team. And who wants to watch

The Sports Page

Dallas Cowboys Cheerleaders. The world-famous Dallas Cowboys Cheerleaders entertain football fans at Texas Stadium. The Cheerleaders are one of the many innovations introduced by the Cowboys that have become a permanent part of NFL football. (Courtesy of Dallas Cowboys Cheerleaders.)

sweaty quarterbacks gulping Gatorade on the sidelines when you can watch dancing girls in sexy costumes?

The Dallas Cowboys Cheerleaders started a national movement, as one pro team after another began adding dance squads. But few people realize how difficult it is not only to be selected, but to be a squad member. Cheerleader preliminary and semifinal auditions are held in April, and finals take place in May. The organization offers eight weeks of dance classes at $15 each to prepare the squads of wannabes.

Cowboys Cheerleaders not only have to be radiant and enthusiastic and possess a great body, they have to be able to leap, kick, swing their hair, do splits and all kinds of acrobatic movements. They don't just stand there and look good. Oh, and they have to either be going to school or working full-time, also.

In 1977 the squad was featured on the "NBC Rock 'n Roll Sports Classic" and the "Osmond Brothers Special" on ABC. They have been on national commercials and were the subject of a made-for-television movie. In addition to appearances on television awards shows and talk shows, the Cheerleaders had their own special on ABC, "The 36 Most Beautiful Girls in Texas."

One of their most popular recent productions is the annual Dallas Cowboys Cheerleaders Calendar and photo shoot that has been the subject of two one-hour specials on ESPN. The calendar is shot in exotic locations such as Jamaica and Cancun. The Cheerleaders have also been featured on NBC's "Entertainment Tonight," "Geraldo," "Donahue," and the "Montel Williams Show."

Why, you might ask, would anyone give up their life to become a DCC (as they call themselves)? And aren't they being exploited by the Cowboys, considering the players' salaries and their lack of one? It is true that the DCC doesn't have much support among feminist groups. And if they should ever start a union—well, watch out.

However, in Dallas and even around the world, being a Dallas Cowboys Cheerleader means instant fame, notoriety, and recognition, plus opportunities to travel and appear at various functions. Being part of this elite group is a great honor and a lifelong dream of thousands of girls. The Cheerleaders not only perform at football games and pose for photo shoots, but they make many personal appearances at corporate functions, private parties, store openings, etc.

The Cheerleaders' musical variety shows have been performed with USO tours, as well as dozens of international tours on behalf of such corporate sponsors as American Airlines and Mitsubishi Motor Corporation. The girls are compensated for their professional appearances, unless it is a charity event.

Auditions take place on a parquet floor in the Texas Club at Texas Stadium in front of seven judges. Contestants perform in groups of six as a cameraman flashes their images on 16 video monitors. According to director Kelli McGonagill, the contestants are judged by appearance, figure, showmanship, and choreographic ability. They are also interviewed and must pass a written test on the Cowboys and current events before they are chosen.

If you make the first cut, you go on with about 150 others to semifinals; of these 150, approximately 45, including veterans, are chosen as "training camp candidates." Of these, approximately 36 will become Cheerleaders, four of those alternates. Veteran Cheerleaders have to audition again each year, although not until the final cuts.

Dallas Cowboys Cheerleaders operate under strict rules. They never stay overnight anywhere without a member of the organizational staff accompanying them. All of their appearances are governed by rigid contractual arrangements to insure safety and image at all times. Many of their appearances are at hospitals, nursing homes, and fund-raising benefits.

Dallas Cowboys Cheerleaders are known not only for their exciting performances, but for their cheerfulness, professionalism, and positive attitudes. They are Dallas' ambassadors all over the world, and although radical feminists may point out that the DCC is a sexist organization and the girls are being exploited, you don't hear any of the Cheerleaders complaining. Indeed, the Cheerleaders are adored around the world, and little girls all over Texas go to sleep dreaming of being a Dallas Cowboys Cheerleader.

But, hey, Cowboys, how about giving these hard-working women a raise?

Section V

3.
Texas Rangers—*Baseball, Not Outlaw*

The Texas Rangers rode into town in 1972 as part of the American League. If you want to be technical, it could be said that the Rangers are more of a Fort Worth team than a Dallas team, because their stadium is in Arlington, which is closer to Fort Worth than Dallas. But Dallas has decided to claim the Rangers as theirs, too, and unfortunately, there's not a whole lot Fort Worth can do about it.

Dallas had baseball long before the Rangers—all the way back in 1886, when both Dallas and Fort Worth entered organized baseball and were Texas League rivals for the next 72 years. The Dallas team, organized as the Dallas Rebels, moved to a park in Oak Cliff known as Rebel Stadium in 1919. The stadium underwent several renovations and twice burned down, once in 1924 and again in 1940.

A new stadium, called Burnett Field, was constructed and opened in 1941, although there were no bleachers for a while after its opening due to wartime material shortages. The team was also renamed and reorganized as the Dallas Eagles.

Burnett Field was the site of countless memorable games during the '40s, '50s, and '60s, the heyday of the minor leagues. Miss Inez Teddlie entertained fans at the organ, keeping a close eye on the game so she could play the appropriate tunes. The theme song of the Dallas Eagles was "Under the Double Eagle March." "Take Me Out to the Ball Game" was played when the Eagles ran out on the field, and home runs brought on strains of "Waitin' for the Robert E. Lee." Often, visiting celebrities would perform a song or two at the game and then go up to the press box for a radio interview.

In order to achieve their goal of bringing a major league franchise to the area, Dallas and Fort Worth had to work together, which has never been easy for the old-time rivals. A Bi-County Sports Committee was formed in 1959 to plan the stadium. After a number of setbacks, construction began in 1964 on Turnpike Stadium, as it was called. The stadium was dedicated on April 23, 1965, when the Dallas-Fort Worth Spurs played their Texas League home opener.

Meanwhile, in 1960, the American League awarded an expansion franchise to Washington, D.C. The team, known as the Washington Senators, was purchased by Robert E. Short in 1968. In 1971 Short received approval from the American League to move the franchise to Arlington, Texas. The team was renamed the "Texas Rangers," in honor of the legendary law enforcement unit.

The first franchise game played in the ballpark, which had been renamed Arlington Stadium, was against the California Angels on April 21, 1972. The Rangers won, 7-6. In 1974 Bradford G. Corbett formed a group and purchased the team from Robert Short.

Throughout the early seasons, the Rangers were noted for starting well and then tapering off as the season progressed. Overall, the young team suffered an unusually high number of injuries that adversely affected the club.

In 1980 Bradford Corbett sold his interest in the Rangers to H.E. "Eddie" Chiles. In 1989 an investor group led by George W. Bush (son of former President Bush) and Edward W. "Rusty" Rose purchased the controlling interest in the ballclub from Eddie Chiles.

When George W. Bush put together the limited partnerships to purchase the Texas Rangers, his stake in the team was only $500,000 of $45 million. However, George W.—as the locals call him—pretty much runs the team, because the other partners are not interested in working with the media. Things were starting to come together for the Rangers.

In 1991 second baseman Julio Franco became the first Texas Ranger to lead the American League in hitting, with a .341 mark that topped the majors and was the best in club history. Despite missing thirty-six days with shoulder and back injuries, pitcher Nolan Ryan was third in the league in strikeouts for 1991 (203) and pitched his seventh career no-hitter against Toronto at Arlington on May 1. On October 30, 1991, the groundbreaking ceremony for a new ballpark took place, but construction didn't actually begin until April 24, 1992.

In 1992 Rangers Managers Tom Grieve and Sandy Johnson hired Kevin Kennedy, former pro player and minor league coach for the Los Angeles Dodgers, to become the Rangers' thirteenth fulltime manager. Another announcement was made that year, a real shocker. On August 31, 1992, the Rangers acquired perhaps the top slugger in the history of baseball, Jose Canseco, from the Oakland A's. Rangers outfielder Ruben Sierra and pitchers Jeff Russell and Bobby Witt went to the A's as part of the trade. The power hitter had spent the entire ten years of his pro career in Oakland.

"Texas is the team of the future," Jose explained to surprised sportscasters. Canseco's first game with the Rangers was September 4, and he attracted large numbers of fans. In the first eight games, he hit .367 (11-30), but only .140 (6-43) in final fourteen games. Unfortunately, Canseco had convinced Manager Kennedy to let him try pitching, and he injured his shoulder.

The 1993 season marked the Rangers' second highest figure in attendance, with over 2,244,616 fans in 79 dates at the final year of Arlington Stadium. The team's overall record was 86-76 (.531); second in A.L. Western Division. Texas was one of five teams in the majors with at least two players with 100 runs scored: Rafael Palmeiro (124) and Juan Gonzalez (105). As a result of injuries, Jose Canseco had the lowest record of his major league career—sixty games, ten home runs, and forty-six RBI. He was sidelined for the final three months of the '93 season after undergoing ligament reconstruction surgery on his right elbow.

The Rangers led the major leagues with 181 home runs, the third highest total in team history, behind 1987 (194) and 1986 (184). Three Rangers hit at least thirty homers: Juan Gonzalez - forty-six, Rafael Palmeiro - thirty-seven, and Dean Palmer - thirty-three.

The year 1993 marked the end of an era for the ball team. It was to be the final season in the old Arlington Stadium, and on February 11, 1993, legendary pitcher Nolan Ryan announced that 1993 would be his final season, bringing an end to the career of a celebrated player who would set fifty-three major league records, including all-time strikeout leader, a record seven no-hitters, and the longest playing period in the major leagues *(see following section)*.

Players and fans were anxious to move to the new ballpark that was being built next to Arlington Stadium. For many years, players had been complaining about the harsh lighting and the wind situation. Sometimes fly balls were unseen by outfielders because of the low-hanging lights, and while everyone in the stands could see where it was going, the poor outfielder was unable to see a thing. The wind patterns caused air to blow crossways and wind to come in through open spots, creating a swirling action. Everybody was ready to go to the new ballpark, which was being touted as a state-of-the-art facility.

On September 12, 1993, Nolan Ryan pitched his final game at Arlington. It was "Nolan Ryan Appreciation Day," and the Minnesota Twins beat the Rangers, 4-2, but Ryan was honored after the game at an on-field ceremony. The last game played at Arlington Stadium was on October 3, 1993, before 41,039 fans. The Royals defeated the Rangers, 4-1. The stadium had hosted major league baseball for 22 years.

The biggest news of the 1994 season was the new facility at Arlington, new uniforms, new logo—and no Nolan. But Rangers fans were in for lots of treats at the new facility. Although there were many grumbles over the name chosen—"The Ballpark in Arlington" just isn't very original, it was said—there were few complaints about the stadium itself.

Designed to look like an old-fashioned ballpark, the new stadium opened April 1, 1994. The ballpark features a natural Bermuda Tifway and rye grass playing field, a granite and brick facade, exposed structural steel, an asymmetrical playing field, and a home run porch in right field. There is also a baseball museum, a children's learning center, an office complex, a youth baseball park, amphitheater, retail and restaurant area, two six-acre lakes, and parks. The stadium seats 49,292 and has computerized snack ordering.

The Rangers' new four-color logo is a light and dark gray Texas Lone Star, enclosed in a red circle that gives the effect of a Texas Ranger marshal's badge. Two baseballs reversed in white with "TEXAS RANGERS BASEBALL CLUB" are enclosed in the circle.

Red has replaced blue as the dominant color of the new uniforms for both home and road. For the first time in Rangers history, the players will wear red caps. New players, new uniforms, new ballpark. And the rest, we hope, will be history.

4.
Nolan Ryan—*The Legend Lives On*

On February 11, 1993, Nolan Ryan called a news conference. At the news conference, he made the announcement that 1993 would be his final season as a major league ball player. This announcement was not unexpected; after all, at the age of 47, he was the oldest player in the major leagues.

What was perhaps unexpected was the sheer magnitude of the Nolan Ryan phenomenon. As soon as the news broke, hundreds, thousands, and eventually hundreds of thousands of fans began to pay respects to this living legend, who had the most strikeouts (5,714) and no-hitters (7) in baseball history. By the end of his career, the man known as "Texas Heat" had set fifty-three major league records and had played the longest of anyone in major league baseball history.

A native Texan, Nolan Ryan grew up in the small town of Alvin, located in southeast Texas. In his autobiography, *Miracle Man*, Ryan says, "There are probably nicer places to grow up than hot and humid and mosquito-infested Alvin, Texas, but for some reason I came back here and will likely die here."

In the spring and summers, young Ryan and his friends made their own baseball diamonds on a vacant lot, using lawn mowers to trim up the infield, then laying bases and building a backstop. There was always a baseball game going on, from sunup to sundown.

"We couldn't get enough baseball," writes Ryan. After he began playing Little League ball, he still played on the vacant lot before and after scheduled practices. In Little League, Ryan made the All-Star team and went on to play in Babe Ruth League and was on the team at Alvin High School.

In high school, Ryan was hitting .700 and was always third or fourth in the lineup, but it was his pitching that set him apart from everyone else. As a senior, he was All-State and won the Outstanding Athlete Award at Alvin High School. Although he didn't know it at the time, he had already been spotted by a big league scout. On June 26, 1965, at the age of eighteen, Ryan signed with the New York Mets and began pitching in the minors.

In the minors, Ryan learned to better control his famous fast ball, and after a little over a year, he was headed to the majors. Military service interrupted his career for six months, then he was back in the minors and suffered an injury to his arm. Ryan was homesick for Texas and for his high school girlfriend, Ruth, and they were married on June 26, 1967.

Nolan Ryan stayed with the Mets another four years but became frustrated missing games because of military duty and having to spend most of his time in the bullpen. Even though the Mets won the 1969 World Series and Ryan was there, he was hardly part of the game and let it be known that he wanted out of his contract. During this period, his father passed away.

The California Angels signed Ryan in a trade with the Mets on December 10, 1971. The month before, Ruth and Nolan's first child, Reid, was born. In California, Ryan had a 183-121 record with a 3.06 ERA in 291 games from 1972 to 1979. In 1973 Ryan pitched two no-hitters in one season. He is California's all-time leader in wins, starts, complete games, innings, shutouts, and strikeouts. His fourth no-hitter was on June 1, 1975, against Baltimore. Ryan holds or shares twenty club records and was inducted into the Angels Hall of Fame and had his number (30) retired in a pregame ceremony at Anaheim Stadium on June 16, 1992.

In Anaheim, Ryan had discovered the value of strength conditioning and began weight training and a strict conditioning regimen that he would follow throughout his career. Ruth and Nolan's other son, Reese, was born in January 1976, and the following spring (1977), their daughter, Wendy, was born. Things were not all good, however. Early in 1979, Reid Ryan, seven years old, was hit by a car and suffered severe internal injuries. That summer, Nolan spent most of his time in the hospital with Reid and Ruth, leaving on road trips only the day before he was scheduled to pitch. Reid lost his spleen and one kidney.

After having problems with the Angels' general manager, Buzzie Bavasi, Nolan was drafted by the Houston Astros and signed with them as a free agent on November 19, 1979. He was headed back to Texas.

With the Astros and now the National League, Ryan was 106-94 with a 3.13 ERA in 282 starts from 1980 to 1988. He was the club's all-time strikeout leader (1866) and ranks in the top five in walks, starts, innings, wins, and ERA. In 1988 Ryan led the National League with 228 strikeouts.

In spite of his spectacular record with the Astros, Ryan was disappointed that he received no feedback from John McMullen, one of the team owners, and very little from Gene Autry, the other owner. Although the money was great, he reports in his autobiography that the obvious lack of care and appreciation made the salary seem empty.

In 1988 Ryan got out from the pitch limit and led the National League in strikeouts. The lack of team spirit continued to cause distress, and word got out that Nolan Ryan was looking. The Giants, Angels, and Rangers were the top contenders—even Japan got into the game and tried to sign him. Nolan signed with the Rangers as a free agent on December 7, 1988.

In his first season with the Rangers, Ryan led the majors in strikeouts and ranked among the A.L. leaders in innings, ERA, and wins. In 1990 he led the A.L. in strikeouts and pitched his sixth career no-hitter on June 11 at Oakland.

In 1991 Ryan was third in the league in strikeouts, fifth in ERA, and seventh in winning percentage, despite missing thirty-six days with injuries. He pitched his seventh career no-hitter against Toronto on May 1 at Arlington Stadium.

Nolan Ryan's 1992 record includes third on the staff in starts, complete games, and strikeouts, in spite of missing six starts due to injuries. He was ejected the only time in his major league career after hitting Oakland's Willie Wilson with a pitch on August 6.

Nolan Ryan's final season, 1993, brought the remarkable player the attention he deserved. Fans flocked to Arlington Stadium and ballparks across the country by the hundreds of thousands to see the extraordinary pitcher. On Sunday, September 12, Ryan was honored with an Appreciation Day. In front of a sellout crowd of 40,105, he and his family received gifts and honors, including the creation of a Nolan Ryan Scholarship Fund.

In addition to being the all-time strikeout leader, Ryan ranks among the lifetime major league leaders in walks, wild pitches, games started, losses, innings, shutouts, wins, ERA, and appearances. He averaged 9.55 strikeouts per 9 innings in his career, joining Sandy Koufax (9.28) as the only pitchers in history to average a strikeout an inning.

On August 4, Ryan was involved in a bench-clearing brawl with Chicago, when Robin Ventura charged the mound after being hit by a ball. In the same game, he fanned Ron Karkovice for his 5,700th career strikeout. Ryan's final major league appearance was on September 22 at the Kingdome in Seattle, when he tore a ligament in his elbow. His last pitch was to Dave Magadan in Seattle, and his last strikeout was Greg Myers, September 17 in California.

Ryan received so many honors during his long career that it is almost impossible to list all of them. Among the major ones are the Man of the Year Award from *The Sporting News* in 1990; Male Athlete of the year from United Press International and the United States Sports Academy; *USA Today* Pro Sportsman of the Year Award; and the cover of *Sports Illustrated* (May 1, 1989).

Ryan's fans saluted him each game, and the likable, modest man on the pitcher's mound acknowledged the crowds before giving the hapless batter at homeplate a sample of his Texas Heat. He was honored on Nolan Ryan Day, September 12 (during Nolan Ryan Appreciation Week) with a parade, a banner contest, and a giant farewell card signed by fans.

October 3, 1993, was Nolan Ryan's last appearance in a Rangers' uniform. It was also the last game played at Arlington Stadium. Ryan and Kansas City's George Brett, who was also playing his last game, exchanged lineup cards prior to the game.

After the game, Ryan, along with the other Rangers selected by fan balloting as the Rangers' All-Time Arlington Stadium Team, were introduced to the crowd. Ryan then took part in a ceremony moving home plate from Arlington Stadium to The Ballpark in Arlington.

Although he has retired from the majors, he will continue to be involved in baseball as special assistant to the president of the Rangers. Ryan owns two banks and operates a ranch in Alvin, Texas, where he lives with his wife and children.

5.
Basketball—*From Diamonds to Mavericks*

In March 1980, Dallas businessman and long-haul trucker Donald Carter was having trouble coming up with a name for his new basketball team, so Dallas radio station WBAP started a Name the Team contest. More than 4,600 entries came in, among them "Wranglers," "Express" and "Mavericks." Mavericks, with 41 entries, won. Although the University of Texas at Arlington was already calling its team the Mavericks, the new backers took the name anyway.

The Dallas Mavericks are relative newcomers to the NBA, having begun as a franchise in 1980. Another Dallas team, the Dallas Diamonds, in 1980-81 became one of the top women's pro basketball teams in the nation, with the most outstanding female player, Nancy Lieberman. Unfortunately, low attendance at the games caused the team to close after their spectacular winning season. Dallas also had an earlier pro basketball team, the Chaparrals, owned by Bob Folsom, that operated until the early seventies, when the franchise was moved to San Antonio and renamed the Spurs.

Section V

In 1979 Norm Sonju spearheaded the expansion drive for a pro basketball team in Dallas. After obtaining the financial backing needed and completing numerous negotiations, the team was formed. Sonju, general manager of the Mavericks, is one of the most experienced executives in the league and has long been involved in the NBA. Along with president and owner Donald Carter, Sonju's goals for the team are to make long-term decisions and recruit young players in order to build the team to be a viable playoff contender.

Working with the city of Dallas, Sonju has enhanced Reunion Arena, where the team plays from early autumn to spring, with a $5 million Sony JumboTron scoreboard, upgraded sound system, and additional seats that include telescopic viewing. On June 10, 1980, Kiki Vandeweghe became the first player selected by Dallas in the college draft. He was traded to Denver December 10, 1980. Under the direction of Head Coach Dick Motta and Assistant Coach Bob Weiss, the Mavericks began playing in September 1980.

Their first preseason game was against Denver on September 20, and Dallas, led by Jerome Whitehead, won 122-98. The Mavericks made their Dallas debut September 26 in the second game of an NBA preseason doubleheader, losing to Philadelphia 113-108. Houston defeated Kansas City 128-106 in the opener. The games, the first basketball games played in Reunion Arena, were before 15,634 fans.

In the past, the Mavericks have made six playoff appearances, reaching the Western Conference Finals in 1988. Dallas made it to the first round of playoffs in 1984, clinching its first ever playoff series with a 105-104 overtime win in game five against the Seattle SuperSonics. Next, the Mavericks were up against the L.A. Lakers at the Western Conference Semi-Finals. The L.A. team won the first two games, then were defeated by Dallas in game three, winning again in game five.

In 1985 the Mavericks went to the first round of playoffs against Portland's Trailblazers, who, after losing the first game, defeated Dallas in each of the last three games. Dallas was once again in the 1986 playoffs and eliminated the Utah Jazz in the first round, 3-1. The Mavericks lost to the Lakers 4-2 in the semifinals. In 1987 John MacLeod replaced Dick Motta as head coach, and the Mavericks reached the Western Conference semifinals. This time, they were defeated by the Seattle Sonics, who won three out of four games played.

Dallas defeated the Houston Rockets in the first round of 1988 playoffs, then went to the semifinals and won four out of six games against the Denver Nuggets. The Mavericks advanced in the finals to play the L.A. Lakers, beating the Lakers in three out of six games, but the Lakers won in game seven. Following their loss to the Lakers, the Mavericks returned to Dallas, where 4,500 faithful fans were waiting to greet them at D/FW airport.

Coach John MacLeod was dismissed and replaced by Richie Adubato during the 1989-90 season, and Dallas made it to the first round of playoffs in 1990, only to be swept for the first time in their playoff history, losing three games to the Portland 'Blazers. The Mavericks were on a downhill slide that tested the perseverance of players and the loyalty of fans.

In 1990-91 the Dallas team ended their 11th NBA season with the largest loss of the season before a sellout crowd in San Antonio. Dallas finished the year 28-54, tying for the second-worst record in franchise history (Mavericks' 1981-82 season was also 28-54 and their 1980-81 season was 15-67).

1991-92 was another dismal season, with Dallas winning 22 games and losing 60, its second-worst record ever. On December 19, 1992, Doug Smith scored a career-high 27 points, although the Mavericks were defeated by the Houston Rockets. On January 13, 1993, Head Coach Richie

Adubato was dismissed and replaced by Assistant Coach Gar Heard.

On March 4, 1993, the Mavericks announced that 10-year NBA veteran Quinn Buckner would take over as head coach upon completion of the NBA finals. Buckner is one of only seven players in basketball history to win NCAA Olympic and NBA titles. On that same date, the Mavericks made another surprise announcement: They had signed holdout first-round draft pick Jim Jackson to a six-year contract. Jackson made his Mavericks debut the following day, scoring six points against the Houston Rockets, but the Mavericks were soundly defeated, 105-86.

On March 10, 1993, veteran guard Randy White scored a career-high 31 points on 10-of-14 shooting against Portland, but the 'Blazers won, 124-96. The team was hurt by numerous player injuries during the season: Sean Rooks, Derek Harper, Doug Smith, Randy White, and Terry Davis. Sean Rooks started a record 68 games (most by a Mavericks rookie) and became the first rookie to win the Favorite Maverick award, which is based on fan balloting. The Dallas team concluded the 1992-93 season with a 11-71 record.

The '93-'94 season showed little improvement. Buckner started the season with no center and his best returning forward, Terry Davis, injured in a car accident. Nevertheless, he had some good players, among them Jim Jackson, Jamal Mashburn, Derek Harper, who was starting his 11th season with the Mavericks, Randy White, veteran guard Tim Legler, guard Lucious Harris, and forward Ron "Popeye" Jones. Mashburn, known as "The Monster Mash," was a unanimous first-team All-America selection in the '92-'93 season.

The 1993-94 season ended with a 13-69 record, only a two-game improvement from the previous year. Head Coach Quinn Buckner was dismissed on May 3, 1994, and the Mavericks rehired Dick Motta, the team's original coach, on May 17, 1994. Motta had left the team seven years earlier.

The Mavericks have come up with other ways besides winning to keep fans happy. The concept of "group preliminary games," that allows business and school teams to play at the Mavericks home court and then watch the pros play, is one of their ideas. Other incentives include a tour of the building and a Dallas Mavericks team photo.

Hang in there, guys and faithful fans. Your time is coming.

6.
Of Ice Hockey and Dallas Stars

The Dallas Stars came crashing into town in the spring of 1993, all the way from Minneapolis, Minnesota. Formerly known as the "North Stars," this National Hockey League team was the first of its kind in Texas. Norman Green, who has owned and governed the team since 1990, was responsible for making the move to the Lone Star State.

The young team has gradually improved over the years, going to the Stanley Cup Finals in 1991 and finishing the '92-'93 season with a 36-38-10 record. Mark Tinordi, #24 and captain of the Dallas Stars, came to the team in a 1988 trade with the New York Rangers. The Stars' best defenseman, Tinordi set career highs in the '92-'93 season by scoring 15 goals, 27 assists, and 42 points. At 6 feet, 4 inches and 205 pounds, Tinordi has become one of the most feared defensemen in the NHL and played in the 1992 All-Star Game. He has served as the Stars captain since 1991. A broken leg in 1994 took Tinordi out of the game for the season.

Perhaps the best-known Dallas Star is center Mike Modano, who was named the Stars' Bill Masterton Award winner as MVP two seasons in a row. Modano, who led the Stars in points in the '91-'92 season (77) and was second in goals (33) and assists (44), was born in Minnesota and came to the Stars from the Prince Albert Raiders in the Western Hockey League. In 1989-90, Modano was named Rookie of the Year by *The Hockey News*.

Head Coach and General Manager Bob Gainey led his Stars to the Stanley Cup Finals (as Campbell Conference champions in 1991), coached in the 1992 All-Star Game, and has consistently raised the team's win totals each year. Gainey, as a defensive forward for the Montreal Canadiens (1973-89), won the Frank J. Selke Award as the league's best defensive forward four years in a row (1978- 81) and in 1979 led the Canadiens to their fourth straight Stanley Cup championship. The talented hockey player hung up his skates in 1989 to begin a coaching career. Bob Gainey was inducted into the Hockey Hall of Fame in 1992.

Although many people don't realize it, ice hockey has been played in Dallas for over fifty years. The first pro hockey game in Texas was played on November 5, 1941, at the Will Rogers Memorial Coliseum in Fort Worth. The Fort Worth Rangers played against the St. Paul Saints for a 2-2 tie in the American Hockey Association season opener.

Not to be outdone, within 24 hours the Dallas Texans made their AHA debut at the Fair Park Ice Arena, also tying 2-2 with the Saints. As might be expected, there was an ongoing rivalry with Fort Worth known as the "Trinity River Rivalry" that entertained minor league hockey fans over 21 winter seasons. The Dallas/Fort Worth battles on ice were notoriously riotous and hard fought.

Hockey playing was quite different back in the old days. There was no glass above the boards, and chicken wire was around the ends behind the goals, causing one Central Hockey League official to remark, "If you got a guy's head up against that screen, he'd come off looking like hamburger." Sticks were not curved, and fans brought cushions to block the pucks.

Between periods, eight or ten kids would go on the ice with metal scrapers and scrape the ice, followed by others

The Sports Page

with big street brooms. Then the ice was hosed down with water. The Dallas team, owned by Clarence Linz, included coach Leroy Goldsworthy, goalie Paul Bibault, Squee Allen, Red McKay, Gord Petrie, Butch Bouchard, Murray Armstrong, and Howie Morenz Jr.

When the NHL expanded in 1967 from six to twelve teams, the Chicago Blackhawks moved their CHL farm team to the State Fair Coliseum in Dallas, which, unfortunately, had no posts. At the same time, Detroit sent the newly created Fort Worth Wings to the Will Rogers Coliseum.

For the next 15 years, the two arch-rivals battled for the Turnpike Trophy, so named after the Dallas/Fort Worth Turnpike (now I-30). The Dallas Blackhawks won the trophy ten times, thanks to the coaching of Bobby Kromm, who inspired his Blackhawks to three league championships and numerous battles with the Wings. Some players who remained in Dallas after their ice careers ended are Moe L'Abbe, Dave Hudson, Greg Vaydick, Doug Shelton, Duane Wylie, and Gord McRae.

A contest between the Wings and 'Hawks in December 1970 has the distinction of being the only game in CHL history to be called with time remaining on the clock. With 39 seconds left to play, Dallas forward Bill Young began fighting with Fort Worth general manager Bob Lemieux in the walkway outside the rink. Referee Alf Lejeune decreed that the last 39 seconds didn't need to be played and called the game.

In 1982 the CHL left the North Texas area, due to the poor economy, but the circuit was restarted in 1992 with the Dallas Freeze and Fort Worth Fire. After over 50 years of ice hockey in Dallas, the sport today is more popular than ever.

Dallas Stars (NHL) 214-GO-STARS (467-8277)
Dallas Freeze (CHL) 214-631-7825

Section V

7. Cotton Bowl

If you are one of those wild and crazy fans who live for the second week in October when Dallas hosts the Texas University-Oklahoma University (Texas-OU) football game (and shoot-out and riot), then you are no doubt familiar with the Cotton Bowl. Located in Fair Park, the huge stadium was built in 1930 and is the city's largest outdoor facility, capable of holding 100,000 people. During the Texas Centennial celebration in 1936, President Franklin D. Roosevelt spoke to a crowd of more than 50,000 gathered in the stadium.

Since 1937, the Cotton Bowl has been known primarily for being the site of the famous football game of the same name that takes place every year on New Year's Day, pitting the Southwest Conference champion against an invited opponent. In conjunction with the football game, a nationally televised parade was traditionally held in downtown Dallas on New Year's Day. Unfortunately, the parade was discontinued in 1992 due to a lack of funds. Of course, some people were happy because they didn't like to stand in the freezing cold even to see a parade.

The Dallas Cowboys and Southern Methodist University Mustangs played home games at the Cotton Bowl for many years until the Cowboys got their own stadium in 1971 (Texas Stadium in Irving) and Ownby Stadium became host to most of SMU's home games. Unless you enjoy fights and brawls, it's best to avoid the area when the Longhorns and Sooners come to town the second weekend in October.

Fair Park—Parry Ave., Cullum Blvd., Fitzhugh Ave., and Washington St.
214-670-8400

SECTION VI

Dallas No-No's: Twelve Things You Should Never Do in Dallas

1. Never, ever criticize the State of Texas (the grandest and best state that ever was in the whole Union), past governors, or members of the Cowboys Ring of Honor. It's okay to criticize present governors, but once their term expires, Texas governors ride off into Southern Governor Heaven, where they can do no wrong. And as far as speaking ill of one in the Ring of Honor, well, that's sacrilege, pal.

2. Don't ever attempt to one-up a Dallasite about anything. You will regret it.

3. Never be caught shopping in Highland Park Village without wearing full makeup and a designer outfit, unless of course, you are very rich and famous, in which case you can wear grunge or anything you like and may even start a trend.

4. Never refuse a man's chili, and don't ask what kind of meat is in it, unless you have a cast-iron stomach. *(Tip: Smile when you swallow it, even though your mouth is afire and your sinuses haven't been so clear since preschool. Say it's the tastiest and hottest stuff you've*

Section VI

ever put in your mouth, and you will make a friend for life.)

5. Don't try to convert a city of carnivores to herbivores. If you insist on being one of them vegetarians, keep it to yourself—or better yet, move to another state.

6. Don't ask the ex-savings & loan officer who used to send you all that business what happened to his Rolex and BMW and why he's driving a rental car and wearing a Timex. And *don't* inquire as to his whereabouts the last 18 months. He will tell you in his own time.

7. Never ridicule a grown man who insists on using a double first name, such as Willy Ray, Benny Joe, etc.

8. Don't offer negative opinions on the cultural life in Dallas unless you attend the events and are knowledgeable about the art form.

9. If you are in town on business, DO NOT criticize the city of Dallas to your host. However, if you are truly a nervy person and can't live with yourself unless you point out something that's wrong with the city, go ahead and do so. At any rate, you've blown the deal, sweetie.

10. If you plan to attend the Cattle Baron's Ball, don't wear jeans.

11. Don't wear dressy attire (sequins, strapless gowns) to the Dallas Symphony. Believe it or not, only business dress is appropriate here.

12. Don't laugh at a Texas accent, no matter how pronounced it may be. Accents are a matter of pride with Texans, even in Dallas. Do whatever it takes—bite your lip or tongue, or think macabre thoughts, until you are back in your hotel room. Then it's okay to howl with laughter and call your friends in Brooklyn to make fun of these Texas hicks.

Galleria's 85-foot tall Christmas tree—tallest indoor tree in Texas. (Courtesy of Galleria.)

Section VI

Mustangs of Las Colinas. Giant mustangs of bronze gallop where real mustangs once roamed free. The Mustangs of Las Colinas is the world's largest equestrian sculpture and commemorates the spirit of those great animals that once lived in "the hills" near Dallas. (Courtesy of the Dallas Convention & Visitors Bureau.)

SECTION VII

Amazing Dallas Trivia: Twenty Little-Known Facts About the Big D

Did you know that...

...1) John Neely Bryan, who is credited as being the founder of Dallas, spent four years living in the Arkansas wilderness with the Indians in order to restore his health after contracting cholera in 1833.

...2) Baylor Medical Center, one of the country's leading hospitals, was begun in 1904 when Colonel C.C. Slaughter, a prominent rancher and the largest taxpayer in Texas, donated the first $50,000 to build a new Baptist Hospital in Dallas.

The hospital, known then as the Texas Baptist Memorial Sanatorium, was built on one of Slaughter's cattle pastures. Directors of the medical facility wished to honor its benefactor by naming the growing hospital for him, but they wisely concluded that "Slaughter Hospital" just didn't have a nice ring to it. The facility was renamed "Baylor Hospital" in 1920.

...3) The original Dallas cowboys were "as wild as the longhorns they drove," according to one writer. During the

Section VII

1870s, the cowboys who visited Dallas would leave their herds nearby to graze, as recorded by one resident, who wrote:

...while they came back and pulled a stampede of their own by racing their horses up and down the town, yelling like Comanches as they fired their guns. Everybody knew that the cowboys meant no harm and that if anyone was hurt, it was an accident. Still the women would gather up their children and crouch with them in the houses until they left town.

...4) A dove lighted on the shoulder of Baptist preacher David Meyers while he was preaching in an arbor near Grapevine in 1846, thus giving rise to the name "Lonesome Dove Baptist Church," a name it holds to this day and made famous by Larry McMurtry's best-selling novel, *Lonesome Dove*. Although the town in the book is fictional, Mr. McMurtry spotted the Lonesome Dove Baptist Church van while dining at a restaurant one day and decided that would be a good name for the town in his novel.

...5) There is a legend that a young girl in an exotic, flowing negligee drowned herself in White Rock Lake because of her broken heart. Sometimes she is said to appear to couples parked around the lake and is known to locals as "The Lady of White Rock Lake."

...6) The MasterCard/Visa idea originated in Dallas, when three shopping centers, Preston Forest, Preston Royal, and Preston Center, got together and issued the "Prestocard," which could be used by shoppers at all three centers. Eventually, the concept was purchased and expanded.

...7) The city of Dallas was the site of a gruesome "Roman Holiday" on May 24-26, 1934, when some estimated 20,000 people turned out to see the bullet-riddled bodies of notorious outlaws Bonnie Parker and Clyde Barrow as they lay in state in two Dallas mortuaries. The notorious couple, who operated out of West Dallas during several years of their crime spree, had been ambushed and killed by Texas Rangers on May 23, 1934, near Arcadia, Louisiana.

Clyde Barrow was interred in the Western Heights Cemetery, and Bonnie Parker was buried in Fishtrap Cemetery in West Dallas, near the slum area where she grew up. The curious mob fought to get to the gravesides, and aviators swooped down to drop flowers on the biers. Even grateful newsboys sent bouquets. Later, Bonnie Parker's body was moved to Crown Hill Memorial Park on Webb Chapel Road.

The 1967 Arthur Penn movie, *Bonnie and Clyde*, starring Faye Dunaway and Warren Beatty, was partially filmed along Upper Greenville in Dallas.

...8) Vera Jane Peers, a.k.a. Jayne Mansfield, grew up in University Park and went through Highland Park High School. The famous "blonde bombshell" actress was killed in a car wreck near New Orleans in 1967.

...9) In the 1960s, Dallas' only coffeehouse (in the beat sense of the term) was in a small building at the corner of Hall and McKinney where Joey Tomato's now stands. Jerry Jeff Walker and Michael Martin Murphy used to play there for $10.00 a night when they were just starting out.

...10) Park Cities, one of the country's first planned communities, was so named because twenty percent of the developed space was to be devoted to parks.

...11) Skillman Avenue was originally named "Lindbergh Lane," after famed aviator Charles Lindbergh. During World War II, when Lindbergh became a somewhat controversial figure through adverse publicity (among other things, he refused to return a medal given to him by

Germany), the city renamed the street "Skillman Avenue," after W.F. Skillman, a Dallas banker.

...12) Fifty years ago, the site of what is now the lobby of the Hyatt Regency Hotel in downtown Dallas was the bed of the Trinity River.

...13) Thanks to the enthusiasm of Dallas civic leaders, the 1936 Texas Centennial was celebrated in Dallas, even though the city had not existed when Texas declared its independence from Mexico. Dallas officials outbid Houston and San Antonio, winning the half-year-long celebration.

...14) In 1876 there was a "grasshopper storm" so great it reputedly stopped the trains between Dallas and Fort Worth.

...15) At least five times during the Texas-OU weekend, Clyde Barrow's 500-lb. gravestone has been stolen from Western Heights Cemetery. Incredibly, it was always found and returned to its place, although the Barrow family had to pay each time to have it hauled back.

...16) Famous actor Tommy Lee Jones attended the exclusive St. Mark's School in Dallas on a football scholarship. It was at St. Mark's that Mr. Jones was introduced to theater.

...17) In 1869 the systematic mass extermination of great buffalo herds in the area caused Dallas to boom as a hide market. An entry from the diary of early settler John B. Billingsley, written in the 1840s, notes the abundance of wild game.
> About the first of June the buffalo came in from the western plains and the prairies were alive with them. Thousands of them were to be seen. Deer, antelope, wild horses and wolves were numerous.

Bear, wild turkeys and all kinds of wild varmints ranged the bottoms and the thickets along the water courses.

...18) In 1966 it was "illegal" for female students to wear slacks at SMU on campus, even in the library. It was, however, acceptable to wear them in the dorms. The "Hockadaisys," as girls of Hockaday School are known, were not permitted to wear trousers as part of their uniform until the late 1970s.

...19) The dugout of John Neely Bryan, founder of Dallas, was located at the spot where, 122 years later, President John F. Kennedy was assassinated.

...20) In the late seventies and early 1980s, rancher Ben Carpenter, owner of a six-thousand-acre spread near the D/FW airport, Hackberry Creek Ranch, found out the land all around his ranch was going to be developed. In order to keep the integrity of the land, Carpenter decided to build himself a city.

The result is Las Colinas, a complete urban center with hills, mesquite trees, a lake, canals, its own transportation system, elegant shopping centers, office buildings, and residential communities. Now, that's a Dallas solution for you.

SECTION VIII

Why Is That? Answers to Ten Petty Questions About Dallas

1. Why is everything so big in Dallas?
   Because it's in Texas, Stupid.

   ♦ ♦ ♦ ♦ ♦

2. Why is there an ongoing rift between Dallas and Fort Worth?
   Some claim it all started when an astute observer pointed out that "Fort Worth is where the West begins, while Dallas is where the East peters out." The origin of this oft-quoted jab is unknown, but ever since anyone can remember, Dallas and Fort Worth have been, for the most part, friendly rivals.
   Fort Worth says all the *real* cowboys live in its boundaries, while Dallas counters that Fort Worth is nothing but a stupid little cowtown. Then Fort Worth points out that Dallasites are snobs, so Dallasites respond that people over in Fort Worth are just hicks. Dallas isn't really a western town, says Fort Worth, and no *gen-u-ine* cowboy would even set the toe of his boot inside the Dallas County line.

Fort Worth, which lies thirty miles to the west of Dallas in Tarrant County, was founded in 1849 and is known for its stockyards, rodeos, and art museums that house astounding collections of original works by such artists as Cezanne, Rembrandt, and Monet, as well as numerous works by renowned western artist Frederic Remington.

Historically, the rivalry between the two cities existed as far back as 1883, when records show that a few years earlier, the *Daily Herald*, a Dallas paper, had "jocosely referred" to its neighbor to the west as "that Micawber of the prairies." Micawber is a character in Charles Dickens' novel, *David Copperfield*, who is very poor, but "lives in optimistic expectation of better fortune."

By the time the Texas and Pacific Railway (T&P) reached Eagle Ford, six miles west of Dallas, in 1873, there was a crisis going on in the economy, so the building of the railway was halted for three years. Fort Worth was hurt economically, and it was said that a substantial number of Fort Worth residents moved to Dallas simply out of frustration. From that time on, it seemed that Fort Worth was always getting the short end of the stick.

In 1883 the Brown Stockings baseball team of Dallas beat Fort Worth's Haymakers 23 to 1, and one of the first recorded football games took place on Thanksgiving Day 1891, when hundreds of spectators watched the Dallas team beat Fort Worth 24 to 11. Rivalry between the two cities became so well known, that one year a "truce" was called on New Year's Day, and newspapers ran a photograph of *Dallas Times Herald* publisher Tom Gooch shaking hands with *Fort Worth Star-Telegram* publisher and civic leader Amon Carter at the Dallas/Tarrant county line.

Perhaps the greatest feat accomplished between the two cities was the construction of the Dallas-Fort Worth Airport, a joint venture that took place only after years of controversy and bickering. Beginning in the 1950s, Amon Carter kept urging that a single airport be built midway between the two cities. Dallas, happy with the convenience of Love Field, would have none of this, so Fort Worth built its own airport. They named it "Amon Carter Field," and Fort Worth leaders optimistically believed that it would eventually replace Love Field.

Dallas decided that Amon Carter Field did indeed pose a threat to Love Field, so the city passed a $12.5 million bond issue to construct a new terminal at Love Field and lengthen its runways. It wasn't long before Carter Field began to decline due to a lack of passengers.

In 1964 the Civil Aeronautics Board (CAB), prompted by Fort Worth, agreed to conduct hearings on the airport controversy. Dallas Mayor Erik Jonsson decided that a brand-new facility should be constructed, because both Love Field and Greater Southwest International Airport, as Carter Field had been renamed, were inadequate.

In 1965 history was made as the two cities agreed to a joint venture (without CAB mandate) of building a new regional airport. When the Greater Dallas-Fort Worth Regional Airport opened in 1973, it was the largest and most modern air facility in the world. Fort Worth's airport had by this time been reduced to little more than a ghost terminal.

One would only hope that after more than a century of bickering, the two cities would once again declare a truce and put this childish belligerence behind them. But Dallas businessmen and businesswomen are still going to Fort Worth to purchase their luxury cars because they can get a better deal over there. Then they take their new luxury autos to the Dallas dealer to get one of his license plate frames to replace the Fort Worth one, because nobody wants to be seen driving around Dallas with "Fort Worth" on their license plates. And if that isn't bad enough....

...Dallas, Fort Worth says, is nothin' but a clump of shiny buildings and shopping centers filled with snooty people, and the only steers over there are a bunch of bronze sculptures.

Hmmmmph!

Dallas responds that it doesn't matter how many art museums Amon Carter's money built and how many original Picassos the city owns, Fort Worth will never be anything more than a big ole' cowtown.

Well, as any Texan will tell you, there's nothing like a good feud to keep the blood stirred up.

♦ ♦ ♦ ♦ ♦

3. What is a tolltag and why is it a Dallas status symbol?

The construction of the Dallas North Tollway during the past decade has tremendously aided the growth of "bedroom" communities, such as Plano and Addison, north of Dallas. This awesome freeway enables working people (and shopping people) to zoom to their downtown Dallas offices in record time. But it costs 25 to 50 cents to pass through each tollgate, and there are a number of tollgates.

As anyone knows, the Dallas businessperson is not one to waste time stopping at tollgates, so the friendly Tollway folks have devised these computerized "tags" that are attached by velcro to the windshield of said commuting vehicle. No more fumbling for quarters.

The tolltag is "read" electronically, and when your allotted amount of forty dollars is used up, the intelligent thing automatically bills your credit card and gives you a fresh start. Talk about efficient!

You can spot tolltaggers whizzing through the tollgates, in specially designated lanes, leaving the parked masses in their wake. If you want to be a member of the commuter elite, you have to buy a tolltag.

Tolltags may be purchased at the Tolltag Store, located at 12300 Inwood Road.

♦ ♦ ♦ ♦ ♦

4. Why does the wind blow so much in Dallas?

You may be surprised to know that the average wind speed in Dallas is 10.8 mph. Even though that doesn't sound like much, visitors to the Big D often comment that it seems windy. Dallas, in fact, *is* windy, even more so than the Windy City itself, Chicago.

Particularly in the summer, the wind patterns across the Central Plains are quite strong. First of all, you don't have the rapidly changing air patterns in summer like you do the rest of the year. Basically, the southwest pattern, known as the "heat low," travels counterclockwise and meets the eastern "Bermuda high," which travels clockwise. The two wind streams cause a funneling "eggbeater" effect, which increases the overall circulation of hot, dry air.

So the next time you're out on the prairies, in the backyard barbecuing, or in the pool, and the hot air is blowing on a Dallas summer night, you might say, "My, this Bermuda high meeting the heat low makes for a rather interesting weather pattern. Rather like an eggbeater effect, wouldn't you say?" Or just say, "Sure is windy tonight."

◆ ◆ ◆ ◆ ◆

5. Why are Dallas freeways given names, such as LBJ, R.L. Thornton, etc.?

Dallas, along with the state of Texas, values its leaders, particularly since the people who founded the city, along with being men and women of great vision, were responsible for its amazing growth. Business and civic leaders made Dallas what it is today, and Dallas likes to show its appreciation.

Granted, they—whoever named these freeways—didn't have the motorists in mind when all this was decided, and more than a few drivers in Dallas have threatened to get their hands on whoever came up with this hare-brained idea. When someone tells you to "Just take R.L. Thornton to Julius Schepps," whip out your trusty *Mapsco* (a necessity for Dallas residents) and match the freeway name with its equivalent numeral.

Here are a few helpful tips to get you started.

Section VIII

LBJ (Lyndon B. Johnson) Freeway = Interstate Highway 635
R.L. Thornton Freeway East = Interstate Highway 30
R.L. Thornton Freeway South = Interstate Highway 35E*
Stemmons Freeway = Interstate Highway 35E*
Julius Schepps Freeway = Interstate Highway 45
Marvin D. Love Freeway = U.S. Highway 67*
Central Expressway = U.S. Highway 75
Woodall Rodgers Freeway = Spur (State Highway) 366
C.F. Hawn Freeway = U.S. Highway 175
Northwest Highway = Spur 224
John W. Carpenter Freeway = State Highways 114 & 183
J. Elmer Weaver Freeway** = U.S. Highway 67*
Preston Road = State Highway 289
Buckner, Ledbetter, Northwest Highway, and Walton Walker Boulevard = Loop 12

---

* Yes, these are duplicate numbers, so you are on your own here.
** This is a real name.

NOTE: "F.M." before a road number means "farm to market" road, a holdover from the days when farmers carted their crops down these paths.

◆ ◆ ◆ ◆ ◆

6. Why do Dallasites dress up so much?

Dallas is known for being glamorous and having lots of beautiful women. Some say it all started in the 1860s and '70s, when Belle Starr, notorious female bandit, would ride the muddy streets of Dallas dressed in a velvet riding gown and plumed hat, her matching revolvers displayed on her hips. Traffic—horses and buggies—came to a halt, and people ran to their doorways to glimpse this bold woman.

Ever since Belle's days, Dallas women have been trying to impress people with traffic-stopping ensembles. Of course, men dress up too, but it isn't considered manly to be

Why is That?

overly concerned about one's looks. In Dallas, you will find that being concerned about your looks is just as important as, well, practically anything else. Even if you're a great-grandmother, you dress to impress.

Alluring Dallas women have been celebrated in song for over a hundred years. Blues tunes from Deep Ellum in the 1920s and '30s were often sung about enticing Dallas women. Even as far back as the 1890s, when Sanger Bros., the well-known department store, carried the latest styles, Dallas was considered a fashion-conscious city.

Of course, when Neiman Marcus arrived in 1907 and began showcasing fashions and convincing Texas women to shop in Texas, rather than New York or Paris, Dallas' reputation as a fashion haven grew. In Dallas, clothing is a multimillion-dollar industry, attracting designers, models, photographers, and others in the world of fashion.

A Dallas woman wears the latest in makeup style, but only in her *personal* colors, of course (one must have one's colors done), dazzling jewelry (even if it's not the real thing), and a coordinated ensemble. The typical Dallas woman carries in her wallet several Glamour Shots to pass out to admirers.

Some might say that there's not much to look at in Dallas except skyscrapers, so people tend to pay more attention to how everybody looks. And you might think this preoccupation with looks is phony and shows a lack of values. Maybe so, but it makes life a lot more interesting, doesn't it?

◆ ◆ ◆ ◆ ◆

7. Why are so many British people attracted to Dallas?

For reasons known and unknown, the British love Texas and everything Texan, especially Dallas. One might wonder why a refined, sophisticated Englishman straight from Heathrow Airport in London would be attracted to a less civilized city like Dallas, where you ask for tea and are given a Mason jar with a straw instead of a dainty cup and saucer (except at the Adolphus or Lady Primrose's). And one might wonder why there are approximately 25,000 Brits working and living permanently in the D/FW area.

The most common reason given is the immense popularity of the "Dallas" TV show. However, history shows that Englishmen dominated life in the Texas Panhandle during the 1800s and that English fiction immortalized the American cowboy as the epitome of virtue, honesty, and decorum—all appealing traits.

The British are credited with bringing barbed wire, steel windmills, and Johnson grass to Texas. AND—hold onto your hats—some authorities report that Texas chili was invented by an Englishman who settled in San Antonio in the 1880s. Apparently, the chap was craving a curry dish he had eaten while in India, so he substituted chili peppers in place of curry.

But why would such refined folks want to *live* in Dallas? Well, reports are that, although Brits have always been attracted to the American West, the TV show "Dallas" indeed put them over the edge. They were fascinated by the glamorous women, the opulence, the palatial houses, the dramatic corporate warfare. The show was extremely popular across the seas, and visitors coming to the States from England soon started adding Dallas and Southfork to their itineraries—or just crossing out New York, San Francisco, and Washington, D.C. and heading straight for the Big D.

They found the climate to be pleasant and mild compared to their harsh winters. And, it may be noted, the attraction is mutual. Texans are impressed by the lovely English accents, the English sense of class and style.

After Caroline Rose Hunt opened her English antique store, Lady Primrose's Shopping the English Countryside, she was advised to open Lady Primrose's Shopping Texas Countrystyle because of requests from English visitors for Texana. The result is a nook that has horseshoe cowboy figures mounted on driftwood, baskets and wreaths of sunflower seed heads, horn chandeliers, and individually designed denim jackets.

Many British people come to Dallas with corporations such as Texas Instruments and EDS, which have offices around the world. Once here, they find that although Americans are fairly materialistic, they (the English) enjoy a smidgen of materialism themselves, and there is no way they could return to England and draw the kind of salaries they get in Dallas. They like the openness of the country and the friendly people and see Dallas as a Land of Opportunity.

There are, however, several British social clubs around Dallas that meet over tea and crumpets once a month or so and pine for the Mother Country.

◆ ◆ ◆ ◆ ◆

8. Why is Sunday School so popular in Dallas?

Dallas, as previously stated, is said to be the "buckle" of the Bible belt, which refers to a group of states stretching across the southern U.S. that are known for fundamentalist religious roots. In spite of being a young city, Dallas has a very strong religious background (*Sec.I:14*), and houses of worship were among the first buildings to be constructed by early settlers.

There are a large number of churches in Dallas County, many of them fundamentalist or nondenominational Bible churches that have traditionally offered Sunday School. One reason Sunday School (or adult Bible study, if you prefer) is well attended is that there are so many religious people in Texas.

Another reason for the popularity of Sunday School is, in a word, "bidness." Many a Dallas church pew is filled with salespeople, car dealers, politicians, and insurance sales— oops, risk management consultants. A large church is a great place to make business contacts. People who weren't habitual church-goers often become involved in church groups after moving to Dallas because the church is a strong institution and very much a part of people's lives in our mobile society.

Think about it. When you become a member of an adult Bible class, you have an instant support group, instant friends, and instant social life. This is especially important if you are new to the community. Most of the large Sunday Schools are not solely social or religious groups; most are actively involved in community projects, from Habitat for Humanity (building houses) to community food banks and shelters. Many good works are performed through the Sunday Schools. And where else can you go on a Sunday morning to eat doughnuts, drink coffee, have friendly conversation, and learn a moral lesson?

Most of Dallas' large congregations have active singles groups. Since Dallas attracts so many single people, they often find attending church is one of the best ways to meet like-minded members of the opposite sex. So check out your local Sunday School. It isn't just for children anymore.

♦ ♦ ♦ ♦ ♦

9. Why, then, is happy hour so well attended?

The average Dallas citizen is thirty years of age, well-educated, hard-working, and hard playing. Many young, single people are drawn to Dallas. Residents are very image conscious, and the city is known for its beautiful people of both sexes—and for its glamorous women.

Of course, singles have to occupy their time after work, so naturally a good number of them end up imbibing spirits with the office gang at a local trendy nightspot. Happy hour isn't limited to singles, and stories abound of husbands who move to the Big D, get stars in their eyes, and end up falling for a gorgeous female coworker.

Wives be warned: There are fast women in these parts who are dazzling and looking for a good time, so do your part by having a little image update of your own. Plain-Jane attire and no makeup just don't cut it here. Naturally, the reverse applies to husbands.

Why is That?

(Pssssssstt.......Don't act surprised if you spot your Sunday School teacher.)

◆ ◆ ◆ ◆ ◆

10. Why is there a hole in the roof at Texas Stadium?

No, it's not so God can watch His team play, as some fans will try to convince you. When Cowboy owner Clint Murchison, Jr. decided to build a new stadium for his team, he wanted the fans to be protected and stay dry but still have the game played in the elements. The result is a giant hole in the roof over the playing field, so that one gets the feel of being outdoors while remaining under a roof.

Texas Stadium was also designed to look full, even when there aren't many people present. The first game played in Texas Stadium was on October 24, 1971, against the New England Patriots. The Cowboys won 44-21, and 65,708 fans were in attendance.

SECTION IX

Dallas Brags

1. World's Largest Equestrian Sculpture—Mustangs at Las Colinas
    You will get a powerful nostalgic feel for the Old West as it can never be again while gazing at the majestic memorial of nine bronze mustangs crossing a stream. When John Neely Bryan first explored the Dallas area, he reached what is now Las Colinas, west of the Trinity, and there found rolling, mesquite-covered hills and herds of wild mustangs that roamed free. It was here that sculptor Robert Glen captured the free spirit of the wild horses.
    5205 N. O'Connor Blvd., Irving
    214-869-9047

2. Largest Urban Arts District in America
    The McKinney Trolley car line is linked with nearly 100 art galleries, antique shops, and restaurants. Dallas' downtown arts district is the largest so-designated area in the United States. The most prominent attractions in the arts district are the Dallas Museum of Art (DMA) and the Morton H. Meyerson Symphony Center. Also, Dallas has over 110 live performances per night.
    DMA—214-922-1200
    Symphony Center—214-871-4000

Section IX

3. Largest Cowboy Ever—Big Tex

Big Tex has been greeting visitors to the Texas State Fair every year since 1952. The 52-foot cowboy was designed and built by Jack Bridges in Kerens, Texas, where he was, of all things, Santa Claus. According to Tex, in 1951 he was attracted to the Big D by the din and glare of the State Fair and decided to give up the North Pole, don a pair of boots, and change his name to Big Tex. Of course, the boots had to be custom made since they are size 70.

Big Tex has been a Dallasite ever since. You might say he's the biggest Dallas fan ever. He greets fair visitors with a friendly "How-dy Folks!" Tex's waist is 23 feet. A 90-gallon hat tops Tex off.

4. More Shopping Centers Per Capita than Any U.S. City

5. Largest Ferris Wheel in the United States—State Fair at Fair Park

The "Star," a 21-story-tall ferris wheel, is in service October 1-24 during the Texas State Fair, located at Fair Park.
214-670-8400

6. More Restaurants Per Capita than New York City—*that's right, NEW YORK CITY!*

7. Largest Permanent Model Train Exhibit in the country—Children's Medical Center

Eight trains run simultaneously in this impressive exhibit over more than 1,000 feet of track, winding around such famous landmarks as Mount Rushmore, the Grand Canyon, and the Dallas skyline. Privately funded, the $400,000 display is located in the lobby of the Children's Medical Center and has proven to be popular among the young patients. But you don't have to be a patient to enjoy the trains.
1935 Motor St.
214-920-2000

Dallas Brags

8. World's Largest Diesel Electric Locomotive—Age of Steam Railroad Museum
   Located at Fair Park, the Age of Steam Railroad Museum is the original site of the 1936 Texas Centennial and offers railroad buffs a wide collection of rail memorabilia, as well as the locomotives on display.
   214-421-8754

9. Largest Children's Library Center in the United States—Dallas Public Library
   Just across the street from Dallas City Hall, the J. Erik Jonsson Central Library houses more than three million items, including the Texas/Dallas History Archives on the seventh floor. The Children's Center is designed so little readers can enjoy books, computers, puppet shows, films, and stories in the Story-telling Village.
   Additionally, there is a library store featuring Texas and Dallas memorabilia, as well as a used book store. Opened in 1982, the Dallas Public Library was architecturally designed to lean inward as the City Hall leans out.
   1515 Young St.
   214-670-1700

10. Largest Banner
    Hung from the roof edge of the Reunion Arena announcing the arrival of the Ringling Bros. Barnum & Bailey Circus, June 29, 1988. The vinyl banner is 350 feet long and 18 feet tall.

11. World's Largest Wholesale Trade Complex—Dallas Market Center

...*and that's enough bragging for now.*

♦ ♦ ♦ ♦ ♦

SECTION X

Dallas Lists

1.
Notable Names

Adams, Nathan—influential Dallas banker whose bank, First National, financed many of the early oil ventures; helped found Scottish Rite Hospital for Crippled Children.
Akard, W.C.C.—early merchant (1864).
Barry, Bryan T.—two-term mayor of Dallas; 1894-95, 1897-98.
Bass, Sam—notorious Dallas train robber; shot to death by Texas Rangers in 1878.
Beeman, John & James J. & family—first Dallas settlers after John Neely Bryan (1842).
Belo, Alfred Horatio—(1839-1901)—*Dallas Morning News* publisher; restored mansion located at the corner of Ross and Harwood; Belo Corporation today is a leading Southwestern media company.
Bennett, William H.—early landowner (1856).
Blaylock, Dr. Louis—capitalist and mayor, 1923-27.
Bopp, Jacob—Swiss colonist (1870), fruit raiser, and vintner.
Brewer, J. Mason—early black historical and biographical writer; author of *Negro Legislators and Their Descen-*

dants (1935); "Juneteenth" (1932); "Old Time Negro Proverbs" (1933); *Negrito* (1933).

Cabell, Earle—twice mayor of Dallas; prominent businessman in family's dairy and retailing business.

Cabell, Gen. W.L. (Old Tige)—Confederate commander and Dallas mayor.

Callaway, Mrs. W.A.—first women's editor of *The Dallas Morning News*; joined staff in 1893 and worked until her death in 1916; wrote under pseudonym of Pauline Periwinkle; instrumental in promoting child welfare and other social projects; pioneer advocate of equal suffrage and founder of both the Dallas and the Texas Federations of Women's Clubs.

Cantagrel, Francois Jean—head of La Reunion Colony Company.

Caruth, Walter Watt & Will—early settlers (1852); two brothers from Kentucky who had a general store at Main and Record; civic leaders.

Cochran, William M.—first county clerk (1846).

Craft, Juanita Jewell (1902-1985)—active in the civil rights movement; organized rural NAACP chapters across Texas in the 1940s and '50s; involved in desegregation of University of Texas Law School, Dallas restaurants and theaters; willed her house to Dallas to develop civil rights programs.

Crockett, John M.—early lawyer (1848) and mayor in 1860; arrived with his law library in his saddlebags.

Crutchfield, Thomas F.—built early Dallas hotel, Crutchfield House, which opened in 1852; menu featured wild game shot by Crutchfield himself.

Dumas, J.P.—surveyor who moved to Dallas with his wife in 1844; platted the original town of Dallas for John Neely Bryan.

Durgan, Elizabeth B. Thomas—organized and sorted the mail beginning in 1846.

Ervay, Henry S.—mayor of Dallas 1870-72 during Reconstruction; refused to step down when radical governor

E.J. Davis attempted to remove city officials; released a hero after state supreme court ruled in his favor.

Exall, Henry—(1848-1913) Virginia calvaryman who moved to Dallas in 1888 and was heavily involved in business and city affairs; bred racehorses on his Lomo Alto farm; attempted to navigate the Trinity River in 1892.

Exall, Mrs. Henry—leader of movement to found public library and permanent art organization.

Field, Thomas W.—built first opera house and famous Oriental Hotel; one of the developers of Oak Cliff.

Fortune, Jan Isbelle—Texas playwright who wrote 52 Texas history plays broadcast on the radio; author of *Cavalcade of Texas*, the historical pageant of Texas shown at the Centennial in 1936; later moved to Hollywood and worked for MGM.

Garrett, Alexander Charles—Episcopalian bishop who served Dallas for half a century and wrote colorful memoirs, including such trials as parishioners spitting tobacco juice on church floors and walls and intrusion of hogs during services; arrived in Dallas in 1873 and conducted funeral service for a murder victim the next day; established St. Mary's College in 1889.

Gaston, William Henry—early banker and developer; rode into Dallas on horseback in 1868, carrying $20,000 in gold specie; instrumental in developing State Fair; reputed to be the model for Confederate Civil War monument in Pioneer Cemetery.

Gooch, Tom C.—editor-in-chief of now-defunct *Dallas Times Herald*.

Good, John J.—led group of angry Dallas residents on July 15, 1852, to seize claim files and maps from the office of Peters Colony agent Henry Oliver Hedgcoxe, resulting in a wild celebration and eventual land title given to colonists; Dallas County provost marshal during Civil War.

Gould, Jay—financier; builder Texas & Pacific Railroad; predicted in 1887 that Dallas' population would reach 150,000 in his lifetime; the "Hundred and Fifty

Section X

Thousand Club," dedicated to promoting the city, was founded after his death in 1892.

Griffith, Mrs. A.B.—first woman in Dallas County to cast a vote for president in 1920.

Guillot, Maxime—Frenchman who stopped in Dallas in 1853 en route to the goldfields in California; established carriage business at northeast corner of Elm and Houston.

Harwood, Alexander—county clerk 1850-51 and 1875-83.

Haskell, Horatio Nelson—alderman of East Dallas in 1883.

Hoblitzelle, Karl St. John—(1879-1967) theater magnate who built the Majestic Theater in 1905; chairman of the board of Republic National Bank 1945-1955.

Hockaday, Ela—opened school for girls in 1913 on Haskell Avenue.

Holland, William Meredith—former judge; first Dallas native to be elected mayor (1911), serving two terms; responsible for creation of White Rock Lake, a 2,200-acre reservoir in East Dallas.

Hughes, Sarah T.—federal district judge appointed by Kennedy; administered oath of office to President Lyndon B. Johnson at Love Field aboard Air Force One, shortly after Kennedy was assassinated.

Jefferson, Blind Lemon—blues singer who played guitar on the streets of Dallas in the World War I era, along with Huddie "Leadbelly" Ledbetter.

Joiner, Columbus Marion "Dad" (1860-1947)—wildcatter working out of Dallas in a one-chair, one-desk office, who, in 1930, penetrated the Austin chalk in East Texas and hit Woodbine sands, striking the greatest pool of oil ever discovered up to that time. The name of the first producing well was the Daisy Bradford No. 3.

Jonsson, Erik—one of the founders of Texas Instruments; mayor 1964-1971; founder of the Goals for Dallas program.

Jones, Preston—Dallas playwright whose *Texas Trilogy* won critical acclaim at the Kennedy Center and had a short Broadway run.

Keating, C.A.—pioneer farm implement dealer; civic leader who helped promote State Fair.

Knight, G.A. (Dude)—early feed merchant.

Lane, John W.—mayor 1862-66; copublisher of the *Herald*; state representative; added rider to a bill that caused the Texas & Pacific railroad to cross the Houston & Texas Central in Dallas, prompting the phenomenal growth and prosperity of Dallas.

Latimer, James Wellington "Weck"—journalist who brought his printing equipment in an oxcart to Dallas in 1849; established first newspaper, the *Cedar Snag*; died from a fall in 1859.

Latimer, Lucy Jordan—wife of James; came to Dallas with her piano—the first in town—in 1849.

Ledbetter, Huddie "Leadbelly"—influential blues singer and songwriter who came to Dallas in the World War I era; strolled the streets of Deep Ellum with his 12-string guitar.

Lemmon, W.H.—realty developer.

Lieberman, Nancy—outstanding professional basketball player with the Dallas Diamonds, 1980-81.

Long, Ben—Swiss who immigrated to Dallas with La Reunion colonists; anglicized his name from "Lang"; mayor of Dallas 1868-70 and 1872-74; had a showdown in 1873 when gambling house proprietors barricaded themselves in the second story of a downtown building and defied the mayor and his deputies for three days and nights. The siege ended in a compromise, celebrated by the smashing of many bottles; shot and mortally wounded in a saloon in 1877 while intervening between a proprietor and a customer named Reynolds.

Marsalis, Thomas L.—wholesale grocer who became flamboyant wheeler-dealer and developer; founder of Oak Cliff.

Martin, J.B. "Springy" (1857-1938)—renowned self-taught artist who came to Texas in 1886 as a cowboy and professional hunter; claimed to have killed the last wild buffalo in the Concho Valley; "discovered" by art world at the age of 77.

McCarroll, Frank—native Kentuckian who came to Dallas in 1890 and settled in Oak Cliff; studied aeronautics and built an airplane in the back of his home on Ninth Avenue; took out patent on retractable landing gear; helped organize Love Field Company after World War I to buy the aviation facility from the Army Air Corps.

McCoy, Colonel John C.—lawyer who came to Dallas in 1845; first practicing attorney; said to be only man in town who did not go to California in 1849 gold rush.

Miller, William Brown—Kentuckian who came to Dallas in 1847 and built log house, with his four slaves, at Hord's Ridge (now Oak Cliff); later constructed a large plantation home, Millermore; widowed in 1855 and raised five daughters; sent for Kentucky teacher, who conducted school for all the girls in the area at Miller's house.

Munger, Robert S.—came to Dallas in 1885 and formed a company for the manufacture of gins, using improvements he had invented and patented; in 1905 developed a 140-acre tract north of East Dallas known as Munger Place.

Onderdonk, Robert J. (1852-1917)—San Antonio artist who moved to Dallas in 1889; established the Dallas Arts Students League at 721 Elm Street in 1893, where he conducted the city's first formal art classes.

Oram, J.M.—Dallas jeweler.

Overton, W.P.—pioneer landowner, builder of first gristmill in county (1846).

Parker, Pat—purported to be the original "Old Black Joe," a character in Stephen Foster's song of the same name; died in the Dallas County poor farm in 1885 at the claimed age of 125 years.

Patterson, J.M.—first general merchant (1846) and later county judge.

Peak, Captain Jefferson—early settler and landowner.

Reaugh, Frank—(1860-1945) artist who came to Texas in a covered wagon in 1876; nationally recognized for his

western paintings; taught art at his studio "El Sibil" in Oak Cliff.
Ross, William W. and Andrew J.—early Dallas landowners.
Routh, Jacob—pioneer North Texas preacher; early abolitionist.
Samuell, Dr. W.W.—bequeathed city $1,000,000 cash and property for park in 1939.
Sanger, Alex & Philip—German immigrants who moved to Dallas and opened Sanger Bros. department store; prominent Dallas citizens.
Slaughter, Christopher Columbus (1837-1919)—extensive landowner who lived in Dallas 1870-1919; successful rancher who was Texas' largest taxpayer; donated land to found Baylor Hospital.
Stemmons, Leslie—developed 10,000 acres of flatland in the Trinity Industrial District, a project his sons, John and Storey Stemmons, continued after his death in 1939.
Stone, Thomas—landowner in 1854.
Thornton, Robert L.—self-made man who started Mercantile National Bank; civic leader known as "Mr. Dallas;" chairman of Texas Centennial Central Exposition; started powerful "Citizens Council" in the 1930s.
Townsend, Thurmond—early black artist; sculpture work locally displayed in the 1930s.
Vail, Dmitri (1903-1991)—well-known Dallas artist who lived in Highland Park; eccentric and controversial in later life.
Webb, Issac B.—one of Dallas' earliest settlers; came from Missouri in 1842; first church met in his home; helped organize building of church known as "Webb's Chapel" in 1846; first school also conducted in his home in 1845.
Welborn, Olin—congressman from Dallas district from 1879 to 1887.
Wozencraft, Frank W.—one of Dallas most popular mayors; called the "boy mayor" because he was elected in 1919 at the age of 26, while still on active duty as a captain following World War I; known for his spirited confrontations with utility companies.

Young, Marilla Ingram—wife of Rev. William C. Young; "Marilla Street" in downtown Dallas named after her.

Zaharias, Mildred Ella "Babe" Didrikson—greatest woman athlete of first half of twentieth century; Dallas team Golden Cyclones won national basketball championship in 1931; won national Amateur Athletic Union women's track team championship in 1932; set world records in 1932 Olympics in javelin throw and 80-meter hurdles; professional golfer, married wrestler George Zaharias.

Zang, J.F.—Oak Cliff land developer; worked to establish a cotton exchange in 1892.

2.
Unusual Dallas Outings

S & D Oyster Company/History Merchant Bookstore

Lunch at the S&D Oyster Company, located at 2701 McKinney Avenue, and you will think you are in New Orleans. Gumbo, oysters, shrimp poboys, and bread pudding, served by quiet waiters in white coats, are only a few of the recommended dishes.

After lunch, walk a few blocks down Routh Street to the History Merchant, a bookstore that specializes in rare books, biographies, and signed collections and caters to the carefree browser. You'll find the History Merchant at 2723 Routh Street, in the back of an older home, and once there, feel free to sit in one of the rocking chairs by the hearth, prop your feet up, and read to your heart's content.

This is especially great for bibliophiles who live in fear of the computer age. It will restore your faith!

S & D Oyster Company—214-880-0111
History Merchant—214-742-5487 (Wed.-Sat. 10-4:30)

McKinney Trolley/Antique Market/Dallas Museum of Art

If you enjoy discovering vintage clothing shops, small restaurants, art galleries, and boutiques and want to see Dallas from a different point of view, then hop on the trolley that runs along McKinney Avenue. Trolley tracks discovered under the pavement have been restored and the original cars renovated. Trolleys ran in Dallas until the 1950s.

Take a nostalgic ride through the arts district on these authentic cars that date from the turn of the century. Red velvet seats, brass railings, and clanging bells will take you back to another era. Cars run every 15-30 minutes along McKinney Avenue. This is a particularly nice way to go to the Dallas Museum of Art, one of the trolley stops.

Forty antique shops make up the Antique Market on the historic trolley route. Fine furniture, lamps, silver pieces, rugs, linens, and jewelry, collected from Texas to the English countryside, are only a few items offered. Additional shops and galleries are within walking distance.

McKinney Trolley - 214-855-0006
McKinney Avenue Antique Market
2710 McKinney Ave.
214-871-1904

Biblical Arts Center

This inspiring and unusual museum utilizes art as a means to help people of all faiths envision the events of the Bible. Operated by a not-for-profit, nondenominational organization, the Biblical Arts Center is constructed in a Romanesque style, reminiscent of Christian-era architecture.

Section X

The limestone entrance is modeled after Paul's Gate in Damascus. Heavy wooden doors and arches and stone columns evoke a feeling of Biblical times. A life-size replica of Christ's Garden Tomb at Calvary is one of the main features.
There are also artworks such as "Rebekah at the Well," "Madonna and Child" and "The Resurrected Christ." Exhibitions range from ancient archaeological artifacts to contemporary spiritual art and are changed every six to eight weeks.
Very nominal group rates make this art museum a pleasant and inspiring destination. The highlight of the Center is the *Miracle at Pentecost*, a giant mural that is unveiled several times a day with a dramatic light and sound presentation.

7500 Park Lane
214-691-4661

Farmer's Market

Four blocks of downtown Dallas filled with all kinds of produce—fruit, vegetables, Texas honey, nuts—and flowers. Also offers organic produce, bread, cheese, and hormone-free beef. Open daily 6-6; 363 days a year.

Bounded by Cadiz & Harwood Sts., Central Expwy. & I-30
214-670-5879

Dollhouse Museum of the Southwest

Not only dolls, but their houses, toys, and paraphernalia that take up a 10-room museum housed in a restored Texas prairie residence. Also features exhibits of private collections, seasonal, collections, and traveling collections. Open Tues.-Sat. 10-4:30; Sun. 10-4

2208 Routh St.
214-969-5502

Telephone Pioneer Museum of Texas

Showcases the evolution of the telephone, from invention to today's state-of-the-art systems. Mon.-Fri. 9:30-4:30

One Bell Plaza—208 S. Akard St. 2nd Floor
214-464-4359

3.
Dallas Firsts

Bank—organized by T.C. Jordan and E.G. Mays some time prior to 1868; one of several private banks operating during Reconstruction.
Brewery—began operation in 1857; proprietor was M. Monduel of La Reunion colony.
County school—opened in Farmers Branch in Dallas County in 1845.
Church building—Built in 1846 in Farmers Branch, near the Issac B. Webb residence. Named "Webb's Chapel," this building was an 18x18 foot log house.
Church service—occurred on March 19, 1844, conducted by Thomas Brown, an itinerant Methodist minister, at the home of William Cochran at Farmers Branch.

Section X

Divorce—1846; Charlotte M. Dalton vs. Joseph Dalton; Charlotte paid costs of the suit and, after winning a decree, married Henderson Couch, foreman of the jury, a few hours later.

Electric lights—Installed in 1882, the first electric lights in Dallas illuminated the Sanger Brothers store and Mayer's Garden.

Electric streetcar—1889.

Golf game—played in 1896.

High school football team—Texas' first high school football team kicked off in 1900 at Dallas High School.

Hotel—the Dallas Tavern, built in 1847 by Henry Harter.

Issue of *Dallas Morning News*—The first issue went to press October 1, 1885.

Jewish congregation—Emanu-El, organized July 1, 1872, from a Hebrew benevolent association.

Newspaper—*The Cedar Snag*, founded in 1849 by James Wellington Latimer using a printing press hauled to the town by ox cart. The newspaper was later renamed *The Dallas Herald*.

Opera house—Field Opera House, built in 1873 at Main, between Austin and Lamar streets; builder Tom Field forgot to include dressing rooms, so performers were forced to climb out a back window and rush to the nearby Grand Windsor Hotel, where they changed costumes.

Rabbi—First permanent rabbi in Dallas was Rabbi A. Suhler of Akron, Ohio, who worked with the Reformed Jewish congregation in 1874.

Sermon—Preached by Thomas Brown, an itinerant Methodist minister, March 19, 1844, at the home of William Cochran at Farmers Branch. The text used was Romans 1:16.

Shopping center—Highland Park Village, built in 1931, was the nation's first shopping center where all the buildings faced inward.

Skyscraper—Though not tall by today's standards, when the six-story North Texas Building was erected in 1888, it was considered the first "skyscraper" in North Texas.

Streets (paved)—Elm and Main streets, paved with bois d'arc (bow wood) from the Trinity River bottoms.

Synagogue—built in 1876 by Emanu-El at Commerce and Field streets.

Telephone—In 1881 the first telephones in Dallas linked the homes of Philip and Alexander Sanger with their store, Sanger Brothers, and the Browder Springs water plant with the downtown fire station.

4.
Dallas Chronology

1542	Luis Moscoso and survivors of DeSoto's Spanish expedition cross northeastern Dallas County, seeking way to Mexico City.
1712	Antoine Crozat and Bernard de La Harpe, Frenchmen from Louisiana, visit Anadarko Indians on the Trinity River.
1760	Roman Catholic missionary, Friar Calahorra y Saenz from Nacogdoches, comes to site of modern Dallas, makes treaties with Indians and changes name of Arkikosa River to Trinity because of its three forks.
1771	Athanase de Mezieres, Frenchman acting for Spaniards, makes treaty with Indians in territories including Dallas, Waco, and Wichita Falls.
1818	Indian battles between Caddo and Cherokee tribes near three forks of Trinity drive Cherokees eastward.

Section X

1837	Nov.—Ten Texas Rangers killed in battle with Indians fifty miles north of present Dallas. Survivors retreated to Dallas, camping first at Turtle Creek, then at present Commerce Street.
1840	John Neely Bryan and Colonel William G. Cooke make separate scouting trips within the present city of Dallas.
1841	Nov.—John Neely Bryan, founder of Dallas, sets up camp on the east bank of the Trinity River, establishing the first permanent settlement.
1842	April—John Beeman and family arrive from nearby Bird's Fort to join Bryan, followed soon by other Bird's Fort colonists.
1842	Issac Webb, along with others from the Peters Colony Company, settle on Mustang (now Farmers) Branch.
1843	A treaty is signed between the Republic of Texas and Indian chiefs at Bird's Fort to make the area safe for settlers.
1844	J.P. Dumas, surveyor, moves to Dallas and lays out original town site. John Neely Bryan is appointed postmaster by Republic of Texas, his log cabin serving as first post office.
1845	Trading post established at Cedar Springs, three miles from Dallas; first school in county is opened at Farmers Branch; William H. Hord residence erected in Oak Cliff. Dallas votes 29-3 for Texas' annexation to the United States.
1846	Dallas County organized, with Dallas as temporary county seat; log courthouse erected; first church congregation organized by Orin Hatch, Methodist minister; first church structure, Webb's Chapel, built at Farmers Branch; first horsepower grist mill erected on west side of river.

Dallas Lists

1847	First hotel, the Dallas Tavern, built by Henry Harter.
1849	J. Wellington (Weck) Latimer, journalist, arrives in Dallas, bringing first piano and printing equipment; establishes the first newspaper, the *Cedar Snag*, later renamed the *Herald*. First cotton gin erected at Farmers Branch.
1850	Dallas made permanent county seat; second courthouse erected. First census reports 2,743 population in county; 430 in town.
1852	Crutchfield House, leading hotel for many years, opens. Cotton first moved from Dallas into commercial channels by J.W. Smith, pioneer merchant; Maxime Guillot builds first carriage-making facility.
1853	First legal hanging: Jane Elkins, a slave; Alexander Cockrell purchases John Neely Bryan's property in Dallas for $7,000.
1855	Alexander Cockrell constructs wooden toll bridge across Trinity; La Reunion colonists begin arriving from Europe.
1856	First stagecoach enters Dallas; city grants first town charter and elects Dr. Samuel B. Pryor first mayor.
1857	M. Monduel of La Reunion French colony establishes first brewery. Subscription library established.
1858	Prominent citizen Alexander Cockrell shot to death in altercation with city marshal; droughts and floods plague Dallas, Trinity bridge collapses.
1859	Sarah Horton Cockrell, widow of Alexander, opens St. Nicholas Hotel; first county fair held by Dallas County Agricultural and Mechanical Association.
1860	Devastating fire destroys most of Dallas business district.

1861	Four Dallas companies form to join the Confederates and march to Austin; Dallas votes 741 to 237 in favor of seceding from the Union.
1865	Civil War ends; John M. Crockett appointed mayor by reconstruction government.
1866	May—Trinity River reaches unprecedented height.
1868	First Dallas bank is organized by Gaston & Camp; steamboat, the *Sallie Haynes*, arrives in Dallas; black voters outnumber white voters in the first election held under Reconstruction; Ku Klux Klan appears.
1869	Systematic mass extermination of the great buffalo herds causes Dallas to boom as hide market.
1870	Population 3,000.
1871	First Dallas County Medical Society organized; Dallas County Bank receives its first state charter.
1872	First train (Houston & Texas Central) arrives in Dallas; Sarah Cockrell has new iron bridge constructed across the Trinity.
1873	Mule-drawn street cars begin operating; second railroad (Texas & Pacific) extended to Dallas; first telegraph service to eastern points established; Field Opera House opens with the Crisp Sisters.
1874	City is illuminated with artificial gas lights for first time.
1876	Dallas County Medical and Surgical Association is formed to succeed Dallas County Medical Society; Dallas Musical Society organized.
1878	Sam Bass and gang are robbing trains all around the Dallas area.
1879	Buckner Orphans Home is founded.

Dallas Lists

1883   Town's first strike, a railway; Dallas Amateur Baseball Association formed; first cotton gin is built; new site selected for post office.

1884   First highway is built—Cedar Springs Road; the Idlewild Club, exclusive social club, is organized; first street paving is laid with bois d'arc.

1885   Oct.—*Dallas Morning News* begins publication.

1886   First State Fair is held; T.L. Marsalis purchases land west of Trinity and begins development of Hord's Ridge (Oak Cliff) the following year.

1887   First history of Dallas County written by John Henry Brown; Dallas joins newly organized Texas Baseball League.

1888   Six-story North Texas Building, touted as the first "skyscraper" in the city, erected; first cotton mill established; *Dallas Times Herald* established by consolidation of *Evening Times* and *Dallas (Evening) Herald*.

1889   First electric street cars begin operation; East Dallas is annexed to Dallas.

1890   Old Red Courthouse erected; Dallas' population 38,067, the largest city in Texas.

1891   Oak Cliff incorporated as a town; first major football game is played between Fort Worth and Dallas.

1893   North Texas National Bank, Central National Bank, and Bankers & Merchants Bank fail in a panic; the steamboat *H.A. Harvey, Jr.*, is launched by the Trinity River Navigation Company.

1894   State National and Ninth National Banks fall in panic; Democratic State Convention meets in Dallas, backs "Cleveland and sound money;" survey of Trinity River by army engineers.

Section X

1895 World's heavyweight fight in Dallas between James J. Corbett and Bob Fitzsimmons is blocked by ban enacted by state legislature.

1896 City votes Republican in presidential race between William McKinley and William Jennings Bryan; cornerstone of Confederate monument is laid in City Park during Confederate State Reunion.

1897 First motion picture shown in Dallas; Buckner Orphans Home burns, killing 20 children; St. Paul's Sanatorium, first modern hospital in Dallas, opens.

1898 Company of Confederate and Union Civil War veterans is formed for service in Spanish-American War; Linz Bros. erects first fireproof building at Main and Martin streets; the Terpsichorean Club, sponsor of annual society balls, is organized.

1899 Feb.—Coldest weather in recorded history of Dallas, 10 degrees below zero; charter granted by the American Federation of Labor to Trades Assembly of Dallas.

1900 The College of Medicine, University of Dallas, is established; Dallas Golf Club (later Dallas Country Club) is organized; funds for public library contributed by Andrew Carnegie; population 42,638.

1901 First cement plant is built (on site of La Reunion colony); Dallas Public Library opens; first art exhibit in library.

1902 April—Confederate veterans' reunion brings 3,000 veterans and 100,000 visitors to city; Dallas assumes world leadership in output of saddles; first art school established by Vivian Aunspaugh; interurban electric lines begin operation.

1904	Oak Cliff residents vote to merge with Dallas; wireless messages are transmitted between Fort Worth and Dallas for the first time.
1905	Majestic Theater is built; Pres. Theodore Roosevelt visits Dallas; Munger Place, restricted residential suburb, opens.
1906	Municipal government adopted by city.
1907	Highland Park subdivision opens; Dallas Cotton Exchange granted charter; first auto license issued to J.M. Oram.; fourteen-story Praetorian building erected; Neiman Marcus opens.
1908	*Aerial Queen*, first airship to fly over Dallas, is brought by carnival; spring flooding of Trinity River causes extensive damage.
1908	Huge Elks' Arch constructed at Main and Akard for Elks' Convention in July; President William Howard Taft visits State Fair.
1910	Lynching of Allen Brooks at Elks' Arch; first flight of heavier-than-air machine in Dallas by Otto Brodie in Curtiss biplane; acute water shortage leads to impounding White Rock Creek water; George E. Kessler employed to devise Trinity River plan; population 92,104.
1911	Dallas selected as site for Southern Methodist University; Elm Street becomes "great white way" by installation of 110 street lamps.
1912	"Dallas Blues" is the first published blues tune, credited to Hart A. Ward. Adolphus Hotel erected; Houston Street viaduct opened, longest concrete bridge in the world; severe outbreak of meningitis results in fumigating of streetcars, ban on public funerals, and quarantines.
1913	County Criminal Courts Building erected.
1914	Dallas awarded Federal Reserve Bank for eleventh district.

Section X

1915	City Welfare Department established; SMU opens.
1916	Union passenger station is erected.
1917	Jan.—first airplane flight made from Love Field; April—patriotic parade held following America's entry into World War I; Sept.—Dallas votes for prohibition; Oct.—saloons close; Nov.—Love Field established as army air training base; 5,000 Dallas men in army.
1918	Camp Dick established at Fair Park; Influenza epidemic taxes hospitals; Nov.—Dallas celebrates armistice ending war.
1919	March—first troops return from overseas to a downtown parade; greatest strike in city's history when building trades throughout North Texas go out with linemen of Dallas Power & Light Co.; voters ratify 18th and 19th federal constitutional amendments.
1920	George E. Kessler revises plan to improve river district; Dallas Little Theater organized; population 158,976.
1922	Magnolia Petroleum Company erects 29-story building; new Ku Klux Klan appears; "bank run" on Security National Bank in Dallas; WRR, first municipal radio broadcasting station established.
1922	Ku Klux Klan candidates carry election in Dallas County.
1923	Railroad tracks removed from Pacific Ave.; Texas Scottish Rite Hospital for crippled children opens; Hiram Wesley, Dallas dentist and imperial wizard of the KKK, greeted by 75,000 citizens at State Fair "Klan Day."
1924	Dallas Little Theater wins Belasco Cup with *Judge Lynch* production; work begins on Lake Dallas reservoir.

Dallas Lists

1925 New Cotton Exchange building built; Half-Century Club formed by fifty-year residents.

1926 May—worst hail storm in Dallas history occurs; Herbert L. Kindred flies first mail plane to Chicago for National Air Transport.

1927 Captain William Erwin of Dallas is lost at sea in attempt to pilot *Spirit of Dallas* airplane from San Francisco to Honolulu; Love Field purchased by city as municipal airport; Santa Fe Building erected.

1928 Groundbreaking for Trinity River levee and reclamation project; first passenger air service between Dallas, San Antonio, and Houston begun by Texas Air Transport; Dallas votes for Herbert Hoover in presidential election.

1929 Dallas Community Trust formed.

1930 "Dad" Joiner discovers largest oil field known 100 miles east of Dallas; Cotton Bowl Stadium erected; Captains Dieudonne Coste and Maurice Bellonte fly from Paris to Dallas for $25,000 prize offered by Colonel William E. Easterwood; population 260,397.

1931 Serious unemployment problems; emergency committee asks $100,000 for relief.

1932 Criminals Clyde Barrow and Bonnie Parker begin their two-year crime spree; city and county relief work programs established.

1933 State Trust and Savings Bank fails to reopen after bank holiday; city votes for repeal of prohibition.

1934 Dallas wins bid for Texas Exposition; outlaws Clyde Barrow and Bonnie Parker slain by Dallas County lawmen and Texas Rangers.

1935 Eighteen striking women garment workers sent to jail after violent outbreak.

Section X

1936   Triple underpass completed, linking Main, Commerce, and Elm streets with Oak Cliff; Museum of Fine Arts at Fair Park opens; Texas Centennial Exposition held at Fair Park; President Franklin D. Roosevelt visits Dallas, along with some 10 million visitors.

1937   Outbreaks of violence after labor strike by millinery workers and Ford assembly plant workers; Governor Allred sends Texas Rangers to Dallas; the Citizens Council, a group of business leaders, is formed.

1938   State Fair of Texas resumes after three-year suspension.

1939   Dallas schoolgirls welcomed home after rescue from *SS Athenia* following torpedo attack in the North Atlantic at the beginning of the Second World War.

1940   North American Aviation opens airplane manufacture plant in Grand Prairie; Adolphus Hotel becomes the world's first hotel to be fully air-conditioned; population est. 380,927.

1943   The Mercantile Bank Building, 31 stories, replaces Magnolia as the city's tallest structure.

1947   Margo Jones founds Theatre '47 repertory group in Dallas.

1953   Robert L. Thornton is elected mayor for first of four terms.

1955   NAACP files suit demanding full integration of public schools; new Dallas library opens.

1957   Deadly tornado strikes Dallas, killing ten and leaving 500 homeless; Dallas-Fort Worth Turnpike opens; Dallas Opera Company opens.

1958   Engineer Jack Kilby, working with Texas Instruments, solves the "tyranny of numbers" that will usher in the computer age.

1960	Two professional football teams come to Dallas, the Dallas Cowboys and the Dallas Texans.
1962	Ross Perot launches EDS.
1963	President John F. Kennedy is assassinated in downtown Dallas, and Texas Governor John Connally is wounded; Dallas Texans move to Kansas City.
1965	Huge oil discovery in Louisiana increases Hunt family fortune.
1967	Texas Instruments invents first electronic handheld calculator using integrated circuits; Jack Ruby, killer of assassin Lee Harvey Oswald, dies of cancer.
1968	Texas Instruments ceases giving free doughnuts to its employees.
1969	Ross Perot makes national news when he attempts to deliver food and supplies to POWs in North Vietnam.
1970	Ford Motor Company closes assembly plant in Dallas.
1972	Texas Rangers baseball team comes to town; Dallas Cowboys defeat Miami and win Super Bowl VI.
1973	Bunker and Herbert begin buying silver; D/FW Regional Airport opens.
1974	H. L. Hunt dies; Ray Hunt launches *D, the Magazine of Dallas*.
1976	Citizens Charter Association, which had long governed Dallas behind closed doors, disbands.
1978	Opening of Reunion Complex by Dallas developer Ray Hunt; debut of television series "Dallas"; Dallas Cowboys win Super Bowl XII against Denver.

Section X

1979	Ross Perot orders rescue of two EDS executives being held in Iran.
1980	A record 80 million Americans tune in to see who shot J.R. Ewing, played by Larry Hagman, on "Dallas," the television series; silver market collapses; Bunker and Herbert Hunt are subpoenaed to testify before Congress; Dallas Mavericks basketball team is formed; population 904,078.
1981	The renovated Adolphus Hotel opens with a four-day celebration; Dallas establishes a municipal Office of Protocol.
1982	Downtown Jonsson Public Library opens; Braniff International Airlines files bankruptcy.
1983	DART (Dallas Area Rapid Transit) endorsed by Dallas voters.
1987	Barney the Dinosaur is hatched in Allen, Texas.
1991	*Dallas Times Herald* ceases publication.
1992	Dallas' favorite billionaire, H. Ross Perot, runs for president; Dr. Joel Gregory of the First Baptist Church resigns; Perot drops out of presidential race; Perot announces that he is back in presidential race.
1993	Dallas Cowboys win Super Bowl XXVII, defeating Bills; all-time strikeout pitcher Nolan Ryan retires; H. Ross Perot starts "United We Stand America," a watchdog political group; Hamon Building of the Dallas Museum of Arts opens; trial of Walker Railey, former Methodist minister accused of strangling his wife in 1987; Dallas Stars ice hockey team arrives from Minnesota.
1994	Dallas Cowboys win Super Bowl second year in a row; Cowboys Head Coach Jimmy Johnson resigns; new Ballpark in Arlington opens.

SECTION XI
Dallas Secrets

1. Where the Rich and Famous Live

Dallas' wealthiest citizens value their privacy, so *Dallas Uncovered* wouldn't think of printing their addresses. However, the following streets and neighborhoods are the havens of such notable Dallas citizens as Ross Perot, Harold Simmons, William Howell, Albert Alberthal, other CEOs of major corporations, and the filthy rich in general. Do be sure to cruise around and check them out.

Preston Hollow Road
Meadowood Lane
Highland Park—the mansions around Exall Lake were built in the 1920s and '30s, when the first oil boom occurred.
Inwood Road
Strait Lane
Willow Bend Country—located ten miles north of Dallas in Plano, this neighborhood is worth the drive just to gawk. These Texas-size homes feature every amenity known to man and would rival any castle—plus, there are often open homes and garage sales on weekends. Willow Bend Properties is a development of the Perot Group. (Take the Dallas North Tollway to Plano; exit

Park Boulevard east [right] and turn left on Willow Bend.)

Lawther Drive—(along White Rock Lake) Mount Vernon, the massive estate of Dallas billionaire H.L. Hunt is on this street.

2. Best-Kept Secret Bargain Stores

Along with the usual outlets, Dallas has some excellent resale shops. Dallas men and women dress well, and when time comes to part with that designer outfit—whether the oil well has run dry, the RTC has come calling, or it's been worn at least once—your typical Dallasite, being the resourceful person that he or she is, turns to resale. Also included are some specialty shops that are not resale, but are great finds. So check them out!

Blue-collar & minority neighborhoods—often have the same clothes as upscale neighborhoods, but at cheaper prices. Plus, you can find one-of-a-kind ethnic attire.

Bock Jewelry Company—fine jewelry at discounted prices. 2300 N. Stemmons Freeway; 214-630-4246

Burlington Coat Factory—linens, coats and designer clothes 121 W. Parker Road, Plano; 214-578-2445

Clotheshorse Anonymous (resale)—written up in *Newsweek*; previously worn couture clothing. 1413 Preston Forest Square; 214-233-6082

Clothes Circuit (resale)—popular recycling center for affluent Highland Park and Preston Hollow residents. 6155 Storey Lane; 214-696-8634

Deno's Shoe Repair—Located in Highland Park Village, this family-run business specializes in custom made exotic-skin belts, purses, shoes, and accessories. For half of what you normally pay, you can select from a variety

of skins, including alligator, camel, etc., and your choice of color, grain, and buckle (but please don't tell this hard-working family who let the cat out of the bag). Highland Park Village; 214-521-1070
Designer Shoe Warehouse 13548 Preston Rd.; 214-233-9931 900 W. Parker Rd.; 214-424-0061
Designer Shops of Southwest Outlet Center (a.k.a. Hillsboro Center)—over 57 famous names, such as Eddie Bauer, Liz Claiborne, Jones New York, Adolfo II, Guess?, Geoffrey Beene, Bass Shoe, Corning/Revere, and many more. 104 Interstate Highway 35, Hillsboro, TX 76645; Call 1-800-969-3767 for directions or info.
Esprit Outlet 2425 McKinney Ave. 214-871-8989
Hillsboro Mall—see Designer Shops of Southwest.
It's A Wrap—whether it's a five-dollar gift or a five-thousand-dollar gift, these cheerful ladies will wrap your special present so well that you hate to open it! 25 Highland Park Village; 214-520-9727
Knox Street Antique Mall—over 100 of Dallas' finest antique dealers. 3313 Knox Street; 214-521-8888
Love Field Antique Mall—antiques, collectibles, classic cars, restaurant. 6500 Cedar Springs at Love Field; 214-357-6500
Neiman Marcus Last Call Sample Shop 2600 Stemmons; 214-630-9820
Syms—best for men. 4770 S. Mockingbird Ln. 214-902-9600
Terry Costa—The place to go for designer clothes—from sequined ballgowns to designer jeans. 1331 Inwood Road (Inwood Trade Center) 214-634-8089
Tuesday Morning—best one at 14621 Inwood Rd. 214-991-1905
Vantage—shoes. 222 Vantage St.; 214-631-1812 (off Wycliff)
Victor Costa Outlet—specialty gowns, dresses, and suits. 100-A Highland Park Village; 214-522-2208 3211 Irving Blvd. 214-634-8089

Section XI

3.
Where the Snobbiest Sales Clerks Work

There are few things that will sour a shopping trip like encountering a clerk who sizes you up and decides that his or her store isn't for you—or drops you like a hot branding iron when his or her favorite Highland Park customer appears in the establishment.

Short of grabbing the guilty "shop girl" by the throat and asking, "Hey, pal, if you're so high and mighty, then how come you have to *work* for a living like the rest of us?" *Dallas Uncovered* decided to go undercover and do a little spying. Here are the results.

Ann Taylor (all stores)—Count on being sized up the minute you cross this towering threshold. You're either an "Ann Taylor Type" or not—and the shrewd salespeople know your category right away. Our spy reported that she loved Ann Taylor, but because she's a size 10, not a size 2, she felt, well, unwanted. Ann Taylor, there are lots of A.T. wannabes out there!

Crate & Barrel—Galleria—Atrocious service every time, but it's still yuppie houseware heaven in there.

Harold's in Highland Park Village and Galleria—This intimidating institution caters to the rich and famous and anybody else willing to spend a couple months' salary on a belt. Unfortunately, our would-be patron only wanted a $65 belt, so she was ignored by the employees counting receipts and arranging merchandise. They seemed to be saying, our meek agent reports, *Why would someone such as yourself bother even setting foot inside our sacred establishment?* You tell us, ladies.

Macy's—Yes, they have great merchandise *and* the best return policies around—but affable? Afraid they haven't quite got the hang of it (and they better, because Nordstrom's is coming to town).

Neiman Marcus (see also friendliest)—Several spies reported being rebuffed at Dallas' most famous store if they aren't well dressed. Dress to the hilt, look like you're rich, and wear lots of jewelry to get the "star" treatment. Considering that rumor has it the NM fortune was made from wives of nouveau-riche Texas oilmen who tried on couture fashions wearing their humble flour-sack undies, we can't help but wonder what Mr. Marcus would have to say about this.

Paul Harris in Valley View Mall—The sales clerks "attacked" our agent when she walked in, determined that she was only browsing, and then ignored her.

Peepers in Highland Park Village—A store featuring sunglasses that cost more than your average used car. "All our glasses here cost much more than the brand you're looking for," sniffed the long-suffering clerk.

Williams-Sonoma—Galleria—Tsk, tsk, tsk. Just because we weren't from Highland Park and were only looking for placemats, not a set of Calphalon or a $19 garlic press, you didn't have to ignore us completely. Customers are people, too!

Never mind, we went to Wal-Mart, where we were warmly greeted and found 99-cent placemats that were perfect! Happy ending, wouldn't you say?

In the Middle:

Dillard's—the only thing we can say is they're inconsistent. We've had friendly, unfriendly, and (most of all) the "I can never find a clerk," complaint. You could do a *lot* better, Dillard's.

Section XI

4.
Where the Friendliest Sales Clerks Work

Dallas Uncovered decided it would not be very nice to point out only the snobby stores, so we are including a few establishments whose welcoming manner and friendly ways put customers at ease, even if they are just old Mom and Pop on their 50th-anniversary trip and want to tell their friends back in Idaho they shopped at Neiman Marcus.

Banana Republic—Galleria, Highland Park Village—here's a bonus: They are not only nice, they're willing to keep your kids!

Bath & Body Works at Prestonwood—We attribute their cheer to less stress in the workplace, or maybe they are breathing all those aroma therapy products. Anyway, these employees make shopping a pleasant experience.

Culwell & Son (all locations)—Oh-so-congenial, it will brighten your day to go in the establishment. Son may even tolerate it as well, since they specialize in exchanging "street-boy wear" for appropriate young gentleman's wear—you know, the kind that's absolutely a must at weddings, funerals, and special occasions. They even do all the tailoring!

First Issue Galleria—These salespeople must love their work and the products they sell. Since we too were enthralled with their merchandise, it turned out to be a mutual admiration. Our secret agent was even given a free tote bag to assuage her hurt feelings when the alarm device was mistakenly left on (an all too-frequent occurrence everywhere).

GAP—Enthusiastic and friendly almost without fail, no matter how many times they have to refold those tops.

Hermes in Highland Park Village—It takes a great deal of courage to walk into this highbrow establishment and say, "Howdy," but that's exactly what our brave spy did, and even though she was overcome by the outrageous prices and found the goods to be less than appealing to her downhome taste, she reports that the natives actually *were* friendly to her and encouraged browsing among the exorbitant selections.

Neiman Marcus—Believe it or not, it was popular in both categories! Guess it depends on who you happen to encounter at the store. Although some "associates" bordered on being too patronizing (she wanted a *shoe*, not a friend for life), others were reported to be downright folksy.

One spy even said a helpful employee spent two hours with her to find and arrange to alter a cocktail dress for a special occasion. Then the customer went down the mall and found *another* dress at another store that she liked much better! The NM clerk cheerfully credited the customer's card, explaining that her main goal was customer satisfaction. Now, that's service.

Polo/Ralph Lauren in Highland Park Village—Okay, the prices are exorbitant, but it won't cost you to breathe the air. Our spy was well received and even offered liquid refreshment as she checked out the oh-so-tasteful goods. Alas, another spy's account was not so complimentary. But that Ralph Lauren fella does have class, don't he?

Victoria's Secret—Galleria, Highland Park Village, Prestonwood—so warm and friendly, he felt right at home! Reported to be especially cordial to male customers, even though they always have that sheepish look. Come on, guys, don't be so embarrassed! It's okay, though, you still have the catalog at home.

5.
You Haven't Lived Until You've…

..........been pelted by hail in a Dallas hailstorm.

..........cut into a sizzling steak at Del Frisco's.

..........watched the ice skaters in the Galleria during the Christmas season.

..........eaten a Dickey's barbecue sandwich on a hot summer day, while guzzling an ice-cold bottled Dr. Pepper.

..........taken a carriage ride through Highland Park at Christmas to see the lights.

..........lunched at The Mansion on Turtle Creek while sitting outdoors.

..........walked through the trees at White Rock Lake.

..........experienced jazz and Dallas nightlife at Beau Nash.

..........watched a norther blow in over the plains.

..........danced at the White Swan Restaurant.

..........wandered through the Midway and exhibitions at the State Fair, watching people and eating turkey legs and sausage-on-a-stick.

..........experienced Afternoon Tea at the Adolphus Hotel.

..........been to Dick's Last Resort on Sunday morning for the "Gospel Brunch," featuring a lively band and singers whose renditions of classic hymns stir up the appreciative audience; also serving an all-you-can-eat brunch; located in the West End.

..........flown into Dallas at night and gotten chills when you spotted the famous skyline, whether it's your first time or your five-hundredth time, ...and know you're home.

♦ ♦ ♦ ♦ ♦

Sources

Dooley, Kirk. *The Book of Texas Bests*. Dallas: Taylor Publishing Company, 1988.
Dooley, Kirk. *Hidden Dallas*. Dallas: Taylor Publishing Company, 1988.
Frost, H. Gordon and John H. Jenkins. *"I'm Frank Hamer": The Life of a Texas Peace Officer*. Austin and New York: The Pemberton Press, 1968.
Galloway, Diane. *The Park Cities: A Photo History*. Mercury Printing & Lithographing Co., Inc., 1989.
Garrett, Judith M. and Erika Sanchez. *Dallas*. 2nd ed. Houston: Gulf Publishing Co., 1992.
Greene, A.C. *Dallas U.S.A.* Austin: Texas Monthly Press, Inc., 1984.
Hurt, Harry. *Texas Rich*. New York: W.W. Norton & Company, Inc., 1981.
Levin, Doron P. *Irreconcilable Differences*. Boston: Little, Brown and Co., 1989.
Margot, Louis, III. *The Dallas Express: A Negro Newspaper: Its History, 1892-1972 & Its Point of View*. diss., East Texas S. University, Dec., 1971.
Mason, Todd. *Perot: An Unauthorized Biography*. Homewood, Illinois: Dow Jones-Irwin, 1990.
McKnight, Mamie L., ed. *First African American Families of Dallas: Creative Survival*. Black Dallas Remembered Steering Committee, Publisher, 1987.
McKnight, Mamie L., ed. *African American Families and Settlements of Dallas: On the Inside Looking Out*. Black Dallas Remembered, Inc., Publisher, 1990.
Payne, Darwin. *Dallas: An Illustrated History*. Woodland Hills, California: Windsor Publications, Inc., 1982.
Perot, Ross. *United We Stand: How We Can Take Back Our Country*. New York: Hyperion, 1992.

Sources

Prince, Robert. *A History of Dallas From a Different Perspective*. Nortex Press, Sunbelt Media, Inc., 1993.
Rumbley, Rose-Mary. *The Unauthorized History of Dallas, Texas*. Austin: Eakin Press, 1991.
Ryan, Nolan and Jerry Jenkins. *Miracle Man: Nolan Ryan, The Autobiography*. Dallas: Word Publishing, 1992.
Shirley, Glenn. *Belle Starr and Her Times*. Norman: University of Oklahoma Press, 1982.
Steele Phillip W. *Starr Tracks: Belle and Pearl Starr*. Gretna, Louisiana: Pelican Publishing Co., Inc., 1989.
Treherne, John. *The Strange History of Bonnie and Clyde*. New York: Stein and Day, Incorporated, Briarcliff Manor, 1985.
Wedgwood, Barbara. *The Demon Inside*. New York, New York: Pocket Books, Simon & Schuster Inc., 1993.
Works Projects Administration. *The WPA Dallas Guide and History*. Ed. Maxine Holmes and Gerald D. Saxon. Dallas: University of North Texas Press, 1992.

Index

A

A.H. Belo Corporation, 160, 237
Abolition, 57
Acroterium, 84
Adams, James Alonzo, 159
Adams, Nathan, 237
Addison, 151
Adolphus Hotel, 46, 77-81, 124, 255, 260, 228, 258, 268
Adubato, Richie, 205-206
African-American art, 67, 69-70
Afternoon Tea, 80, 143, 268
Age of Steam Railroad Museum, 75, 235
Aikman, Troy, 184-187, 189
Akard, W.C.C., 237
Allen, Texas, 260
Allison, Wick, 175
American Football League, 131
Amon Carter Museum, 68
Anderson Bonner Park, 145
Ann Taylor, 264
Antique Market, 245
Arizona Slim, 121-122
Arlington Stadium, 195-197, 201-203
Armstrong, John S., 12
Armstrong, Mrs. John S., 101
Art Museums, 65-70
Arts and Letters Live, 67-68
Arts District Theater, 74
Ash, Mary Kay, 143-144
Atrium Cafe, 68
Attitude, Dallas, 1-2
Aviation, 99-100

B

Baby Bop, 146
Baker Hotel, 78, 124
Ballpark in Arlington, 197, 203, 260
Banana Republic, 266
Barney the Dinosaur, 145-149, 260
Barrow, Blanche, 29-32
Barrow, Buck, 29-32
Barrow, Clyde, 25-34, 217-218, 257
Barrow gang, 29-34
Barry, Bryan T., 237
Bass, Sam, 237, 252
Bath & Body Works, 266
Baylor Medical Center, 60, 215, 243
Beau Nash, 142, 268
Beeman, James, 237
Beeman, John, 63, 237, 250
Beeman, Margaret, 119
Bell Tower, Old Red Courthouse, 169-171
Belo, Alfred Horatio, 237
Belo Corporation, 160, 237
Bennett, William H., 237
Biblical Arts Center, 245-246
Big Tex, 234
Billingsley, John, 53-54, 118-119, 218
Bill Masterson Award, 207
Bird's Fort, 118, 250
Black Dallas Remembered, Inc., 82, 165
Black Elephant Theater, 70
Black magic, 7, 56
Blaylock, Dr. Louis, 237
Blues singers, 8, 10-11, 165, 227, 241, 255
Bock Jewelry Company, 262
Bone, The, 9
Bonner, Anderson, 145
Bopp, Jacob, 237
Bovis, Ann, 62
Bovis, Lou, 62
Braniff International Airlines, 172-173, 260
Brewer, J. Mason, 237-238
Bridges, 95

271

Index

Bridwell Library, 38, 40
Bright, H.R. "Bum," 182
British, 227-229
Brooks, Allen, 169-171, 255
Brown, John Henry, 253
Brown, Thomas, 247, 248
Bryan, John Neely
  Background, 116-120, 215
  Dallas name, 152-153
  Founding of Dallas, 2, 41, 53, 116-120, 233, 250-251
  Log cabin, 86, 219
  Trinity River navigation, 92-93
Bryan, Margaret Beeman, 117, 119
Buckner Orphans Home, 86, 252, 254
Buckner, Quinn, 206
Buffalo
  art, 68
  herds, 218, 252
  hides, 63, 218, 252
Bunker, Lyda, 122
Burleson, Hattie C., 168
Burlington Coat Factory, 262
Burnett Field, 194
Busch, Adolphus, 77, 81
Bush, George W., 195
Bush, George, 115
Butcher Pen Road, 60

C

C.M.E., 57
Cabell, Earle, 238
Cabell, W.L., 238
California Crossing, 104
Callaway, Mrs. W.A., 238
Calvin Klein, 6, 64
Canseco, Jose, 196
Cantagrel, Francois Jean, 238
Carpenter, Ben, 219
Carter, Amon, 68, 222-224
Carter, Donald, 203-204
Caruth, Walter, 238
Caruth, William, 101, 238
Catholic Church, 56
Cattle Baron's Ball, 212
Cedar Snag, 248, 251
Cedar Springs, 63, 152, 250
Cedar Springs Road, 253

Celebrity Restaurant & Bakery, 5, 64
Cement City, 26
Central Expressway, 6, 8, 45, 50-51, 64, 81-83, 226
Century Room, 78, 80
Chambers, Joseph R., 148
Chaparrals, 203
Cheek, James, 4
Cheerleaders, Dallas Cowboys, 180, 190-193
Chiapparone, Paul, 111-112
Chiles, H.E. "Eddie," 195
Chili, 211, 228
Christian Church, 54
Christianity, 52-59, 245-246, 250
Christian preachers, 52-59, 168, 247, 250
Churches, 52-59, 247, 250
Church of Christ, 54
Civil War, 6, 57, 70, 150, 162, 239, 252, 254
Clinton, Bill, 115, 147
Clock Tower on Courthouse, 169-171
Clothes Circuit, 262
Clotheshorse Anonymous, 262
Club Dada, 9
Cochran, William, 53, 238, 247
Cockrell, Alexander, 149-151, 251
Cockrell, Sarah, 149-151, 251-252
Coffee's Trading Station, 41-42
Colored Methodist Episcopal Church, 57
Communism, 68-69, 126, 128
Connally, Governor John, 79, 90, 259,
Connally, Nellie, 79, 90
Considerant, Victor, 155-158
Cook, David, 4, 12
Corbett, Bradford, 195
Cotton Bowl, 78, 178, 210
  Parade, 79
  Stadium, 46, 257
Cotton Club, 7-8
Courthouse Bell, 169-171
Clock Tower, 169-171
  Dallas County, 83-85, 95, 150
  Old Red, 83-85, 105, 119, 253

Index

Cowan, Nell, 31
Cowboys, 215-216, 221
Cowboys Ring of Honor, 180-181, 184, 211
Craddock Theater, 71-72
Craft, Juanita Jewell, 238
Crate & Barrel, 264
Crescent Court, 12, 142-143
Crescent Complex, 65, 142-143
Criswell College, 58
Criswell, Dr. W.A., 58, 127-128
Crockett, John M., 238, 252
Crutchfield House, 238, 251
Crutchfield, Thomas F., 238
Culture, 65-76, 212
Culwell & Son, 266

D

D, the Magazine of Dallas, 136, 174-175, 259
D/FW Airport, 219, 223, 259
Da Boyz, 187-189
Daisy Bradford No. 3, 124, 240
Dallas Alley, 46, 47
Dallas Blues Society, 8
Dallas
  Ballet, 71, 74
  Convention Center, 104
  Convention and Visitors Bureau, 104
  County Historical Commission, 85
  County Jail, 24
  Courthouse, 81, 83-86, 93, 95, 105
  Cowboys, 191
  Cowboys Cheerleaders, 180, 190-193
  Cowboys (football), 177-189, 231, 259-260
  Culture, 65-75, 212
  Fire of 1860, 57, 160-163, 251
  Flood of 1908, 94-95
  Fort Worth feud, 68, 208-209, 221-224
  Hall, 101-102
  Historical Society, 158
  Market Center, 2, 235
  Museum of Art, 66-70, 98, 131, 233, 245, 260
  North Tollway, 64, 224, 261
  Opera, 71-72, 258
  Public Library, 254
  Religion, 52-59, 229-230
  Shopping, 63-65, 262-267
  Skyline, 14-17
  Symphony, 72, 74, 98, 212
  Theater, 70-75, 256
Dallas Black Dance Theatre, 74
Dallas Blackhawks, 209
Dallas Bridge Company, 150
Dallas Daily Times, 159
Dallas Diamonds, 203, 241
Dallas Eagles, 194
Dallas Express, 167-169
Dallas/Fort Worth Airport, 2, 222-223
Dallas Freeze, 209
Dallas Gazette, 7
Dallas, George Mifflin, 152-153
Dallasmania, 18-20
Dallas Mavericks, 203-207, 260
Dallas Morning News, 39, 52, 128, 159-160, 237-238, 248, 253
Dallas Morning News Arts Hotline, 75
Dallas Rebels, 194
Dallas Stars, 207-209
Dallas Texans, 131, 177, 208, 259
Dallas Theatre, 72, 74
Dallas Times Herald, 159-160, 239, 248, 253, 260
"Dallas" TV show, 17-20, 87-88, 139, 228, 259-260
Dancers Unlimited, 74
Davis, Terry, 206
Dayton, John, 174
Dealey, George Bannerman, 90
Dealey Plaza, 89-92, 94-95, 117
Deep Ellum, 6-11, 162, 165, 227, 241, 268
Del Frisco's, 268
Deno's Shoe Repair, 262
DeShazer, Dennis, 146
Designer Shoe Warehouse, 263
Designer Shops of Southwest Outlet Center, 263

Index

D/FW Airport, 2, 222-223
Dick's Last Resort, 268
Dickey's Barbecue, 50-52, 286
Dickey III, T.D., 50
Dickey, Jr., T.D., 50-52
Dickey, Ollie, 51
Dickey, Roland, 50-51
Dickey, Sr., Travis D., 50
Dillard's, 265
Distinguished Writers, 67-68
DMA, 66-70, 98, 233, 245, 260
Dollhouse Museum of the Southwest, 246-247
Dorsett, Tony, 183
Doughnuts, 44
Dr. Pepper, 268
Dumas, J.P., 119, 238, 250
Durgan, Elizabeth, B. 238

E

Eagle Ford, 222
EDS, 42, 98, 109-112, 229, 259-260
Electronic Data Systems Corporation, 42, 98, 109-112, 229, 259-260
Elks' Arch, 170-172, 255
Elks' Club, 172
Elm Street, 6-11, 47, 71, 89, 91, 162, 249, 258
Emancipation, 57
Emerson, Cecil, 40
England, 142
Englishmen, 227-229
Ervay, Henry S., 238
Esprit Outlet, 263
Eugene McDermott Concert Hall, 98
Ewing, J.R., 17-20, 121, 139, 260
Exall, Henry, 239
Exall Lake, 261
Exall, Mrs. Henry, 239
Exxon Corporation, 2, 97

F

Facts Forum, 126-127
Fair Park, 69, 72, 74-75, 178, 210, 234-235, 256, 258
Farmer's Market, 246

Farmers Branch, 53, 247, 250, 251
Field Opera House, 71, 248, 252
Field, Thomas W., 71, 239, 248
Fire of 1860, 57, 160-163, 251
First Baptist Church, 52, 58, 127
First Baptist Hard Rock Cafe, 103
First Issue, 266
First United Methodist Church, 34-41
Fishtrap Cemetery, 34, 158, 217
Flood of 1908, 94-95
Follett, Ken, 112
Folsom, Bob, 203
Fondren Library, 38, 40
Fort Worth, 3, 68, 98, 102, 105, 194, 253, 255
  Art museums, 68
  Ballet, 174
Fort Worth-Dallas feud, 68, 208-209, 221-224
Fort Worth Spurs, 195
Fortune, Jan Isbelle, 239
Fourier, Charles, 155
Fourierism, 16, 155
Franco, Julio, 195
Freedman's Cemetery, 81-83
Freedman's Towns, 6, 45, 57, 81, 162-166, 167
French colonists, 155-158
French Room, 80
Friends of Old Red, 85
Frogtown, 45
Frontiers of Flight Museum, 99-100, 173

G

Gainey, Bob, 208
Galleria, 63, 65, 213, 264, 266-267
Galleria Wonderland Express, 63
Gambling, 7, 52, 55
Gap, 6, 64, 266
Garrett, Alexander Charles, 239
Gaston, William Henry, 239
Gaylord, Bill, 111-112
General Motors, 108, 112-113
Geophysical Service, 43
Glen, Robert, 233
Golden Corridor, 42
Gonzalez, Juan, 196-197

Index

Gooch, Tom C., 239
Good, John J., 239
Gospel Brunch, 268
Gould, Jay, 239
Grasshoppers, 157, 218
Grassy knoll, 90
Greater Dallas/Fort Worth Airport, 2, 222-223
Green, Cecil, 43
Greene, A.C., 104
Green, Norman, 207
Greenville Avenue, 62, 217
Gregory, Dr. Joel, 52, 260
Grieve, Tom, 196
Griffith, Mrs. A.B., 240
Guillot, Maxime, 56, 240, 251
Gypsy Tea Room Cafe, 9

H

H.L. Hunt, Inc., 124
Hagman, Larry, 17-20, 260
Hamer, Frank, 32
Hamilton, Raymond, 27-28
Hamon Building, 66, 260
Hamon, Nancy (Mrs. Jake), 66
Hangings, 84
Hard Rock Cafe, 103
Harold's, 5, 64, 264
Harper, Alvin, 185-187
Harper, Derek, 206
Harston, Sheriff Dan, 24
Harwood, Alexander, 240
Haskell, Horatio Nelson, 240
Heard, Gar, 206
Hermes, 5, 266
Hester, A.V., 59
Highland Park, 3, 11-14, 42, 124, 132, 211, 217, 243, 255, 261, 268
Highland Park High School, 217
Highland Park Methodist Church, 102
Highland Park Village Shopping Center, 4-5, 12, 72, 211, 248, 262-267
Hill, Margaret Hunt, 140
Hillsboro Mall, 263
Hinton, Ted, 26, 32
History Merchant, 244

History of Aviation Collection, 99-100
HLH Products, 127, 129, 131, 134
Hoblitzelle, Karl, 71, 240
Hockaday, Ela, 240
Hockaday School, 3, 219
Holland, William, 240
Horchow Auditorium, 68
Hord's Ridge, 149, 242, 253
Hord, William H., 250
Horton, Sarah, 149
Hotel Adolphus, 77-81, 124, 260, 258, 268
Hot pan men, 165
Houston and Texas Central Railroad, 93, 120
Houston, Sam, 119
Howley, Chuck, 180
Hughes, Sarah T., 240
Hunt Oil, 124-125, 127, 131-133, 135, 139, 141
Hunt Energy Corporation, 133, 139, 141
Hunt, Caroline Rose, 122, 129, 134, 140-143, 228
Hunt family, 121-143, 259
 D magazine, 175
 "Hassie," 122, 125, 127
 Helen LaKelley, 126
 H.L., 121-141, 177, 259, 262
 Margaret, 122, 140
 Reunion Complex, 135-136
 Ruth June, 126
 Ruth Wright, 125-127, 132, 134
 Silver market, 135-140
 Swanee Grace, 126
Hunt, Lamar, 123, 129, 131-132, 134, 138, 141, 177
Hunt, Lyda Bunker, 121-127, 141
Hunt, Nelson Bunker, 123, 128, 131-141, 259-260
Hunt, Norma (Mrs. Lamar), 131, 134
Hunt, Ray, 16, 126-127, 132-133, 135-137, 139, 158, 175, 259
Hunt, William Herbert, 123, 128-141, 259-260
Hyatt Regency Hotel, 16, 104, 218
Hyer, Robert Stewart, 101-102

Index

I
IBM, 109-110
Ice Hockey, 207-209
Indian attacks, 119
Ingels, Prosper A., 78
Irvin, Michael, 185-187
It's A Wrap, 263

J
J.C. Penney, 42, 97
J. Erik Jonsson Public Library, 235, 260
J & J Blues Bar, 8
James, Jesse, 22
Jazz singers, 6, 8, 165
Jefferson, Blind Lemon, 8, 240
Jewish congregation, 56
Jewish settlers, 248
Johnson, Jimmy, 177, 184, 187-189, 260
Johnson, Sandy, 196
Johnston, Daryl, 186
Jonsson, Erik, 43, 223, 240
Joiner, C.M. "Dad," 124-125, 240, 257
Jones, Jerry, 177, 183, 184, 189
Jones, Margo, 72-74, 258
Jones, Preston, 240
Jones, Ron "Popeye," 206
Jones, Tommy Lee, 68, 218
Jones, W.D., 29-32
Jordan, Lee Roy, 184
July, Bill, 23

K
Kalita Humphreys Theater, 74
Karcher, J. Clarence "Doc," 43
Keating, C.A., 241
Keller, Henry, 151
Keller Springs Road, 151
Kennedy assassination, 18, 79, 128-129, 219, 240, 259
Kennedy, John F., 79, 88-92, 128-129, 219, 259
Kennedy, Kevin, 196
Kessler, George E., 94-96, 255-256
Kessler Plan, 94-96
Kilby, Jack, 42-45, 258

King, William Elisha, 167-169
Kinne, Norman, 39-40
Knight, G.A., 241
Knox Street Antique Mall, 263
Ku Klux Klan, 163-164, 168, 252, 256

L
Lady Primrose's, 142-143, 228
Lake Texoma, 42
Lambert, Jr., Joe, 13
Landry, Tom, 178-184
Lane, John, W., 241
La Reunion Colony, 16, 26, 136, 155-158, 238, 241, 247, 251-254
Las Colinas, 64-65, 214, 219, 233
Latimer, James Wellington, 241-248, 251
Latimer, Lucy Jordan, 241
Lawrence, Harding, 172
LBJ Freeway, 64, 107, 225-226
Leach, Sheryl, 146
Ledbetter, A.A., 170
Ledbetter, Huddie "Leadbelly," 8, 241
Lee, Frania Tye, 123-125, 137
Left Brain, Right Brain, 9
Lemmon, W.H., 241
Library, J. Erik Jonsson, 235, 260
Lieberman, Nancy, 203, 241
LIFELINE, 127, 129, 131
Lilly, Bob, 179-181
Limestone, 158
Lindbergh, Charles, 78, 217
Loco weed, 8
Lonesome Dove Baptist Church, 216
Long, Ben, 158, 241
LouAnn's, 62
Love Field Antique Mall, 263
Love Field, 34, 89-100, 173, 223, 240, 242, 256
Lovers Lane, 62
Lower Greenville, 62
Lynching, 84, 168-171, 255
Lyons Group, 148
Lyric Opera of Dallas, 71

Index

M

MacLeod, John, 205
Macy's, 264
Magnolia Oil, 15, 258
Magnolia Petroleum Company, 256, 14
Magnolia Petroleum Building, 20-21
Majestic Theater, 71, 240, 255
Mandalay Canal, 64
Mansfield, Jayne, 217
Mansion on Turtle Creek, 142, 268
Marcus, Herbert, 48
Marcus, Sr., Herbert, 47
Marcus, Stanley, 48-49
Marsalis, Thomas L., 241
Martin, J.B., 241
Martin, Kelvin, 185
Mary Kay Cosmetics, 143-144
Maryland, Russell, 184-185
Mashburn, Jamal, 206
Massoud, Charles, 36-37
Mavericks, Dallas, 203-207
McCarroll, Frank, 242
McCoy, John C., 242
McDermott, Eugene, 43, 98
McDermott, Mrs. Eugene, 97
McGonagill, Kelli, 193
McKinney Avenue, 103, 217, 244, 263
McKinney Trolley, 103, 233, 245
McMath, J.B., 21
Meadows Foundation, 60-61, 69
Meadows Museum of Art, 70, 103
Meadows School of the Arts, 69, 102
Mercantile Bank Building, 258
Meredith, Don, 178, 180
Meyerson, Morton, 96-98, 112, 116
Microchip, 43
Miller, Jr., Henry S., 5
Miller, William Brown, 242
Mobil Oil, 20
Mobil Pegasus, 20-21
Mockingbird Lane, 4, 62, 263
Modano, Mike, 207
Moore, Andrew M., 150
Morton H. Meyerson Symphony Center, 74, 96-98, 233
Motta, Dick, 204-206

Mount Vernon, 125-126, 129-130, 132, 262
Muggle smokers, 8
Mulder, Doug, 38, 40
Multivibrator, 43
Munger, Robert S., 242
Murchison, Jr., Clint, 178, 182-183, 231
Murphy, Michael Martin, 217
Mustangs of Las Colinas, 214, 233

N

NAFTA, 116
NationsBank Plaza, 14, 17
Neiman, A.L., 47
Neiman, Carrie Marcus, 47
Neiman Marcus, 47-50, 64, 227, 255, 265, 267
Neiman Marcus Last Call Sample Shop, 263
Newspaper, 159-160
Newton, Nate, 186
Nicolai, Bill, 37, 39, 41
Nicolai, Billie Jo, 35, 37, 39, 41
No Pass, No Play, 112
Northpark Mall, 64-65, 72
Novacek, Jay, 184-186
Nussbaumer, Dorothea Boll, 60
Nussbaumer, Jacob, 60, 158

O

Oak Cliff, 194, 239, 241-244, 250, 253, 255
Oak Cliff Presbyterian Church, 59
Oak Lawn District, 173
Oakley, Adeline, 35
Oil drilling, 122-125, 129
Oil exploration, 122-125, 129, 134
Old Red Courthouse, 83-86, 95, 105, 119, 253
    Clock Tower, 169-171
Onderdonk, Robert J., 242
On Wings of Eagles, 112
Opera, 71-72, 248, 258
Oram, J.M., 242, 255
Orlopp, M.A., 83
Oswald, Lee Harvey, 89, 91, 129, 259

Index

Overton, W.P., 242
Owens, J.H., 7
Ownby Stadium, 210

P

Palmeiro, Rafael, 196-179
Palmer, Dean, 197
Papillon, Lucy, 37-41
Park Cities, 4-5, 11-14, 175, 217
Parker, Bonnie, 25-34, 217, 257
Parker, Kathy, 146
Parker, Pat, 242
Patrizio's, 64
Patterson, J. M., 242
Paul Harris, 265
Peak, Jefferson, 242
Pearson, Drew, 179
Peepers, 265
Peers, Vera Jane, 217
Pegasus, 14-15, 20-21
Pei, I.M., 97
Performing Arts, 70-75
Perkins, Don, 178, 180
Perot, H. Ross, 107-116, 121, 259-261
   Dickey's Barbecue, 51-52,
   EDS, 109-112
   General Motors, 108, 112-113
   Headquarters, 107-108
   Hostage rescue, 111-112
   IBM, 109-110
   Meyerson, Mort, 96-98, 112, 116
   Morton H. Meyerson Symphony Center, 96-98
   NAFTA, 116
   Politics, 107-108, 112-116
   POWs, 111
   Presidential race, 51-52, 113-116
   United We Stand America, 116
Perot, Margot Birmingham, 109
Perotistas, 115
Perot Systems Corporation, 116
Peters Colony, 86, 118, 250
Pioneer Cemetery, 104, 239
Pioneer Plaza, 104-106
Plano, 42, 51, 261-262
Pleasant Mound Methodist Church, 59
Polo/Ralph Lauren, 6, 64, 267

Prather, Hugh, 4, 6, 12
Preston Road, 4, 30, 41-42, 64, 104, 226
Prestonwood Town Center, 64-65, 266
Primrose's, 65
Pryor, Charles, 160
Pryor, Dr. Samuel B., 251
Pumpkin Air, 142
Pyles, Stephan, 174

Q

Quantrill, William, 22
Queen Anne style houses, 60-61

R

Racial strife, 57-58, 161-163, 169-171
Railey, Margaret "Peggy," 34-41
Railey, Walker, 34-41, 260
Railroad, 6, 93-94, 120, 163, 222, 252
Ray, Ruth Eileen, 125-127
Reaugh, Frank, 242
Rebel Stadium, 194
Reed, Jim, 23
Religion, 52-59, 229-230
Renfro, Mel, 181
Republic National Bank, 240
Reunion Complex, 16, 96, 104, 135-136, 155, 158, 204, 235, 259
Reves, Emery, 66
Reves, Wendy, 66
Richardson, 42, 131, 148
Ring of Honor, 180-181, 184, 211
Rogers, Richard, 144
Root Square Gang, 26
Rose, Edward W. "Rusty," 195
Rosewood Hotel Group, 142
Ross, Andrew J., 243
Ross, William, 243
Routhier, Steve, 103
Routh, Jacob, 243
Routh Street, 57, 103, 173, 244-245
Routh Street Cafe, 173-174
Ruby, Jack, 129, 259
Ryan, Nolan, 196-203, 260
Ryan, Ruth, 199-200

Index

S

S & D Oyster Company, 244
Samuell-Grand Park Amphitheater, 74
Samuell, Dr. W.W., 243
Sands, Caroline Hunt, 129
Sands, Loyd, 141
Sanger, Alexander, 243, 249
Sanger Bros., 243, 248-249
Sanger, Philip, 243, 249
Savardan, Dr. Eugene, 157-158
Schoellkopf, Hugo "Buddy," 141-142
School Book Depository, 89-91
Schramm, Tex, 183-185
Scyene Road, 21
Shakespeare Under the Stars, 74
Shawnee Cattle Trail, 104
Shirley, Edwin "Eddie," 23
Shirley, John, 22
Shirley, Myra Maybelle, 21-23
Shirley, Pearl, 22-23
Shopping, 63-65, 248
Sierra, Ruben, 196
Silver market, 135-140
Simons, Bull, 111-112
Singleton Road, 158
Sixth Floor Museum, 88-90
Skillman Avenue, 217-218
Skillman, W.F., 218
Skyline, 14-17
Slaughter, Christopher Columbus, 215, 243
Slavery, 6, 56-57, 162
Sliger, Gale, 79
Smith, Dr. A.P., 59
Smith, Emmitt, 184-189
Smith, Roger, 112, 115
SMU *(see Southern Methodist University)*
Sonju, Norm, 204
Southern Methodist University, 62, 146
    Founding, 101-103, 255-256
    Meadows School of the Arts, 69
    Mustangs, 210
    Park Cities, 12-13
    Walker Railey trial, 35, 38, 40

Southfork Ranch, 18, 20, 87-88, 228
St. Nicholas Hotel, 150, 218, 251
Stanley Korshak, 65
Starr, Belle, 21-23, 226
Starr, James July, 23
Starr, Sam, 23
Starr, Tom, 23
State Fair of Texas, 74, 78, 164, 234, 239, 241, 255, 258, 268
Staubach, Roger, 179, 182
Stemmons, Leslie, 243
Stepnoski, Mark, 186
Stone, Thomas, 243
Suhler, Rabbi A., 56, 248
Summers, Robert, 104
Sunday School, 58, 229-232
Super Bowl, 178-182, 184, 186, 189-190, 259-260
Super Bowl Victory Parade, 187-188
Swiss Avenue, 26, 60-61, 167
Swiss colonists, 155-158, 241
Switzer, Barry, 189
Symphony, 72, 96-98
Syms, 263
Synagogues, 249

T

Tarrant County, 222
Telephone Pioneer Museum of Texas, 247
Terry Costa, 263
Texas-Oklahoma University feud, 46, 78-79, 210, 218
Texas Baptist Memorial Sanatorium, 215
Texas Bound, 67-68
Texas Centennial, 210, 218, 235, 239, 243, 258
Texas Department of Transportation, 81-83
Texas Heat, 199, 202
Texas Instruments, 42-45, 97, 240, 258-259
Texas Rangers, 194-198, 201-203, 259
Texas School Book Depository, 89-91
Texas Stadium, 178, 180-184, 186, 190-191, 193, 229, 231

Index

Texas State Fair, *(see State Fair)*
Thatched Cottage Pantry, 142-143
Theater, 70-75
Thornton, Robert L., 225-226, 243, 258
Thornton, Roy, 26
TI, 42-45, 97, 240, 258-259
Tinordi, Mark, 207
Tollway, 64, 261, 224
Townsend, Thurmond, 243
Trinity Industrial District, 96, 243
Trinity River Navigation Company, 93, 253
Trinity River, 13, 16, 41, 53, 81-82, 86, 91-96, 104, 116-119, 149-150, 152, 156, 158, 161, 218, 233, 239, 249-252, 255, 257
Trinity River Rivalry, 208-209
Tuesday Morning, 263
Turnpike Stadium, 195
Turnpike Trophy, 209
Turtle Creek, 13, 74, 250
TxDOT, 81-83
Tye, Frania, 123-125, 137

U

Union Terminal, 135-136
United We Stand America, 116, 260
University of Texas-Oklahoma University feud, 46, 78-79
University Park, 11-14, 132, 217
UT-OU game, 46, 78-79

V

Vail, Dmitri, 243
Valley Ranch, 182-183
Valley View Center, 64-65, 72, 265
Vandeweghe, Kiki, 204
Vantage, 263
Vaughan, Stevie Ray, 103
Vencil, "Ma," 100
Vencil, Troy, 100
Victor Costa Outlet, 263
Victoria's Secret, 267
Voodoo, 56

W

W. W. Peak & Brothers Drug Store, 160
Walker, Herschel, 184
Walker, Jerry Jeff, 217
Warren Commission, 91-92, 129
Washington, James, 189
Watson, Edgar, 23
Webb's Chapel, 53, 243, 250
Webb Chapel Road, 217
Webb, Issac B., 53, 243, 247, 250
Weiss, Bob, 294
Welborn, Olin, 243
Wells, Mary, 172-173
West End, 45-46, 79, 268
Westin Hotel, 63
Whitehead, Jerome, 204
White, Randy, 206
White Rock Creek, 145, 255
White Rock Lake, 125, 216, 240, 262, 268
White Swan Restaurant, 268
Wild at Heart, 9
Wiley College, 57
Williams-Sonoma, 265
Williams Square, 64
Wilson, Frederick P., 60-61
Wilson, Henrietta Frichot, 60
Wilson Historic District, 60-61
Wise, Wes, 175
Wish-I-Wish Company, 7
World War I, 100, 163, 242-243
World War II, 100, 258
Wozencraft, Frank W., 243
Wright, Ray Lee, 126-127
Wynne, Bedford, 178

Y

Yarrington, Diane, 36, 39
Yarrington, John, 36, 39
Younger's Bend, 23
Younger brothers, 22
Young, Marilla Ingram, 244

Z

Zaharias, Mildred "Babe" Didrikson, 244
Zang, J.F., 244